CHARGER
MUSCLE PORTFOLIO
— 1966 - 1974 —

Compiled by R.M.Clarke

ISBN 1 85520 2611

BROOKLANDS BOOKS LTD.
P.O. BOX 146, COBHAM,
SURREY, KT11 1LG. UK

Printed in Hong Kong

A-DC66MP

Brooklands Books

MOTORING

BROOKLANDS ROAD TEST SERIES

Abarth Gold Portfolio 1950-1971
AC Ace & Aceca 1953-1983
Alfa Romeo Giulietta Gold Portfolio 1954-1965
Alfa Romeo Giulia Coupés 1963-1976
Alfa Romeo Giulia Coupés Gold Port. 1963-1976
Alfa Romeo Spider 1966-1990
Alfa Romeo Spider Gold Portfolio 1966-1991
Alfa Romeo Alfasud 1972-1984
Alfa Romeo Alfetta Gold Portfolio 1972-1987
Alfa Romeo Alfetta GTV6 1980-1986
Allard Gold Portfolio 1937-1959
Alvis Gold Portfolio 1919-1967
AMX & Javelin Muscle Portfolio 1968-1974
Armstrong Siddeley Gold Portfolio 1945-1960
Aston Martin Gold Portfolio 1948-1971
Aston Martin Gold Portfolio 1972-1985
Aston Martin Gold Portfolio 1985-1995
Audi Quattro Gold Portfolio 1980-1991
Austin A30 & A35 1951-1962
Austin Healey 100 & 100/6 Gold Port. 1952-1959
Austin Healey 3000 Gold Portfolio 1959-1967
Austin Healey Sprite Gold Portfolio 1958-1971
Barracuda Muscle Portfolio 1964-1974
BMW 1600 Collection No.1 1966-1981
BMW 2002 Gold Portfolio 1968-1976
BMW 316, 318, 320 (4 cyl.) Gold Port. 1975-1990
BMW 320, 323, 325 (6 cyl.) Gold Port. 1977-1990
BMW M Series Performance Portfolio 1976-1993
BMW 5 Series Gold Portfolio 1981-1987
BMW 6 Series Gold Portfolio 1976-1989
Bricklin Gold Portfolio 1974-1975
Bristol Cars Gold Portfolio 1946-1992
Buick Automobiles 1947-1960
Buick Muscle Cars 1965-1970
Cadillac Allanté 1986-1993
Cadillac Automobiles 1949-1959
Cadillac Automobiles 1960-1969
Caprice 1965-1976 ☆ Limited Edition
Charger Muscle Portfolio 1966-1974
Checker ☆ Limited Edition
Chevrolet 1955-1957
Impala & SS Muscle Portfolio 1958-1972
Chevrolet Corvair 1959-1969
Chevy II & Nova SS Muscle Portfolio 1962-1974
Chevy El Camino & SS 1959-1987
Chevelle & SS Muscle Portfolio 1964-1972
Chevrolet Muscle Cars 1966-1971
Chevy Blazer 1969-1981
Chevrolet Corvette Gold Portfolio 1953-1962
Chevrolet Corvette Sting Ray Gold Port. 1963-1967
Chevrolet Corvette Gold Portfolio 1968-1977
High Performance Corvettes 1983-1989
Camaro Muscle Portfolio 1967-1973
Chevrolet Camaro & Z28 1973-1981
High Performance Camaros 1982-1988
Chrysler 300 Gold Portfolio 1955-1970
Chrysler Valiant 1960-1962
Citroen Traction Avant Gold Portfolio 1934-1957
Citroen 2CV Gold Portfolio 1948-1989
Citroen DS & ID 1955-1975
Citroen DS & ID Gold Portfolio 1955-1975
Citroen SM 1970-1975
Cobras & Replicas 1962-1983
Shelby Cobra Gold Portfolio 1962-1969
Cobras & Cobra Replicas Gold Portfolio 1962-1989
Cunningham Automobiles 1951-1955
Daimler SP250 Sports & V-8 250 Saloon Gold P. 1959-1969
Datsun Roadsters 1962-1971
Datsun 240Z 1970-1973
Datsun 280Z & ZX 1975-1983
DeLorean Gold Portfolio 1977-1995
Dodge Muscle Cars 1967-1970
Dodge Viper on the Road
Edsel 1957-1960 ☆ Limited Edition
ERA Gold Portfolio 1934-1994
Excalibur Collection No.1 1952-1981
Facel Vega 1954-1964
Ferrari 1947-1957 ☆ Limited Edition
Ferrari 1958-1963 ☆ Limited Edition
Ferrari Dino 1965-1974
Ferrari Dino 308 & Mondial Gold Portfolio1974-1985
Ferrari 328 • 348 • Mondial Gold Portfolio 1986-1994
Fiat 500 Gold Portfolio 1936-1972
Fiat 600 & 850 Gold Portfolio 1955-1972
Fiat Pininfarina 124 & 2000 Spider 1968-1985
Fiat X1/9 Gold Portfolio1973-1989
Fiat Abarth Performance Portfolio 1972-1987
Ford Consul, Zephyr, Zodiac Mk.I & II 1950-1962
Ford Zephyr, Zodiac, Executive, Mk.III & Mk.IV 1962-1971
Ford Cortina 1600E & GT 1967-1970
High Performance Capris Gold Portfolio 1969-1987
Capri Muscle Portfolio 1974-1987
High Performance Fiestas 1979-1991
High Performance Escorts Mk.I 1968-1974
High Performance Escorts Mk.II 1975-1980
High Performance Escorts 1980-1985
High Performance Escorts 1985-1990
High Performance Sierras & Merkurs
Gold Portfolio 1983-1990
Ford Automobiles 1949-1959
Ford Fairlane 1955-1970
Ford Ranchero 1957-1959
Ford Thunderbird 1955-1957
Ford Thunderbird 1958-1963
Ford GT40 Gold Portfolio 1964-1987
Ford Bronco 1966-1977
Ford Bronco 1978-1988
Goggomobil ☆ Limited Edition
Holden 1948-1962
Honda CRX 1983-1987
Imperial 1955-1970 ☆ Limited Edition
International Scout Gold Portfolio 1961-1980
Isetta Gold Portfolio 1953-1964
Iso & Bizzarrini Gold Portfolio 1962-1974
Kaiser • Frazer 1946-1955 ☆ Limited Edition
Jaguar and SS Gold Portfolio 1931-1951
Jaguar XK120, 140, 150 Gold Port. 1948-1960
Jaguar Mk.VII, VIII, IX, X, 420 Gold Port. 1950-1970
Jaguar Mk.1 & Mk.2 Gold Portfolio 1959-1969
Jaguar E-Type Gold Portfolio 1961-1971
Jaguar E-Type V-12 1971-1975
Jaguar S-Type & 420 ☆ Limited Edition
Jaguar XJ12, XJ5.3, V12 Gold Portfolio 1972-1990
Jaguar XJ6 Series I & II Gold Portfolio 1968-1979
Jaguar XJ6 Series III Perf. Portfolio 1979-1986
Jaguar XJ6 Gold Portfolio 1986-1994
Jaguar XJS Gold Portfolio 1975-1988
Jaguar XJS Gold Portfolio 1988-1995
Jeep CJ5 & CJ6 1960-1976
Jeep CJ5 & CJ7 1976-1986
Jensen Interceptor Gold Portfolio 1966-1986
Jensen Healey 1972-1976
Lagonda Gold Portfolio 1919-1964
Lancia Aurelia & Flaminia Gold Portfolio 1950-1970
Lancia Fulvia Gold Portfolio 1963-1976
Lancia Beta Gold Portfolio 1972-1984
Lancia Delta Gold Portfolio 1979-1994
Lancia Stratos 1972-1985
Land Rover Series I 1948-1958
Land Rover Series II & IIa 1958-1971
Land Rover Series III 1971-1985
Land Rover 90 110 Defender Gold Portfolio 1983-1994
Land Rover Discovery 1989-1994
Land Rover Story Part One 1948-1971
Lincoln Gold Portfolio 1949-1960
Lincoln Continental 1961-1969
Lincoln Continental 1969-1976
Lotus Sports Racers Gold Portfolio 1953-1965
Lotus Seven Gold Portfolio 1957-1974
Lotus Caterham Seven Gold Portfolio 1974-1995
Lotus Elan Gold Portfolio 1962-1974
Lotus Elan Collection No. 2 1963-1972
Lotus Elan & SE 1989-1992
Lotus Europa Gold Portfolio 1966-1975
Lotus Elite & Eclat 1974-1982
Lotus Turbo Esprit 1980-1986
Maserati 1965-1970
Matra 1965-1983 ☆ Limited Edition
Mazda Miata MX-5 Performance Portfolio 1989-1996
Mazda RX-7 Gold Portfolio 1978-1991
Mercedes 190 & 300 SL 1954-1963
Mercedes G Wagen 1981-1994
Mercedes S & 600 1965-1972
Mercedes S Class 1972-1979
Mercedes 230 • 250 • 280SL Gold Portfolio 1963-1971
Mercedes SLs & SLCs Gold Portfolio 1971-1989
Mercedes SLs Performance Portfolio 1989-1994
Mercury Muscle Cars 1966-1971
Messerschmitt Gold Portfolio 1954-1964
MG Gold Portfolio 1929-1939
MG TA & TC Gold Portfolio 1936-1949
MG TD & TF Gold Portfolio 1949-1955
MGA & Twin Cam Gold Portfolio 1955-1962
MG Midget Gold Portfolio 1961-1979
MGB Roadsters 1962-1980
MGB MGC & V8 Gold Portfolio 1962-1980
MGB GT 1965-1980
MGC & MGB GT V8 ☆ Limited Edition
MG Y-Type & Magnette ZA/ZB ☆ Limited Edition
Mini Gold Portfolio 1959-1969
Mini Gold Portfolio 1969-1980
High Performance Minis Gold Portfolio 1960-1973
Mini Cooper Gold Portfolio 1961-1971
Mini Moke Gold Portfolio 1964-1994
Morgan Three-Wheeler Gold Portfolio 1910-1952
Morgan Plus 4 & Four 4 Gold Portfolio 1936-1967
Morgan Cars 1960-1970
Morgan Cars Gold Portfolio 1968-1989
Morris Minor Collection No. 1 1948-1980
Shelby Mustang Muscle Portfolio 1965-1970
High Performance Mustang IIs 1974-1978
High Performance Mustangs 1982-1988
Nash & Nash-Healey 1949-1957 ☆ Limited Edition
Nash-Austin Metropolitan Gold Portfolio 1954-1962
Oldsmobile Automobiles 1955-1963
Oldsmobile Toronado 1966-1978
Opel GT Gold Portfolio 1968-1973
Opel Manta 1970-1975 ☆ Limited Edition
Packard Gold Portfolio 1946-1958
Pantera Gold Portfolio 1970-1989
Panther Gold Portfolio 1972-1990
Pontiac Tempest & GTO 1961-1965
Firebird & Trans-Am Muscle Portfolio 1973-1981
High Performance Firebirds 1982-1988
Pontiac Fiero 1984-1988
Porsche 356 Gold Portfolio 1953-1965
Porsche 911 1965-1969
Porsche 911 1970-1972
Porsche 911 1973-1977
Porsche 911 SC & Turbo Gold Portfolio 1978-1983
Porsche 911 Carrera & Turbo Gold Port. 1984-1989
Porsche 924 Gold Portfolio 1975-1988
Porsche 928 Performance Portfolio 1977-1994
Porsche 944 Gold Portfolio 1981-1991
Range Rover Gold Portfolio 1970-1985
Range Rover Gold Portfolio 1986-1995
Reliant Scimitar 1964-1986
Renault Alpine Gold Portfolio 1958-1994
Riley Gold Portfolio 1924-1939
Rolls Royce Silver Cloud & Bentley 'S' Series
Gold Portfolio 1955-1965
Rolls Royce Silver Shadow Gold Port. 1965-1980
Rolls Royce & Bentley Gold Port. 1980-1989
Rover P4 1949-1959
Rover P4 1955-1964
Rover 3 & 3.5 Litre Gold Portfolio 1958-1973
Rover 2000 & 2200 1963-1977
Rover 3500 & Vitesse 1976-1986
Saab Sonett Collection No.1 1966-1974
Saab Turbo 1976-1983
Studebaker Gold Portfolio 1947-1966
Studebaker Hawks & Larks 1956-1963
Avanti 1962-1990
Sunbeam Tiger & Alpine Gold Portfolio 1959-1967
Triumph Dolomite Sprint ☆ Limited Edition
Triumph TR2 & TR3 Gold Portfolio 1952-1961
Triumph TR4, TR5, TR250 1961-1968
Triumph TR6 Gold Portfolio 1969-1976
Triumph TR7 & TR8 Gold Portfolio 1975-1982
Triumph Herald 1959-1971
Triumph Vitesse 1962-1971
Triumph Spitfire Gold Portfolio 1962-1980
Triumph 2000, 2.5, 2500 1963-1977
Triumph GT6 Gold Portfolio 1966-1974
Triumph Stag Gold Portfolio 1970-1977
TVR Gold Portfolio 1959-1986
TVR Performance Portfolio 1986-1994
VW Beetle Gold Portfolio 1935-1967
VW Beetle Gold Portfolio 1968-1991
VW Beetle Collection No.1 1970-1982
VW Karmann Ghia 1955-1982
VW Bus, Camper, Van 1954-1967
VW Bus, Camper, Van 1968-1979
VW Bus, Camper, Van 1979-1989
VW Scirocco 1974-1981
VW Golf GTI 1976-1986
Volvo PV444 & PV544 1945-1965
Volvo Amazon-120 Gold Portfolio 1956-1970
Volvo 1800 Gold Portfolio 1960-1973
Volvo 140 & 160 Series Gold Portfolio 1966-1975
Westfield ☆ Limited Edition

Forty Years of Selling Volvo

BROOKLANDS ROAD & TRACK SERIES

Road & Track on Alfa Romeo 1964-1970
Road & Track on Alfa Romeo 1971-1976
Road & Track on Aston Martin 1962-1990
R & T on Auburn Cord and Duesenburg 1952-84
Road & Track on Audi & Auto Union 1952-1980
Road & Track on Audi & Auto Union 1980-1986
Road & Track on Austin Healey 1953-1970
Road & Track on BMW Cars 1966-1974
Road & Track on BMW Cars 1975-1978
Road & Track on BMW Cars 1979-1983
R & T on Cobra, Shelby & Ford GT40 1962-1992
Road & Track on Corvette 1953-1967
Road & Track on Corvette 1968-1982
Road & Track on Corvette 1982-1986
Road & Track on Corvette 1986-1990
Road & Track on Ferrari 1975-1981
Road & Track on Ferrari 1981-1984
Road & Track on Ferrari 1984-1988
Road & Track on Fiat Sports Cars 1968-1987
Road & Track on Jaguar 1950-1960
Road & Track on Jaguar 1961-1968
Road & Track on Jaguar 1968-1974
Road & Track on Jaguar 1974-1982
Road & Track on Jaguar 1983-1989
Road & Track on Lamborghini 1964-1985
Road & Track on Lotus 1972-1981
Road & Track on Maserati 1975-1983
R & T on Mazda RX-7 & MX-5 Miata 1986-1991
Road & Track on Mercedes 1952-1962
Road & Track on Mercedes 1963-1970
Road & Track on Mercedes 1971-1979
Road & Track on Mercedes 1980-1987
Road & Track on MG Sports Cars 1949-1961
Road & Track on MG Sports Cars 1962-1980
Road & Track on Mustang 1964-1977
R & T on Nissan 300-ZX & Turbo 1984-1989
Road & Track on Pontiac 1960-1983
Road & Track on Porsche 1951-1967
Road & Track on Porsche 1968-1971
Road & Track on Porsche 1972-1975
Road & Track on Porsche 1975-1978
Road & Track on Porsche 1985-1988
R & T on Rolls Royce & Bentley 1950-1965
R & T on Rolls Royce & Bentley 1966-1984
Road & Track on Saab 1972-1992
R & T on Toyota Sports & GT Cars 1966-1984
R & T on Triumph Sports Cars 1953-1967
R & T on Triumph Sports Cars 1967-1974
R & T on Triumph Sports Cars 1974-1982
Road & Track on Volkswagen 1951-1968
Road & Track on Volkswagen 1968-1978
Road & Track on Volkswagen 1978-1985
Road & Track on Volvo 1957-1974
Road & Track on Volvo 1977-1994
R & T - Henry Manney at Large & Abroad
R & T - Peter Egan's "Side Glances"
R & T - Peter Egan "At Large"

BROOKLANDS CAR AND DRIVER SERIES

Car and Driver on BMW 1955-1977
Car and Driver on BMW 1977-1985
C and D on Cobra, Shelby & Ford GT40 1963-84
Car and Driver on Corvette 1978-1982
Car and Driver on Corvette 1983-1988
C and D on Datsun Z 1600 & 2000 1966-1984
Car and Driver on Ferrari 1955-1962
Car and Driver on Ferrari 1963-1975
Car and Driver on Ferrari 1976-1983
Car and Driver on Mopar 1956-1967
Car and Driver on Mopar 1968-1975
Car and Driver on Mustang 1964-1972
Car and Driver on Pontiac 1961-1975
Car and Driver on Porsche 1955-1962
Car and Driver on Porsche 1963-1970
Car and Driver on Porsche 1970-1976
Car and Driver on Porsche 1977-1981
Car and Driver on Porsche 1982-1986
Car and Driver on Saab 1956-1985
Car and Driver on Volvo 1955-1986

BROOKLANDS PRACTICAL CLASSICS SERIES

PC on Austin A40 Restoration
PC on Land Rover Restoration
PC on Metalworking in Restoration
PC on Midget/Sprite Restoration
PC on MGB Restoration
PC on Sunbeam Rapier Restoration
PC on Triumph Herald/Vitesse
PC on Spitfire Restoration
PC on 1930s Car Restoration

BROOKLANDS HOT ROD 'MUSCLECAR & HI-PO ENGINES' SERIES

Chevy 265 & 283
Chevy 302 & 327
Chevy 348 & 409
Chevy 350 & 400
Chevy 396 & 427
Chevy 454 thru 512
Chrysler Hemi
Chrysler 273, 318, 340 & 360
Chrysler 361, 383, 400, 413, 426, 440
Ford 289, 302, Boss 302 & 351W
Ford 351C & Boss 351
Ford Big Block

BROOKLANDS RESTORATION SERIES

Auto Restoration Tips & Techniques
Basic Bodywork Tips & Techniques
Camaro Restoration Tips & Techniques
Chevrolet High Performance Tips & Techniques
Chevy Engine Swapping Tips & Techniques
Chevy-GMC Pickup Repair
Chrysler Engine Swapping Tips & Techniques
Engine Swapping Tips & Techniques
Ford Pickup Repair
Land Rover Restoration Tips & Techniques
MG 'T' Series Restoration Guide
MGA Restoration Guide
Mustang Restoration Tips & Techniques

MOTORCYCLING

BROOKLANDS ROAD TEST SERIES

AJS & Matchless Gold Portfolio 1945-1966
BSA Twins A7 & A10 Gold Portfolio 1946-1962
BSA Twins A50 & A65 Gold Portfolio 1962-1973
BMW Motorcycles Gold Portfolio 1950-1971
BMW Motorcycles Gold Portfolio 1971-1976
Ducati Gold Portfolio 1960-1974
Ducati Gold Portfolio 1974-1978
Ducati Gold Portfolio 1978-1982
Laverda Gold Portfolio 1967-1977
Moto Guzzi Gold Portfolio 1949-1973
Norton Commando Gold Portfolio 1968-1977
Triumph Bonneville Gold Portfolio 1959-1983

BROOKLANDS CYCLE WORLD SERIES

Cycle World on BMW 1974-1980
Cycle World on BMW 1981-1986
Cycle World on Ducati 1982-1991
Cycle World on Harley-Davidson 1962-1968
Cycle World on Harley-Davidson 1978-1983
Cycle World on Harley-Davidson 1983-1987
Cycle World on Harley-Davidson 1987-1990
Cycle World on Harley-Davidson 1990-1992
Cycle World on Honda 1962-1967
Cycle World on Honda 1968-1971
Cycle World on Honda 1971-1974
Cycle World on Husqvarna 1966-1976
Cycle World on Husqvarna 1977-1984
Cycle World on Kawasaki 1966-1971
Cycle World on Kawasaki Off-Road Bikes 1972-1979
Cycle World on Kawasaki Street Bikes 1972-1976
Cycle World on Norton 1962-1971
Cycle World on Suzuki 1962-1970
Cycle World on Suzuki Off-Road Bikes 1971-1976
Cycle World on Suzuki Street Bikes 1971-1976
Cycle World on Triumph 1967-1972
Cycle World on Yamaha 1962-1969
Cycle World on Yamaha Off-Road Bikes 1970-1974
Cycle World on Yamaha Street Bikes 1970-1974

MILITARY

BROOKLANDS MILITARY VEHICLES SERIES

Allied Military Vehicles No.2 1941-1946
Complete WW2 Military Jeep Manual
Dodge Military Vehicles No.1 1940-1945
Hail To The Jeep
Military & Civilian Amphibians 1940-1990
Off Road Jeeps: Civ. & Mil. 1944-1971
US Military Vehicles 1941-1945
US Army Military Vehicles WW2-TM9-2800
VW Kubelwagen Military Portfolio 1940-1990
WW 2 Jeep Military Portfolio 1941-1945

RACING

Le Mans - The Jaguar Years - 1949-1957
Le Mans - The Ferrari Years - 1958-1965
Le Mans - The Ford & Matra Years - 1966-1974

CONTENTS

ACKNOWLEDGEMENTS

It is some nine years since we published our first book on the Charger: *Dodge Charger 1966-1974* - in fact it proved so popular that we had to reprint it no fewer than three times. When the need came for a fifth printing we decided to search out new material and upgrade the book to a Muscle Portfolio. Over 50% of the articles and road tests found here did not appear in the original book.

Without the understanding and co-operation of the world's leading magazine publishers, we would be unable to produce volumes such as this. We are pleased to record our sincere thanks to those who have made it possible for us to reissue their copyright material. For this volume, those thanks go to the managements of *Buyer's Guide, Car and Driver, Car Craft, Car Life, Classic American, Hi-Peformance Cars, Hot Rod, Modern Motor, Motor, Motorcade, Motor Trend, Road Test* and *Special Interest Autos*.

R. M. Clarke

Dodge were a little later than other automakers to follow the Mustang with a sporty fastback of their own, but when they announced the Charger in the middle of the 1966 season, they made sure it had power aplenty. Top option on the new model, based on the 117-inch wheelbase of the much-respected Coronet sedan, was the 425bhp 426 Street Hemi motor.

Between 1966 and 1974, Chargers always showed well at the NASCAR superspeedways, and they always had just the right blend of style and performance to stand out on the street, too. Not for nothing was it a Charger R/T 440 which featured in the famous *Bullitt* car chase - even though Steve McQueen's Mustang ultimately kept ahead of it.

The first-generation Charger was replaced by a more curvaceous new model for 1968, the first one to feature the formidable 440 Magnum motor. It was from this second-generation Charger that the Dodge division created its astonishing Daytona Charger in 1969, the winged monster designed for NASCAR, who's regulations insist that similar models must be made available to the general public.

Minor cosmetic changes kept the second-generation model looking fresh until Dodge reorganised their intermediate ranges for 1971, moving the Charger to a 115-inch wheelbase in an attempt to minimise weight gain as emissions control regulations took their toll on engine outputs. The writing was already on the wall by 1972, when the Hemi ceased to be an option and all engines were tuned for low-lead gasoline, but the Charger remained a credible muscle car until 1974. After that, the Charger name was transferred to a personal luxury line, and the great muscle car tradition was broken.

The Charger belongs to a breed of car we shall never see again. But it lives on in the hands of enthusiasts who lovingly restore and run these classic examples of American muscle. For all of them and for the countless fans who would have a Charger if only they could, this book is essential reading.

James Taylor

DODGE CHARGER

The Dodge Charger is being heralded as an "all-new" car. Although less than that, it is still a lot newer than some others with restyled bodies.

A little over two years ago, Dodge started showing a special one-of-a-kind show car called the Charger II. This experimental prototype had a full-width grille, disappearing headlights and a long, sloping fastback roofline that ended in pointed rear fenders that stuck out some six to eight inches beyond the rear deck. The automobile that evolved from it is as much like a prototype show car as a production model could possibly be.

Bill Brownlee, Dodge's chief stylist and Burt Bouwkamp, chief engineer and product-planning manager had a lot to do with it and the Charger reflects their outlook, as well it should. Brownlee is a young man who likes the outdoors. One of his favorite hobbies is riding motorcycles. He likes bikes that are light, responsive and have maximum performance; these characteristics are reflected in his Charger. He also likes mechanical things that are functional as well as being beautiful.

If Dodge employees had been allowed to compete in a recent "Press Gymkhana" held to introduce the Charger to West Coast automotive writers, Burt Bouwkamp would have won first prize. As it tran-

spired they didn't allow his time around the course to count so managing editor, Dick Brashear took top honors. But Burt is a first rate driver and can handle a wheel with the best. He knows what he wants in an automobile and, as product planner, he usually gets it.

These are two men, among many responsible for the Dodge Charger. Although it's not a completely new automobile; (it shares many components with the popular Coronet, an already good automobile). It has its share of innovations and should have a wide appeal in the much sought after Specialty car market.

WHERE IT FITS

The Charger is squared off against the Mustang GT, Fairlane GT and GTA, Comet Cyclone and all the GM Things, (4-4-2, Skylark GS, Chevelle SS, and Pontiac GTO). Dodge dealers are biting off a big chunk and comparing it with such specialty cars as the Riviera, Thunderbird, and Toronado in their local newspaper ads. In the realm of yes or no comparisons of maximum horsepower, transmission options, torsion bar suspension, unibody construction, safety rim wheels, battery-saving alternator and 5-year/50,000-mile warranty, only the Mustang has more than one "yes" answer. Of course this is what's called selective reasoning, but it does show where dealers are setting their sights and the Charger is priced way below all cars mentioned except the Mustang.

Why, in this specialty car field would prospective buyers pick a Charger over the others? Its base price of $3146.00 F.O.B. Detroit places it competitively in the market, but if you want power steering, windows and brakes, you'll have to up that to $3372.00. Air conditioning will bump the price another $338.00. And that price is with the standard 318 cubic-inch V-8 engine and standard 3-speed manual transmission. Albeit an all-new, all synchromesh unit. For the Chrysler 4-speed manual or Torqueflite, you'll have to pay even more out of the old tin can you've got buried in the back yard.

WHAT IT HAS

One thing Charger has, (or more correctly, will have soon) is the much touted 426 cubic inch Hemi-head V-8 that claims a modest 425 horsepower. The ROAD TEST staff feel that this is a bit much for the average car buyer, even in this specialty car idiom. Unless you just have to blow off every thing else on the road; and have no doubts that the Hemi will do just that, you'll be much happier with Dodge's

other choices; which are the 361 265 hp and 383 325 hp cubic inch V-8s.

We doubt that many buyers will order the 318 or the 426 engines. The 426 Hemi has oodles of power, but it's all at the high end, right along with the torque. Keeping the revs up is mandatory and this kind of driving just isn't going to lend itself to stop and go conditions. The "GO" boys will, however, love it.

As sure as taxes, the 361 and the 383 will be the engine you'll see most often when a Charger's hood is raised. But the great image of the Hemi shines overhead, regardless of what lies under the hood.

By the same token we probably won't see more than a handful of Chargers with the standard 3-speed manual transmission; it just isn't that kind of car. Most buyers won't think twice before ordering the optional 4-speed manual gearbox at $184.00 or Chrysler's excellent Torqueflite automatic for $206.00 extra. Dodge's 4-speed manual transmission is both ahead of, and behind those offered by the competition. In strength, positive feel and quietness, it's ahead. Ford and GM's boxes tend to be weaker and to loosen up after hard use in the area of linkage. On the other hand, theirs shift a bit easier and have a shorter throw. We rate the Dodge unit as about equal in the overall picture.

Flow-through fresh air system uses adjustable front vents and slot under deck lid for entry and exit. Rubber flaps cover holes in deck frame.

Now, when it comes to automatics, there isn't a finer, more positive, more responsive, or smoother unit on the market. It shifts exactly at the right time, gives perfect engine-to-wheel coordination on exact command from the throttle and has very little slippage.

The Charger's suspension system is the well-proven Dodge configuration of torsion bars in front and leaf springs at the rear. Even though there's a stiffer suspension package offered as an option, the ROAD TEST staff can, for once, recommend the standard suspension for almost any kind of driving.

The standard suspension Charger is perfectly predictable in all situations, at all speeds and its spring balance is nearly perfect. In corners it has a lot of body roll, but this has little effect on its predictable handling characteristics. It does nothing out of the ordinary when pressed hard in turns and gives the driver a feeling of sureness and stability. At the same time, there isn't too much harshness in the ride. It is quite comfor-

Novel interior has full-length console over driveshaft tunnel, individual seats which fold down for additional luggage space. Interior communicates with trunk.

table over most any surface.

Suspension action during braking is notable without much nose-dive and with good control as is shown with our recorded deceleration rate of 26 ft./sec.^{2}

The 383 cubic inch, automatic transmission Charger tips the scales at 3990 pounds. With 2170 pounds of this on the front wheels and 1820 pounds over the rear for a 54.5/45.5 weight distribution. When compared with the 4110-pound Chevrolet Caprice that puts 2330 pounds of its weight over the front wheels (57/43) the Charger looks well-balanced by comparison.

The Charger standard brakes are drums of ten-inch diameter with 2½-inch width shoes which give it a total swept area of 314 square inches. Somewhat ahead of cars of similar weight and size in lining area the Charger also profits

Handling of Charger is notable for vehicle in this class. Stiffer suspension than stock model (shown) is available but is not considered mandatory. Deceleration rate and braking attitude rate "good." Larger (7.75) tires are recommended to improve overall character.

by the extra cooling benefits of its brake drum location. Lots of cooling air gets to these units and they are acceptable brakes—for drums. A peak stopping rate of 28 ft./sec.^{2} was hit and would have been better with more rubber on the ground. Brake fade wasn't a factor and it isn't often we can say this. Optional 7.75 x 14 tires would have been superior to the 7.35 x 14 tires that are standard.

Dodge is working hard to come up with a set of optional disc brakes for the front end of their intermediates; Coronets and Chargers. Since discs are available on Darts and full-sized Dodges, it shouldn't be long before they're offered on the more popular Coronets. Hemi-engined Chargers will come with the extra-large Chrysler or "Police" brakes in addition to the reinforced heavy-duty drive train and suspension that comes standard with the Hemi engine. Metallic linings are extra-cost options.

You can't get disc brakes on any GM Thing except the Corvette, but the Mustangs, Marlins, Barracudas and Thunderbirds have them either as options or, in the T-Bird's case, as standard equipment.

INTERIOR APPOINTMENTS

When it comes to utility, the Charger stands alone. It sits on a longer (117-inch), wheelbase than any of the other fastbacks and has a bigger load-carrying capacity and more room for stuff.

Each of its twin rear bucket seats will fold down for loading such trivia as skis, surfboards or extra-bulky items, and its extra length means you can get

Full-circle instruments are used in Charger. Tachometer, which can be read easily, oil pressure gage and ammeter are included.

Peak deceleration rate of 28 ft./sec.^{2} was recorded during brake tests. Big drum brakes are used on standard models, larger Chrysler brakes will be fitted to 426 cubic inch "Hemi" model.

Bucket seats in Charger appeal to staff because of maximum thigh support. Rear seats are identical to front, rate high. Relationship of brake pedal to throttle is proper for quick transfer of foot. Clutch release and engagement is exceptionally smooth, shift lever is long, 4-speed action is firmer than other transmissions.

that expensive sporting equipment inside, and lock it up. If you're carrying extra-long objects like surfboards, one passenger can still ride behind the driver with the bulky objects occupying the other side of the car. Unlike the Barracuda, the Charger doesn't have a rail that keeps luggage from sliding forward, but the bolsters of the carpeted rear seatbacks serve to keep things from sliding too far forward.

So, the Charger can either carry two people and lots of luggage or four people and a little less. Whichever way you go you can surely "take it with you" in a Charger, especially if your sporting interests run toward skiing or surfing, or, perhaps you just like a car that you can stretch out and sleep in if the mood moves you.

Another plus in the Charger's favor is its use of Chrysler's unit-body construction. The reinforced body structure around that big rear window helps make it a rattle-free automobile. You can also expect less cowl shake, hood vibration, but somewhat more road noise than GM cars with their separate body-frame construction.

Another Charger feature is its interior ventilation system. Front vents pressurized the cabin and stale air exits through small openings covered by rubber flaps, in the trunk partition and a vent under the deck lid. The trunk is sealed by a rubber extrusion and has a fold-down "security panel." This lets owners either hide some smaller items from sight or open the entire area by folding the panel down for more storage room in the fully carpeted area immediately behind the rear seats.

When it comes to interior room the Charger is a cut above its competition. Four people ride comfortably in four bucket seats with adequate head, leg and hip room in back and more than enough in front. Both pairs of seats are separated by consoles.

The Charger's dash is in keeping with its sporty nature. It is completely different from the standard Coronets with four, big, round chrome trimmed dials right in front of the driver. A tachometer, right where you can see and use it, is standard. Instrumentation isn't perfect, but it isn't the worst—especially at night when the numerals light up on tach and speedometer and the bright red pointers show against a blue glow of numbers.

That's when the disappearing headlights come out too. An over-riding switch is provided for those who

Glove compartment in Charger is above average in size. Rear seat headroom is adequate, fastback gives impression of much more space. Spare is hidden beneath neatly carpeted trunk floor.

want to show their lenses all the time. Should either, or both of the rotating electric motors fail for some reason you can manually lock the headlights in open position by loosening the screws on the motor mounting straps and do the job by hand.

Chargers use a new one-piece headliner of molded fiberglass panel that has improved sound-deadening qualities. Scratch and soil-resistant the material is easily cleaned with soap and water. This shows good thinking in product planning since this body style lends itself to carrying things much more so than standard sedans and is more likely to be subjected to gouges and scratches on the headliner.

When it comes to visibility the fastback design has inherent weak points; mainly the blind spot created by the right-hand panel behind the right rear window. A standard outside rear view mirror helps out on the left side. The rear window goes all the way across the car, sweeping up slightly on each side and incurs a minimum rear vision problem for this type body configuration. However, objects placed behind the rear seats readily reflect in the almost flat backlight window and make it difficult to see through. A rear window defroster is an extra-cost option on the Charger.

HOW DOES IT RATE?

The ROAD TEST staff feels that the Charger represents a better than average buy when compared to what the competition has to offer. Its extremely wide range of engines from 230 hp, 318 V-8 to 425 hp Hemi-head and its three choices of transmissions plus a wide variety of rear axle ratios help lend it to the specialty car buyer with performance uppermost in his mind.

It is still a Coronet, but its unusual front and rear-end treatment sets it apart. Evolving from the pre-war fastback and torpedo style schools, the Charger concept of automotive design combines utility with a sporting flavor. A well-balanced automobile, the Charger handles in a predictable manner and has better than average brakes with stronger options in the offing. Its trunk opening is larger and more useful than that of Marlin and its inside dimensions and carrying space "one-up" the Barracuda and Mustang fastbacks in both passenger comfort and utility. Thus far GM intermediates have no ammunition to fight back with and still stick to their half-fastback design with a trunk and a back seat, but no attempt to combine the two.

Ford is supposed to have a fastback in the offing, but it looks like the Charger has the jump on the market.

The Charger concept is one designed by men of action for others from the same mold. Although it isn't named after an animal or race course where it will never compete, the Charger is setting the stage for the competition as the first of the intermediate fastbacks. At a total price of around $3500.00 for the average unit, it represents a good selection.

Car's service card, similar to credit card, is placed in engine compartment pocket for safe-keeping.

GENERAL SPECIFICATIONS

Wheel base	117	Brake type	drum	Clutch dia.	10.5
O. A. Length	203.5	Swept area, sq. in.	314	Std. ratios	
Width	75.3	Tire size	735 x 14	4th	
Height	53	Steering, turns		3rd	1.00:1
Ground clearance	5.2	Manual	5.4	2nd	1.83:1
Curb weight	3380	Power	3.5	1st	3.02:1
Weight dist.	55/45	Turning circle	44'	Diff. ratio	2.94:1

ENGINE

Type	(426) V-8 Hemi
Bore	4.25
Stroke	3.75
Disp. cu. in.	426
Comp. ratio	10.25
BHP @ rpm	425/5000
Torque @ rpm	490/4000

OPTIONAL TRANS.

4th	1.00:1
3rd	1.39:1
2nd	1.91:1
1st	2.66:1

AUTOMATIC

3rd range	1.00:1
2nd range	1.45:1
1st range	2.45:1

ENGINE

Type	(383) V-8 ohv
Bore	4.25
Stroke	3.38
Disp. cu. in.	383
Comp. ratio	10.0
BHP @ rpm	325/4800
Torque @ rpm	425/2800

ENGINE

Type	(318) V-8 ohv
Bore	3.91
Stroke	3.31
Disp. cu. in.	318
Comp. ratio	9.0
BHP @ rpm	230/4400
Torque @ rpm	340/2400

ENGINE

Type	(361) V-8 ohv
Bore	4.12
Stroke	3.38
Disp. cu. in.	361
Comp. ratio	9.0
BHP @ rpm	265/4400
Torque @ rpm	380/2400

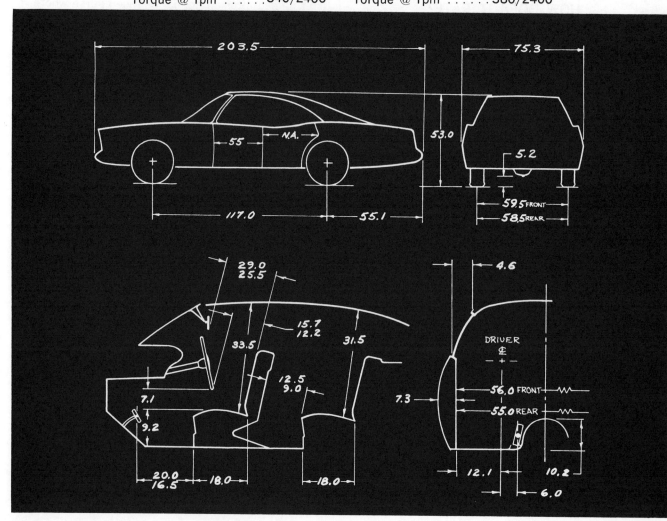

HOW THEY COMPARE

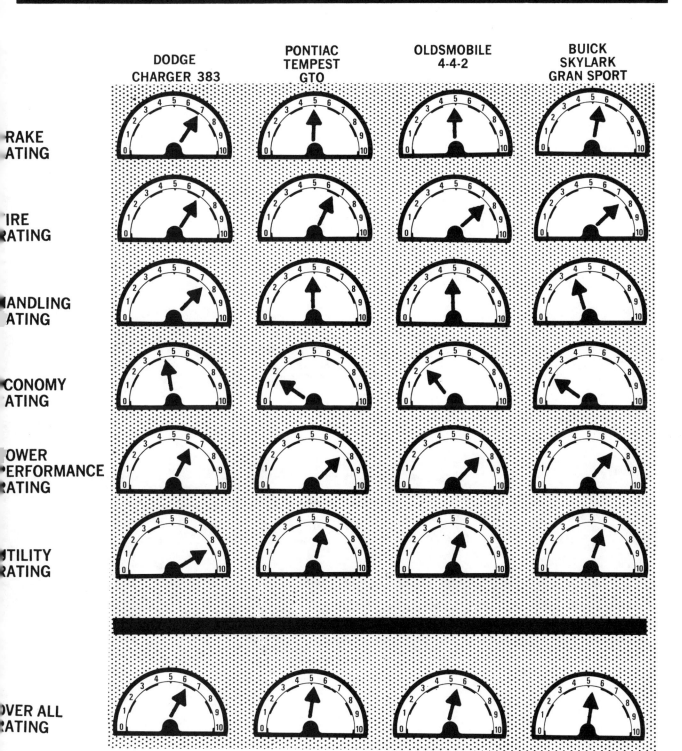

	DODGE CHARGER 383	PONTIAC TEMPEST GTO	OLDSMOBILE 4-4-2	BUICK SKYLARK GRAN SPORT
BRAKE RATING				
TIRE RATING				
HANDLING RATING				
ECONOMY RATING				
POWER PERFORMANCE RATING				
UTILITY RATING				
OVER ALL RATING				

DODGE'S CHARGING CHARGER

Instead of jumping on the bandwagon, it leads the parade

WHEN MT FIRST HEARD that Dodge would introduce a fastback based on the Coronet, we were understandably apprehensive of seeing another hastily styled car, cobbled together just for a free ride on Detroit's current stylewagon. Our fears were allayed a full year ago by the Charger II, a one-of-a-kind show car obviously built to measure public opinion. Enthusiastic reaction at four major shows as well as private samplings from, of all people, 400 mainline Philadelphians clearly indicated that all Dodge had to do was put on some practical bumpers and start production. ● We road-tested the first production Charger and in eyeing it from every angle, nowhere could we find evidence of that compromise so evident in some of the other recently introduced fastbacks. The interior is fully as esthetically pleasing as the exterior. There are very comfortable, full-sized bucket seats for four but no more. These are divided front and rear by a console that runs the length of the passenger compartment. The rear seat backs are carpeted and can be individually folded down flush with a similarly carpeted utility area behind the seats, forming a storage area long enough for the traditional 4 by 8-foot piece of plywood. The rear central arm rest also folds over, and a trap door leading to the

by John Ethridge
Technical Editor

luggage compartment drops down to make a large flat area much like that in a Barracuda. ● The vinyl upholstery, stitched in narrow horizontal pleats, the one-piece vacuum-formed, foam-filled ABS plastic door panels, the fiberglass/non-woven nylon headlining, and the brushed bright metal trim harmoniously blend together to make a truly neat interior. It should be easy to keep it looking that way, because, according to Dodge, even the headliner can be washed with soap and water. ● There's a full set of instruments to inform the driver, including, glory be, a 6000-rpm tachometer right in front of his eyes. Somebody deserves great credit for breaking with tradition and not putting it on the console underneath the dash where only grandma, who probably thought it was a clock anyway, could see it from the back seat. And now *she'll* have less trouble telling time, because the instrument occupying that hallowed spot *is* a clock. ● If you have something under your hood that tempts thieves, which may well be the case with the Charger, the inside hood release makes their job more difficult. We wonder if this heralds a revival of inside hood releases, which have been mostly absent since the time fastbacks were last popular. Manufacturers had dropped them for economy's

sake. ● Standard engine for the Charger is the 230-hp "318" V-8 with 2-barrel. There's also a 2-barrel, 265-hp "361" and a 4-barrel, 325-hp "383" as in our test car offered as options. What'll really get you out of Dullsville in a haze of rubber smoke is the top engine option, the "426-hemi." This street version of Dodge's racing engine uses two 4-barrel carbs with staged linkage to permit idling and low-speed running on the two primary barrels of the rear carb only. Slotted pistons for thermal and noise control, lower compression (10.25 to 1), a manifold heat riser, cast-iron headers, and stellite-faced exhaust valves tame down the engine to make it durable enough to come under the 5-year/50,000-mile warranty. It's conservatively rated at 425 hp at 5000 rpm with the standard cam. A "maximum performance" bump-stick is optional, increasing the output an unspecified amount. ● Four-speed manual shift is available with all engines save the "318," and you can have the 3-speed TorqueFlite automatic with all powerplants, including the hemi. ● With the hemi, you get 11-inch-diameter by 3-inch-wide brakes in front and 11 by 2½ in the rear. These manually adjusted brakes are optional with the "383" engine. Standard brakes

continued

The eyes have it, whether wide awake, half closed, or asleep. Two electric motors, working through 4.5:1 gears, rotate lamps.

CHARGER

are self-adjusting 10 by 2½ front and rear. Standard tire size is 7.35 x 14, with 7.75 optional. Although there was no mention in preliminary literature, we think it's reasonable to presume that 8.25 x 14 HS tires will be offered, same as with the Coronet. Dodge tells us that discs (stiff suspension, too) are in the works for the Charger. Most likely, 15-inch wheels will come, also.

Plans for the Charger go even further. If all goes well, these call for a mini-hemi, a "426" de-stroked to 405 cubic inches, being installed in a well shocked and suspended Charger set up for road courses and complying with NASCAR's intermediate category.

First off, Dodge plans to lob two or three of these small bombs into the D-zone. In this case, D stands for Dan Gurney, the zone is Riverside, and H-hour's the MOTOR TREND 500 on January 23. Dan, whose loyalty has been with Ford, has held unquestioned sway in that sector for lo these many years. The boys from Hamtramck would like nothing better than to occupy that redoubt. Of course they're troubled, as always, by fears that should they come up with any truly lethal weapon, the Geneva Convention (meeting in Daytona) might change the rules, leaving them with something to either convert to peaceful uses or dispose of as radioactive waste. Just the thought of these cars slithering down the esses is thrilling. They should add considerable spice to the event.

On first getting into our test car, we discovered someone had "Uncle Tom-ed" the TorqueFlite transmission. The two shifts occurred at only 3400 and 3700 rpm, making the car slower off the line than a snail on a treadmill. Fortunately, this box allows manual shifting, which is the way we got the times recorded.

About the only quarrel we could pick with the car is over vision through the rear-view mirror. Either it's too high up, or the top of the rear window's too low down. We could see 300 or 400 yards behind us, but not the horizon or that patrolman stalking us about a half-mile behind. We think lowering the mirror a bit would cure the problem.

The roll-over headlamps do it in a reasonably short time, and are the first we've seen that look as nice out as they do in. The car's quiet, even at 100 mph. The flow-through ventilation system works, allowing you to shut out noise.

If the price (which should hover at $3500) is right, we don't see how Dodge can miss with this car. **/MT**

Peek inside Charger reveals plush vinyled and carpeted furnishings, done in sporty, personalized style with utilitarian flair. All passengers benefit from rests for both arms. The bottom photo catches the aft compartment in a cargo-carrying posture.

Rubber flap valves exhaust passenger compartment via plenum chamber under rear window, prevent entry of dust and moisture.

A familiar object in new surroundings, Dodge's 325-hp "383" supplies ample urge. Hemi will fit for those who want more go.

LOOK AT IT FROM WHERE YOU MAY, YOU WON'T FIND AN UNGAINLY OR AWKWARD ASPECT — PROOF OF THE CHARGER'S SUPERIORITY IN STYLING.

CHARGER ACCESSORY PRICE LIST*

"361" 2-bbl. engine	$ 87.75
"383" 4-bbl. engine**	149.60
Manual 4-speed transmission	184.20
TorqueFlite	206.30
Sure-Grip differential	37.60
Power brakes	41.75
Power steering	84.35
Air conditioner	338.45
Radio	57.35
Electric window lifts	100.25
Rallye suspension	25.65
Clean-air package	25.00
Whitewall tires	32.70
Electric clock	15.30
Tinted body glass (all)	39.50
Tinted windshield only	21.20
Bumper guards, front & rear	30.85

*Prices based on Coronet. Charger prices NA at press-time.
**"426" 4-bbl. and "426-hemi" offered; prices NA.

DODGE CHARGER
2-door, 4-passenger fastback

OPTIONS ON TEST CAR: TorqueFlite automatic transmission, power brakes and steering, radio, misc. access.
BASE PRICE: NA
PRICE AS TESTED: NA
ODOMETER READING AT START OF TEST: 767 miles
RECOMMENDED ENGINE RED LINE: 5200 rpm

PERFORMANCE

ACCELERATION (2 aboard)

0-30 mph	3.3 secs.
0-45 mph	5.8
0-60 mph	8.9

PASSING TIMES AND DISTANCES

40-60 mph	4.8 secs., 352 ft.
50-70 mph	5.6 secs., 492 ft.

Standing start ¼-mile 16.3 secs. and 85 mph.
Speeds in gears @ shift points

1st	49 mph @ 5000 rpm	3rd	106 mph @ 4700 rpm
2nd	85 mph @ 5000 rpm		(observed)

Speedometer Error on Test Car

Car's speedometer reading	31	47	52	63	73	85
Weston electric speedometer	30	45	50	60	70	80

Observed mph per 1000 rpm in top gear .... 22.5 mph
Stopping Distances — from 30 mph, 35 ft.; from 60 mph, 175 ft.

SPECIFICATIONS FROM MANUFACTURER

Engine
Ohv V-8
Bore: 4.25 ins.
Stroke: 3.38 ins.
Displacement: 383 cu. ins.
Compression ratio: 10.0:1
Horsepower: 325 @ 4800 rpm
Horsepower per cubic inch: 0.85
Torque: 425 lbs.-ft. @ 2800 rpm
Carburetion: 1 4-bbl.
Ignition: 12-volt coil

Gearbox
TorqueFlite 3-speed automatic; console-mounted lever

Driveshaft
1-piece, open tube

Differential
Hypoid with Sure-Grip limited slip
Standard ratio: 3.23:1

Suspension
Front: Independent, lateral, non-parallel control arms with torsion bars, telescopic shocks
Rear: Solid axle with semi-elliptical leaf springs, telescopic shocks

Steering
Rack and sector, with integral power assist
Turning diameter: 40.9 ft.
Turns lock to lock: 3.5

Wheels and Tires
14 x 5.5 JK 5-stud, steel disc wheels
7.75x14 (7.35x14 standard) tires

Brakes
Hydraulic, duo-servo, self-adjusting; cast-iron drums
Front: 10-in. dia.x2.5 ins. wide
Rear: 10-in. dia.x2.5 ins. wide
Effective lining area: 195.2 sq. ins.
Swept drum area: 314.2 sq. ins.

Body and Frame
Unit construction
Wheelbase: 117.0 ins.
Track: front, 59.5 ins.; rear, 58.5 ins.
Overall length: 203.6 ins.
Overall width: 75.3 ins.
Overall height: 53.0 ins.
Curb weight: 3760 lbs.

LEADER OF THE REBELLION...
THE CHARGER

Return with us now to those thrilling days of

yesteryear . . . when out of the past come

the thundering hoofbeats of the great horse, Silver . . . .

THE COMING thing in car design, according to Dodge Division, is the specialty car of intermediate size. A body style that harks back to the late '30s and early '40s, in modernized form, returns as a Charger II to challenge the silver-studded segment of the affluent society. It comes none too soon to capitalize on the phenomenal growth in interest in high Camp.

MIGHTY STALLION or mild mare, the choice of character for the Charger is made by specifying engine capacity. Though the 383-cu. in. V-8 developing 325 bhp is standard, Dodge's majestic 426-cu. in. Street Hemi echoes across the plains along with a hearty cry of "Hi Yo Silver, Away!" The graceful, broad back of the gleaming white Charger invites lolling upon as well as riding under. Torpedo-backed body may be used on NASCAR circuit this season.

THE CHARGER

NO MERE saddlebag, this copious trunk can be opened into the passenger compartment for carrying longer loads. A full-width taillight spreads its broad-beamed signal for stops or turns. In the business office beyond the wood-grained wheel, all instruments are in front of the driver.

UTILIZING THE regular Coronet body, the Charger II is a new model patterned after last year's show car which tested public reaction. Headlights, mounted in pivoting grille sections, roll upward out of sight.

ROOF-SIDE ridges sweeping from windshield to rear bumper create a novel rear window. Glass is formed into a broad W-shaped curve. Flap-covered internal outlets along the trunk opening exhaust stale cabin air. Individual backs of rear bucket seats fold forward in any combination.

The Hemi was never in better shape

Beauty and the beast. That's a sleek Dodge Charger with come-hither fastback styling and a deep-breathing 426 Street Hemi growling under the hood. Looks like a pampered thoroughbred, comes on like Genghis Khan. Got to be the toughest combination on the road. And good news: The optional Street Hemi comes in a package deal with heavy-duty suspension, 4-ply nylon Blue Streak tires, and big 11-inch brakes to put you safely and firmly in control. To keep an even tighter rein on Charger (or Coronet), new front disc brakes are now optional. If you're looking for a "charger" that looks great, with go and handling to match, look no further than Dodge Charger. See your nearest Dodge dealer; he'll introduce you to the hot new leader of the Dodge Rebellion.

Dodge Charger

DODGE DIVISION **CHRYSLER** MOTORS CORPORATION

Dodge Charger—named *"Top Performance Car of the Year"* by CARS magazine.

by Eric Dahlquist / *technical editor*

Attention! Beat the troops to station. One if by land, two if by sea, and all that. In case you didn't know it, there is a rebellion underway in our country, aimed at attracting supporters from all factions, left and right. At least that's what the Dodge boys hope will be the effect of their advertising to allow further flanking movements on the competition in the medium-price field.

Hottest secret weapon in their stratagem bag is a sporty, new, full-sized fastback dubbed the Charger from an earlier machine of the same name that was shown around the country last year. It takes about a season longer to bring out a new design this way, exhibiting an advance prototype, but it allows the distinct advantage of accurately pre-gauging public acceptance. The fact of the matter is that some critics assayed the original one-off Charger as a bit too bulbous in a few spots. Evidently word got back to the farm because the finished car that we previewed at Riverside International Raceway early in October appeared to be a happier blend and anything but bulbous.

On a full-sized car with such a profile, there is always hanging on a single stroke of the designer's pencil the danger that the finished form will be mediocre rather than chic. But when the sheet metal was added to the Charger, it was given clean definition by recessing the rear window and deck area slightly in contrast to thin perimeter "rails" that flank either side. The outer edges of the glass, then, curl upward, flowing into the "rails." This tack slims out the top as does radiusing the rear wheel wells to match the front.

The Charger shares a common body shell with the Coronet, which has a 117-inch wheelbase and 203-inch over-all length. Total width is an identical 75 inches, as is height at 53, to a normal hardtop. Despite these similarities there's not much chance that you'll be apt to confuse the two cars. The Charger's single most arresting feature is as anticipated — that natty fastback roof that swoops at a rakish angle to the taillight.

Ah yes, we said the taillight, singular, and this is not a grammatical error, for one red ribbon of plastic stretches across the back, allowing fender-to-fender light. Underneath the plastic there are six bulbs to provide illumination in a single bank when braking or when the headlights are on. The turn signal indicators operate in banks of three for the appropriate side and no sequential arrangement is used, although it would be a natural step for a setup like this. Don't be surprised if it comes along later as a feature.

The grille chapter is twofold. First, it's one of the best uncluttered fronts ever put up by a manufacturer and second, Dodge joins the ranks of the hidden, folded-away-when-not-in-use headlight group. But they're one up. You see, the grille is comprised of a raft of die-cast chrome uprights, some which conceal nothing and others the quad lights. From even close range you can't tell where the lights are unless, of course, the switch is actuated, at which time they slowly rotate into position. Even then the lamping doesn't disrupt the over-all grille design. As an aside, it should be noted that there is a red warning light to tell the driver when the headlights are not open, besides a toggle

RIGHT — Down with Charger's seat backs and trunk separation and there's for things like sheet plywood.

BELOW RIGHT — Sculptured top sweeps to one piece plastic taillight.

BOTTOM RIGHT — All instruments are housed in shiny, round nacelles.

It's half-year introduction time again and Dodge is on the march with a sleek four-passenger fastback, a basket of power options and luxuriant interiors that invite you to come join the rebellion

CHARGER

photography: Eric Dahlquist, Dodge Corp.

switch to allow the lights to be exposed even though the switch might be off.

Charger interiors will surely set a standard of comparison because of their tasteful execution and design. The seating plan is arranged for four individuals with an armrest-cum-console configuration that runs the full length of the cockpit. Front buckets are of the new clamshell structure, stitched in slender, horizontal, vinyl-material pleats. And the rear seat backs fold down; the trunk separation does too and it's surfboard city-like room if you need it.

Standard Coronet instrumentation was well laid out as it was but the Charger goes it one better with four round, chromed nacelles that house, from left, alternator and gasoline meter, speedometer, 6000 rpm electric tach and temperature and oil pressure indicators. It's gaugeville and it's great, especially with glare-free, electroluminescent lighting and bold design. Another feature that gets a kudo or two is the wide-mouth glovebox and its door, which, when opened down, provides a nice spot, with recesses yet, for coffee or milk shake containers or what-have-you. Finally, the air circulation properties of the passenger compartment are enhanced greatly by two rubber-flapped ducts that exhaust stale air into the atmosphere. The "flaps" act as one-way air valves to eliminate the possibility of dust entering the interior when no air is escaping.

The standard powerplant for the Charger is the 318 cubic inch V8 with 2-barrel carburetor rated at 230 horsepower but the Silver Metallic machine with which we made hot laps around the course had the 383 cuber mit quad (325 horse), dual exhausts

and unsilenced air-cleaner. Other choices are the 361-inch V8 at 265 ponies and the 426 hemi-hummer for max belt. Should you order this last tidbit, you will also get all the good things like stiffer springs, larger brakes and such that were described in detail last month in the "street-hemi" road test.

Charger transmissioning offers a standard 3-speed manual with 3.02 low gear and an optional Torqueflite. 2.94 rear axle gears are supplied for both but you can get a 3.23 or, just for the manual, 3.55, at no extra cost. Brake linings are the 10x2.5-inch variety and the new, deep-dish-type 5½-inch rims with 7.35x14 skins of various makes fitted.

So off we went, Managing Editor Don Evans, Feature Editor Dick Wells, Associate Editor Jim McFarland and I, to wring out the Charger in the afternoon we had alloted to us. The car was without benefit of anything but entirely stock suspension and it showed as soon as we shot into the first turn, which happened to be the number nine sweeper. At above sixty there was a noticeable amount of understeer, but decreasing the speed a bit cured this, and bumping the tire pressure would have helped also. You wouldn't normally run into such a situation at this speed on the street but just to be sure an addition of the available .88-inch anti-sway bar would be well taken. On the same day we also had the opportunity of trying out a hemi-equipped Coronet that had the stiffer suspension parts and this really gets the job done with no bad aftertaste, blasting through the serpentine sequence with confidence. Its manners are so good and its

Continued on following page

CHARGER

power so abundant that you can actually quite successfully steer with the throttle.

The fact that the Charger offers the whole hemi ball of wax as optional equipment is especially interesting because you'd have the unique styling, the tremendous performance and the handling to go with it. The combo is probably one of the best, most practical packages ever beamed at the sporty-oriented individual.

Standard braking is on a par with the Charger's 383 propulsive force but front-wheel discs can be had if you like. We did not have the opportunity to weigh the car out at the track, but taking the Coronet similarly equipped, it ought to go 3700 pounds at the curb or thereabouts. In terms of the quarter-mile yardstick, this meant a best elapsed time of 16.28 seconds with a terminal velocity of 85

miles per hour. Jazzing up the engine compartment to 426 territory will improve this measurably, and what with the slippery shape, we wouldn't rule out the sight of a Charger or two making it around some of the NASCAR banked ovals during the season. And, because of the machine's distinctness, it might not make a bad exhibition or match racer.

We have a dream-wheel here at the office that will reasonably predict a car's performance from a given set of statistics like weight, horsepower, axle ratio, and tire size. One thing it cannot tell us, however, is whether a certain model will be a success or not but, all things equal, we make a wild guess that the Chargers may do just that, right to the head of the middle-class personal car field.

TOP — Wide mouth grille cavity is filled with numerous glittering uprights and four headlights when the switch is on. Flip the toggle off and the lights do a neat 180. ABOVE — Into the boondocks with vigor, Charger exposes another facet of its unique sporting character. RIGHT — 383 cubic inch powerplant in test vehicle is one of but many power choices available. Most interesting of all is 426 hemi that complements car's classy cast.

DODGE CHARGER MAJOR SPECIFICATIONS

ENGINES	BORE	STROKE	DISPLACEMENT	HORSEPOWER	TORQUE	COMPRESSION RATIO	FUEL
*(1)V-8 (2-bbl.)	3.91	3.31	318 cu. in.	230 @ 4400	340 @ 2400	9.0 to 1	Regular
V-8 (2-bbl.)	4.12	3.38	361 cu. in.	265 @ 4400	380 @ 2400	9.0 to 1	Regular
*(2)V-8 (4-bbl.)	4.25	3.38	383 cu. in.	325 @ 4800	425 @ 2800	10.0 to 1	Premium
*(3)V-8 2-4 bbl.)	4.25	3.75	426 cu. in.	425 @ 5000	490 @ 4000	10.0 to 1	Premium

*(1) Standard Engine   *(2) With Dual Exhaust and Unsilenced Air Cleaner   *(3) With Special Camshaft, Dual Exhaust, Unsilenced Air Cleaner Maximum Performance Camshaft Also Available

OVERALL:	Height: 53.0″ Length: 203.6″ Width: 75.3″ (Loaded)	**LEGROOM,**	Rear: 33.3″ Front: 41.6″	**TIRE PRESSURE,**	Rear: 24 lbs. Front: 24 lbs.
WHEELBASE:	117.0″	**TREAD,**	Rear: 58.5″ Front: 59.5″	**FUEL TANK CAPACITY:**	19 gals.
HEADROOM:	(Effective) Rear: 36.5″ Front: 37.7″	**TURNING CIRCLE,**	Curb-to-Curb: 40.9 ft.	**CRANKCASE CAPACITY:**	4 qts. (5 qts. w/426 engine)
SEAT HEIGHT:	Rear: 9.9″ Front: 8.6″	**TIRE SIZE:**	7.35 x 14	**COOLING SYSTEM CAPACITY** (Standard Engine) With Heater: Without Heater:	21 qts. 20 qts.

MARLiN
& CHARGER

Caught in the middle, but far from homeless, are the Marlin from AMC and Dodge's Charger. Neither has the compactness of the basic sports-personal archtypes such as Mustang and Camaro, nor the posh elegance to social climb their way into the company of the luxury-personals: Eldorado, Riviera, et al. Nor, it should be added, do they attempt to.

Each is looking for its own home in this fast-growing market. Most likely competition (in philosophy rather than sales volume) comes from Cougar and Firebird, both upgraded variations of smaller cars but with more of a performance image. Both aim at the driver who wants a sporty-type car, but who doesn't want to give up room and comfort and isn't ready to move into the more expensive category.

Charger assumes that the man interested in such a car also wants performance and will spring for bigger engines. American Motors takes a more conservative view of Marlin's prospective buyer, believing him more interested in the sporty look rather than the sporty reality. Both are large cars which fill *all* of the average marked parking space but neither drives like a monster, so they have some justification in claiming the sporty image.

The Charger, which had a late introduction in 1966, makes no external changes for 1967. The Marlin has been with us since 1965, when it received a rather chilly reception from the buying public. To offset this and to restore the sense of freshness it has an all-new front-end treatment but still retains the tapering fasback so reminiscent of the Tucker.

Seeking a corner of this market untouched by the competition, AMC emphasizes Marlin as a sports-personal car for the entire family. This isn't quite the contradiction in terms that it seems, for the head of the family spends a fair part of the day alone in the car. It is the only sports/personal car capable of transporting six adults, so a family with several children does not have to be a 2-car family, though it probably will be anyway.

Neither has shied away from controversial styling. Both are fastbacks, considered to be the sportiest shape and the most "in," thanks to the Sting Ray and several generations of Ferrari. They have their own distinctive interpretations of the form, and as with anything different, provoke much dispute over what is really a matter of personal taste. Not even the Camaro-Firebird shell inspires such a polarization of opinion.

Powertrain & Performance

Competition-oriented Dodge built up Charger's image as a hot one on both the NASCAR and USAC circuits in 1966 and moves that image to the street with engine options including the 426-cu.-in. Hemi that sometimes terrorizes Ford on the super-speedways. The sound of the 425-hp Hemi when fired up is unmistakeable; it gives goose pimples to enthusiasts and fits to the competition. It isn't really loud, just powerful and authoritative. Only the Shelby GT 350 and 500 offer a comparable sound.

With barely enough miles on the clock to permit high-speed driving, we turned the Hemi-Charger loose on the drag strip at Carlsbad. E.T.s ran in the mid-14-second bracket and our best trap speed was 100.33. All of this was in a genuine, unprepared street machine without benefit of cheater slicks. For comparison, the same car with the standard 318-cu.-in., 230-hp engine was more than two seconds and 25 mph away. The 383-cu.-in. engine option produced a 16.5 quarter at over 86 mph. The very rare 440 option ran close to the Hemi and may be a bit faster out of the hole.

We had the most time in the 383 and found it to be a very reasonable compromise. Ours had the 4-bbl. carb and, while it didn't burn any rubber unless we really made it do so, we were never starved for power with 325 horses. In 2-bbl. form, the same engine claims 270-hp which burns less gas, but isn't nearly as exciting to drive. This doesn't mean the smaller engines are slugs; they do take some of the charge out of the Charger, but even the 318 is peppy. The 318, for example, has enough power to cruise all day as fast as the law allows, taking most changes of gradient in stride, even if it can't accelerate as fast as the Hemi. The driver of a 318 is more aware of steep hills and must be more judicious about passing than his Hemi-mounted friend, although neither may care about standing quarters and stoplight-winternationals.

American Motors, which has eschewed any kind of competition in the past (but may change its mind under new management), offers nothing bigger than 343-cu.-in. in 235- and 280-hp versions. This puts the hottest Marlin in about the same class as the Charger with the 2-bbl. 383, a thought borne out by the performance tests. There was little to choose between them on the strip. The standard Marlin V-8 is a 200-hp engine of 290-cu.-in.

However, AMC has recently introduced a hot cam kit consisting of a high-lift, long-duration camshaft, competition-type hydraulic lifters, heavier valve springs with dampers and other valve train components for Olivers who want to twist more out of the V-8s. There are occasional rumors of a 390-cu.-in. engine being offered, but this hasn't come to pass.

Unlike Charger, Marlin offers a 6. In fact, they offer a pair of them. The difference between the 145- and 155-hp versions is a 1- versus 2-bbl. carburetor; both displace 232 cubic inches. The performance of these engines in our tests will start no rush of hot rodders to AMC showrooms, but they were not intended to. It was flat-out impossible to burn rubber (not surprising, since the biggest V-8 couldn't either), which made for a long, thoughtful 20-second plus ride down the strip. Even more thought-provoking is the problem of trying to accelerate into a hole in another lane of expressway traffic.

Who would buy such an engine? Someone who wants a sporty car, but belongs to the growing legion which commutes ever increasing distances from the suburbs to the city, while paying more and more for gas. So far, however, these people seem more inclined to solve their dilemma with a Mustang 6 or an import — and Marlin 6 sales are very low.

Handling, Steering & Stopping

Getting a Charger or Marlin around a turn is no great problem. Neither is a real sports car in this respect, but they don't throw the driver any curves either. On the straight we were pleased to notice that both were suitably shocked. There was none of the wallow that makes a long trip seem even longer.

If one of the cars is better than the rest, it is the Charger 318 by virtue of its weight distribution. With the small V-8, it comes very close to 50-50 distribution. Going to the bigger engines steals some of this, but even the Hemi version, which adds over 300 pounds to

Performance is part of the Charger image. Here our Hemi-powered test car is shown charging out of the hole at the drag strip. Stopping power was equally impressive.

Marlin profile shows how esthetic qualities of fastback are employed on a larger car.

From this angle Marlin (above) and Charger look almost identical. Biggest difference is the Charger's better rear visibility, thanks to full-width rear window, but both are restricted compared to notchbacks despite great glass area. Charger has bigger trunk.

MARLIN & CHARGER

Marlin rear seat (above) was meant to hold three. Charger has rear buckets, but various fold-down combinations lend versatility to luggage/passenger capacity.

the front end and more than 400 to the whole car, had no strong tendency to push the front end.

The Marlins also handled well compared to the opposition and far better than the other AMC products we've driven. Again, weight distribution is a major part of the story, for the 6 felt better than the V-8, at least going into a turn. But, lack of torque sometimes gave us a moment getting out of the turn.

Stopping the cars was an interesting problem. We've often found that a small-engine car with drums stops better than the same car with a bigger engine and discs. This proved out in the Marlins where the drum-braked 6 pulled up slightly shorter at 60 mph than the V-8 with power discs, though not as straight.

The Dodges were even more interesting and less predictable. The 318 stopped in an almost straight line in 147 feet; eight less than the best Marlin. This was with drums. The 383, also with drums, took eight feet more, the same as the Marlin 6. No surprise so far. The Hemi-Charger with discs did the same test in an amazing 133 feet, despite its greater front-end weight. The only conclusions we'll attempt to draw are that the bigger engine cars really need discs, and don't count on being able to stop faster than the car in front of you unless you know his engine and brakes.

Space, Comfort & Convenience

Both Marlin and Charger have done better than average by the driver and front-seat passenger. All the seat and upholstery variations we tried were comfortable, although we would give the edge to the Charger's buckets over the full-width seat that permits the Marlin to bill itself as a 6-passenger personal car. We also have some second thoughts about the fancy cloth that is standard in the Marlin. How fancy will it look in two years or so? The vinyl upholstery in the Charger has the texture and feel of real leather. The vinyl in the Marlin has a basket weave embossed on it which leaves room for some air to circulate and gives a non-skid effect. Instruments and controls are well laid out on both cars.

The problem of headroom for rear-seat passengers is the petard on which the fastbacks of the '40s were hoisted. The concept of the sports-personal car is that the rear seat will be used only occasionally. We might add that that occasional passenger had better be less than 5-foot-8 and forget about wearing a hat. This was equally true of both cars, although part of their total bulk is

doubtless due to the attempt to give the back-seat passenger as much room as possible. Neither does he have much foot room; he fairs better in the Marlin.

As far as luggage space is concerned, it's less a space problem than it is getting to it. The deck opening in the Marlin is very small to fit inside the trim strips. We were just barely able to load our 5th wheel through it and getting at the space is also tricky. Charger has a bigger deck lid, but a combination body stiffener-sill intrudes into the opening.

Best & Worst Features

The best feature of the Charger is that it offers stages of performance geared to attract the largest possible number of buyers. The bottom of the range has been chosen so as not to detract from the performance image by providing an engine no smaller than the majority are likely to want or be happy with, while putting engines at the top of the range as hot as any offered. Marlin has gone the other way and stuck with smaller, more economical engines. For the buyer who must be practical they

have given him something more exciting than the 2-door sedan he is used to.

Other appealing features were the Marlin's reclining seats, well worth the extra $44.65 to anyone who travels long distances on a forced-march schedule, and Charger's fold-down rear seats which augment the luggage compartment for those who hate to travel light. Both cars have excellent instrument lighting with shrouding that eliminates all straight-ahead glare.

Both suffer another fastback curse; restricted rear visibility. Rear windows are large, but the sloped angle limits the view to a slim slot. The Charger, with a wider window, has a slight edge, but neither is as good as the Mustang.

Even with their biggest engine options, neither has the pretensions of sports car performance that the Sting Ray or Shelby cars (or even the hot Mustangs, Camaros and Firebirds) can claim. Both hedge short of being luxury cars. But even being betwixt and between, each seeks a special part of the market, though not the same one.

—Bob Schilling

Charger

BODY STYLES	2-dr. fastback coupe
WHEELBASE	117.0 ins.
TRACK	59.3 ins. front; 58.5 ins. rear
OVERALL	Length: 203.6 ins.; width: 75.3 ins.; height: 53.8 ins.
TURNING DIAMETER	40.9 ft. curb-to-curb
GAS CAPACITY	19 gals.
SUSPENSION	Independent front with torsion bars; 1-piece rear axle, leaf springs
BRAKES	Drums standard; front discs optional
CONSTRUCTION	Unitized body and frame
ENGINES	230-hp V-8, 318-cu.-in. standard, 270- and 325-hp V-8s, 383-cu.-in., 375-hp V-8, 440-cu.-in. and 425-hp V-8, 426-cu.-in. Hemi optional
TRANSMISSIONS	3-spd. manual standard, 4-spd. manual and 3-spd. automatic optional

MANUFACTURER'S SUGGESTED RETAIL PRICE $3128.00

Performance

ACCELERATION (2 aboard)

	318	383	440	426 Hemi
	230 hp	325 hp	375 hp	425 hp
0-60	10.9 secs.	8.9 secs.	8.0 secs.	7.6 secs.
¼-mile	18.6 secs.	16.5 secs.	15.5 secs.	14.4 secs.
	76 mph	86.4 mph	93 mph	100 mph

BRAKING from 60 mph: 147 ft. 155 ft. 140 ft.* 133 ft.* (*disc front brakes)

MILEAGE — Avg. city: 13.3 mpg 12.1 mpg 11.7 mpg 11.7 mpg
Avg. highway: 17.9 mpg 15.2 mpg 14.4 mpg 14.6 mpg

Marlin

BODY STYLES	2-dr. fastback coupe
WHEELBASE	118.0 ins.
TRACK	58.6 ins. front; 58.5 ins. rear
OVERALL	Length: 201.5 ins.; width: 78.4 ins.; height: 53.8 ins.
TURNING DIAMETER	39.0 ft., curb-to-curb
GAS CAPACITY	21.5 gals.
SUSPENSION	Independent front, 1-piece rear axle; coil springs all wheels; heavy duty optional
BRAKES	Drums standard, front discs optional
CONSTRUCTION	Unitized body and frame
ENGINES	145-hp L-6 232-cu.-in. or 200-hp, V-8 290-cu.-in. standard; 155-hp L-6, 232-hp, 235- or 280-hp V-8, 343-cu.-in. optional

TRANSMISSIONS	3-spd. manual standard, 3-spd. manual with o'drive, Flash-O-Matic, Shift Command, or 4-spd. manual optional

MANUFACTURER'S SUGGESTED RETAIL PRICE $2859.00

Performance

ACCELERATION (2 aboard)

	L-6, 232-cu.-in.	V-8 343-cu.-in.
	155 hp	289 hp
0-60 mph	15.4 secs.	9.6 secs.
¼-mile	20.3 secs., 68 mph	17.6 secs., 82 mph
BRAKING	from 60 mph: 156 ft.	161 ft.
MILEAGE	Avg. city: 17.3 mpg	15.3 mpg
	Avg. highway: 20.4 mpg	17.6 mpg

CAR and DRIVER ROAD TEST

DODGE CHARGER

Detroit's latest
fastback is a neat
package of proven
components, but the
best of the Charger
is·yet to come!

You've got to admit that "Charger" is a pretty neat name for an automobile. It's gutsy sounding, and best of all, it brings about a refreshing departure from the current Detroit fashion of naming so-called sporting vehicles after various members of *Regna Animalis*.

An occasional wild horse is fine, and maybe even a predatory fish or two, but being aware of the bandwagon instinct that flourishes in the Motor City, we have recurrent nightmares of minor executives by the dozen, poring through zoology texts seeking new car names. Hopefully, those volumes will be closed with the introduction of the Charger.

This new vehicle is the latest Detroit entrant into the burgeoning field of fastbacks. After falling out of style during the 1940s, the sloping roofline began its. renaissance with the introduction of the Plymouth Barracuda in 1964. Hard on its heels came the Mustang 2+2 and the Rambler Marlin, and now the Charger. When Chrysler Corporation developed the Barracuda, management gave Dodge Division the option of marketing its own version with different trim work or developing a completely new sports model on the 117-inch Coronet wheelbase. Recalling the thundering failure when Plymouth and Dodge joined to market the near-identical Valiants and Lancers, the Dodge boys chose to develop their own ver-

sion, even though it would mean a one-year delay in getting the automobile on the market.

Dodge had planned to get the Charger into production as a late arrival in the 1965 lineup, but production difficulties delayed its debut until the 1966 model year. This forced Dodge to make a minor adjustment in their promotional strategy, because the entire line of '66s was intended to reflect the "Charger look." Obviously, this was a bit difficult to accomplish as long as the regular models were going to reach the public before the Charger, but the fact remains that there is a strong generic resemblance between the Charger and the entire intermediate-sized Coronet lineup.

Despite the fact that one of the Charger's major styling features is a grille with concealed headlights, the entire frontal treatment has a strong Coronet flavor. This is due primarily to the fact that the same long, narrow rectangle encloses the grillework on both cars, and when the headlights are exposed on the Charger, it looks like a Coronet. The disappearing headlights on the Charger are electrically powered, and operate automatically when the lights are turned on and off. However, they can be left permanently exposed merely by snapping another switch on the Charger instrument panel.

The artistic challenge of placing a streamlined, fastback shape on a wheelbase of 117 inches is not inconsequential and Dodge Chief Stylist William Brownlie and his staff were generally successful in pulling it off. The car looks fine in profile, though it does seem to sit rather high on the suspension. Viewed from a three-quarters front angle, the Charger has a decidedly narrow look about it, but this certainly isn't pronounced enough to offend anyone's sensibilities. There is nothing garish about the Charger; aside from some subdued reliefs in the forward section of the rear fenders, the sides of the car are crisp, simple and tasteful. A cynic recently described the Charger as a "good-looking Marlin," but that isn't a fair appraisal. To be sure, the basic shapes of the two cars are similar, but all of the flashy spaceship styling of the Marlin is lacking in the Charger, and it is to Dodge's everlasting credit that they resisted the temptation to dapple its exterior with the customary chromium frosting.

Our only strong objection to the

styling of the Charger involves the wheel covers. They are an uninspired version of the standard phony wheel discs, complete with phony knock-off hubs. With a new trend toward functional wheels without decoration of any kind, it is a bit disappointing that Dodge is sticking with the same old hokum. It may be that the company will make the custom Cragar wheels available as an option (as with the Dart and Coronet series), and they would make a welcome addition to the line.

The interior provides a rather pleasant environment for four peo-

ple—and no more. Carrying the console to its ultimate conclusion, the right-hand seats are separated from the left by a high ridge that runs the entire length of the passenger compartment like a backbone. This means that accommodations are limited to four persons under all conditions. The rear seat-backs fold down—as with the other Detroit fastbacks—and plenty of utility space is available in the back. We found the headroom in the rear to be adequate for adults, though the seating is not what you would describe as sumptuous. The seat-backs are too low and too upright and the footroom is too limited for really comfortable travel by a person more than six feet tall. On the positive side, the designers have placed the sloping rear window far enough aft so the rear passengers are adequately protected from the sun. Several of the new fastbacks have such large glass areas over the rear seats that the passengers get the impression that they are traveling in a solarium. Not so with the Charger.

Up front, the instrument panel layout is basically Coronet, though the idiot lights of the regular line have given way to a full set of dials, including a tachometer. The panel styling just misses being outstanding, due primarily to a trifle too much chrome. We would have liked the starkly efficient brand of instrumentation found on the Corvette and the 1966 Barracuda Formula S, but you can't have everything.

The seating position is fine and the relationship between the pedals, the steering wheel and the console-mounted shift lever is excellent. Our only complaint involves the optional ersatz wood-rim steering wheel, and the same thing goes for other brands in the industry. With the new sporty wheels has come a tendency to relocate the horn button on the steering wheel hub, where a hand must be removed from the rim to reach it. While *C/D* does not subscribe to the "honk and be damned" school of driving, there are numerous situations where a blast on the

horn can reduce the danger of an accident. Therefore, the horn should be reachable—preferably with the thumbs—without having to steer one-handed. We love the new wood-rim wheels, but let's hope that Detroit sees fit to integrate horn rings into them in the near future.

The Charger is the first vehicle to use a new one-piece headliner made from molded fiberglas. Its surface is a special nylon fabric that is both scratch and soot resistant, while the fiberglas is supposed to provide outstanding temperature and sound insulation.

Naturally you can expect a great deal of noise from Dodge about the "all new" Charger, but the fact remains that it is really a jazzed-up Coronet. In addition to the chassis and wheelbase, the Charger shares the same suspension, powerplants and brakes with its parent car. In fact, its body has practically the

same dimensions as a Coronet two-door hardtop. It is six-tenths of an inch longer than the Coronet (203.6 inches), while both models have an identical girth (75.3 inches).

This similarity is in itself not a bad thing, because the components that have been lifted from the Coronet are in themselves properly, if conventionally, designed. The suspension is standard Chrysler, with torsion bars up front and leaf springs at the rear. The brakes are drums, 10 x 2½ inches, fore and aft. This setup is not particularly great, and look for Dodge to announce disc brakes for the Charger (and the entire Dodge Coronet and Plymouth Belvedere lines as well) about the same time the fabled 426 Hemi is offered as an option, in mid-February.

The basic Charger engine is the old reliable 318 cubic inch V-8, equipped with a two-barrel carburetor and rated at a pallid 230 horse-

power. Our test car contained the optional 383-cubic inch four-barrel, developing 325 horsepower. The engine was coupled to the outstanding Chrysler Corporation three-speed Torque-Flite automatic transmission, though the Corporation's equally effective four-speed is also available. A manual three-speed is standard equipment on the Charger.

Ignition timing varies slightly between the 383s set up for automatic and manual transmission duty, with the latter having a decidedly fiercer feel. Our test car lacked the potent throb that one comes to expect from the 383 four-barrel set-up. Though the difference in performance is negligible, there is a certain appeal, based on the impression of power, from the unit set up for the manual transmission, and we frankly missed it on our test car.

Because of its strong heritage, it would be a denial of all logic if the Charger didn't feel like a Coronet on the road. Indeed it does feel like a Coronet, and that, we suppose, should not be interpreted as a drawback. The Dodge Coronet is a well-engineered, medium-sized vehicle with a properly located beam rear axle and sensible weight distribution. The Charger is a good automobile, make no mistake about it, but we had somehow expected more when we first got behind the wheel. Maybe it's because the sporty styling conjured up the fantasy of all sorts of exotic engineering underneath. At any rate, we failed to get terribly turned on with the car during our initial tests. It wasn't that we disliked it, it was just the fact that we'd been there before—in an ordinary Coronet.

The Charger runs a true and relatively silent course at 100 mph, with considerably less wind noise than most of the Chrysler line. It corners with grace, if not great style, and it provides a good, workaday balance between powerplant, transmission and suspension. But like we said, why shouldn't it, the Coronet being what it is?

There is no question that any reservations about the Charger based on blandness would have been nonexistent had the test car been equipped with the Hemi. This engine, the very mention of which makes bold men pause to wonder, is maybe the most exciting powerplant to arrive on the American market since the supercharged Duesenberg straight-eight. It is rated at a ludicrously conservative 425 horsepower—primarily to keep the

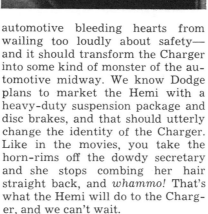

automotive bleeding hearts from wailing too loudly about safety—and it should transform the Charger into some kind of monster of the automotive midway. We know Dodge plans to market the Hemi with a heavy-duty suspension package and disc brakes, and that should utterly change the identity of the Charger. Like in the movies, you take the horn-rims off the dowdy secretary and she stops combing her hair straight back, and *whammo!* That's what the Hemi will do to the Charger, and we can't wait.

As it is, the car is designed to penetrate the market somewhere in the over-$3000 category. This means it will be slightly more expensive than the Mustang GT and the Formula S Barracuda, but highly competitive with the Fairlane GT/A, the Chevelle 396 and the Pontiac GTO. In its stock form, the Charger won't have the steam to compete in this league, though the 383 with four-speed, *et al,* should be a contender. But then, we have the Hemi on the horizon, don't we?

The Dodge Charger is basically a performance automobile, and the market in which it will either succeed or fail is that which responds to exaggerated emphasis on raw horsepower and the inherent glamour of speed. Therefore we question the reason for marketing the car

with the 318 or the similarly-tame 361 engines at all. Plymouth initially made the mistake of making the Barracuda emit what the corporation officials liked to call "broad appeal," and was later forced to jazz the car up with the Formula S option. We know the Dodge management is not about to write the Charger off on such a basis, but it is possible that an unerring adherence to the performance line would be the best way to market the car. It might narrow the appeal of the Charger slightly, but the glitter of excitement it would cast on the rest of the Dodge line, from the economy sizes to the plush Polaras, might more than compensate for any loss in sales. With the Chargers expected to bear the burden of Dodge's NASCAR racing fortunes in 1966, the case for stacking the deck in favor of performance becomes even stronger. The Charger will run in NASCAR's "intermediate" class, with a destroked 405 cu.in. Hemi. Wind-tunnel tests have indicated the car's shape is indeed slippery—there's little question it'll be a contender at Daytona and Charlotte. Performance like this *has* to be exploitable in the showroom.

At any rate, please hurry up with that Hemi. **c/D**

Specifications overleaf

DODGE CHARGER

Manufacturer: Dodge Division
Chrysler Corporation
Detroit 31, Michigan

Price as tested: $3471.83 FOB Detroit

ACCELERATION

Zero to	Seconds
30 mph	3.2
40 mph	4.3
50 mph	5.7
60 mph	7.8
70 mph	10.2
80 mph	13.1
90 mph	16.9
100 mph	21.8
Standing ¼ mile	88 mph in 16.2

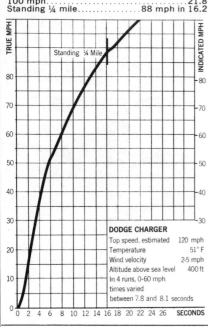

DODGE CHARGER

Top speed, estimated	120 mph
Temperature	51° F
Wind velocity	2-5 mph
Altitude above sea level	400 ft

In 4 runs, 0-60 mph times varied between 7.8 and 8.1 seconds

ENGINE

Water-cooled V-8, cast iron block, 5 main bearings
Bore x stroke.4.25 x 3.38 in, 108.9 x 86.6 mm
Displacement.................383 cu. in, 6277 cc
Compression ratio..................10.0 to one
Carburetion..........Single downdraft 4-barrel
Valve gear. Pushrod-operated overhead valves, hydraulic lifters
Power (SAE)...........325 bhp @ 4800 rpm
Torque...........425 lbs-ft @ 2800 rpm
Specific power output........85 bhp per cu. in, 51.8 bhp per liter
Usable range of engine speeds.500–5500 rpm
Electrical system...12-volt, 70 amp-hr battery, 400W alternator
Fuel recommended.................Premium
Mileage........................12–16 mpg
Range on 19-gallon tank.......228–304 miles

DRIVE TRAIN

Transmission. 3-speed automatic, plus torque converter

Gear	Ratio	Overall	mph/1000 rpm	Max mph
Rev	2.20	7.11	−10.6	−58
1st	2.45	7.91	9.5	52
2nd	1.45	4.68	16.1	89
3rd	1.00	3.23	23.3	120

Final drive ratio.................3.23 to one

CHASSIS

Wheelbase.........................117.0 in
Track.................F 59.5 R 58.5 in
Length...........................203.6 in
Width.............................75.3 in
Height............................54.3 in
Ground Clearance....................5.8 in
Curb Weight.....................3650 lbs
Test Weight.....................3840 lbs
Weight distribution front/rear.........51/49%
Pounds per bhp (test weight).............11.81
Suspension F: Ind., unequal-length wishbones, torsion bars, stabilizer bar
R: Beam axle, semi-elliptic leaf springs
Brakes.............10-in drums front and rear, 340.2 sq in swept area
Steering.................Rack and sector
Turns, lock to lock..................3.5
Turning circle.....................40.9 ft
Tires and wheels........7.35-14 on 5.5-in rim

CHECK LIST

ENGINE

Starting	Good
Response	Good
Noise	Good
Vibration	Good

DRIVE TRAIN

Clutch action	—
Transmission linkage	—
Synchromesh action	—
Power-to-ground transmission	Fair

BRAKES

Response	Good
Pedal pressure	Good
Fade resistance	Fair
Smoothness	Very Good
Directional stability	Good

STEERING

Response	Good
Accuracy	Very Good
Feedback	Good
Road feel	Fair

SUSPENSION

Harshness control	Very Good
Roll stiffness	Good
Tracking	Good
Pitch control	Good
Shock damping	Very Good

CONTROLS

Location	Good
Relationship	Very Good
Small controls	Good

INTERIOR

Visibility	Good
Instrumentation	Good
Lighting	Good
Entry/exit	Very Good
Front seating comfort	Good
Front seating room	Good
Rear seating comfort	Fair
Rear seating room	Fair
Storage space	Excellent
Wind noise	Good
Road noise	Good

WEATHER PROTECTION

Heater	Very Good
Defroster	Good
Ventilation	Good
Weather sealing	Fair
Windshield wiper action	Good

QUALITY CONTROL

Materials, exterior	Good
Materials, interior	Good
Exterior finish	Good
Interior finish	Good
Hardware and trim	Fair

GENERAL

Service accessibility	Fair
Luggage space	Very Good
Bumper protection	Fair
Exterior lighting	Good
Resistance to crosswinds	Good

EVEN CUSTER COULDN'T MUSTER
A STAMPEDE LIKE THIS

Dodge Charger musters enough horses, with optional 426 Hemi V8 or 440-Magnum, to mount up a whole cavalry troop. And then some. Along with each of these smooth, powerful, responsive performers, you get a whole package of special handling equipment to make America's first full-sized fastback behave like a thoroughbred: heavy-duty suspension, high-performance nylon tires, and big 11-inch brakes (with discs optional up front). Every Charger has a dash-mounted tach, front buckets and fold-down rear seats, full-width taillights, plus disappearing head lamps that blend beautifully with the front end styling. Check it out for yourself . . . Dodge Charger, a balanced automobile engineered for the enthusiast.

It's Dodge Rebellion Operation '67

'67 Dodge Charger

DODGE DIVISION    CHRYSLER MOTORS CORPORATION

Dodge's Fastback Fullback Plays Offense and Defense

SCOREBOARD LIGHTS read: "Third down, three yards to go." In the huddle, the quarterback earnestly calls the play. Across the stadium that die-hard fan blows his bugle once again. "Ta-da-da-dah-da-daaah!" The partisan crowd responds with one roaring voice, "CHARRRRRGE!"

The quarterback takes the snap and hands off to the fullback who bulls his way through the crush of straining bodies, straight up the middle for that three yards and inches to spare. The crowd bellows approval.

As professional football fullbacks provide excitement, so do the automotive fastback fullbacks from Dodge. The enthusiast who desires to play the game can huddle with his Dodge dealer and call on the player of the year, that big, strong, tough fullback, the Hemi/Charger. Ever afterward as he tramps down on the Hemi/Charger's accelerator pedal, the owner will hear that bugled "Ta-da-da-dah-da-daaah!"

and his lips will automatically, silently form that word, "CHARRRRRGE!"

Driving the Dodge Hemi/Charger is like quarterbacking the Green Bay Packers. Call the play, and the job gets done with great speed, strength and agility. The power and speed of the Hemi/Charger stem directly from what is underhood—simply the current NASCAR champion engine in its twin 4-barrel-carburetored, 10.25:1 compression street form. In this tune, the 426-cu. in. engine is rated at 425 bhp at 5000 rpm (110 mph), with torque delivery maximum of 490 lb.-ft. at 4000 rpm (89 mph), but proves eminently tractable for the street and singularly tenacious for the strip.

In addition to the Hemi/Charger, Dodge Division makes available engine options to create the Demi/Charger and the Magna/Charger. The Demi category includes Chargers powered by the 2-barrel carburetored, 318-cu. in./230-bhp engine, or 383-cu. in. V-8s

rated at 270 bhp in single 2-barrel trim or 325-bhp with a single 4-barrel carburetor. The Magna/Charger is distinguished by installation of the largest of all Chrysler Corp. engines, the 440-cu. in. V-8, rated at 375 bhp with one 4-barrel carburetor.

But for brute strength for a Charger, the 426-cu. in. hemispherical combustion chamber engine is the choice. Its cylinder block, for example, carries special reinforcement at the main bearing webs, and main bearings No. 2, 3 and 4 are secured with horizontal tiebolts through the sides of the block to the bearing caps. Heads have additional tie-downs by special studs and nuts that are tightened from inside the tappet chamber. Domed pistons are of extruded aluminum.

The Hemi's crankshaft is forged from carbon steel. Added strength comes in the form of shot-peened fillets and a special nitriding dip to harden the entire surface of the crank to aid in resistance to fatigue. Extra-wide oil grooves in main bearings help protect this strength in high speed operation.

The high lift camshaft, driven off the forward end of the crank by a dou-

CAR LIFE
ROAD TEST

the primary throttle blades of the forward carburetor to remain closed until the rear carburetor's primary blades are 40% open. After this point is reached, both sets of primary blades travel in unison, reaching full open position simultaneously. The secondary barrels of both carburetors are velocity actuated by the flow of incoming air. Weights hold the valves closed until the air velocity pressure drop overcomes the counterweights and the secondaries swing open.

Manifold and carburetors are isolated from the top of the cylinder block by a heat shield that minimizes transfer of heat from engine oil to the incoming fuel/air charge. Heat riser tubes, when the engine is cold, carry hot exhaust gasses through heat passages in the intake manifold. As engine heat increases, a thermostatically controlled valve reduces gas flow through the riser tubes, thus regulating mixture temperature for smoother warmup operation.

Gasses from the engine's internal activity are dumped through cast iron exhaust headers and thence into dual 2.5-in. exhaust pipes. A 4-speed manual gearbox is available with the Hemi engine, but a TorqueFlite 3-speed automatic was fitted to CAR LIFE's test Charger.

If the engine can be likened to a fullback, then this transmission must be compared to the fleet halfback who can run the sweeps and the tricky veers on quick-openers, who can catch flare passes and the bomb, who can run the pass option and who comes in to kick the extra points as well. The TorqueFlite transmission, if allowed to remain in "Drive" position, shifts for itself, plays the field, chooses the right gear for trickling through traffic, passing on a short stretch of straight, or snarling up the dragstrip for automatic gear change quarter-mile times of under 15 sec. But, when called upon by the driver to do so, the transmission can be held in first and second gears for so long as is desired. CL, with some prudence, chose 6000 rpm as the manual shift point for the automatic and therewith recorded top time in acceleration runs conducted at Carlsbad (Calif.) Raceway.

WHEN A PLYMOUTH Satellite with a similar Street Hemi engine underhood was tested (CL, July '66) the transmission's torque converter maximum ratio at stall was 2.2:1. Automatics being installed with the Hemi engines in Chrysler Corp. cars now have torque converter maximum ratio at stall of 2.0:1. This means the 1967 TorqueFlite unit is a little tighter and is inclined toward creep at engine idle—but to some enthusiasts, converter creep means a more responsive,

ble roller chain, is made of hardened cast iron and is specially coated for protection from scuffing. Valve duration and timing aim not only at smooth operation at low engine speeds for normal street and highway operation, but also at efficient high speed breathing and top power output.

The valve train itself is made up of mechanical tappets, tubular pushrods and forged steel rocker arms, all designed for light weight with maximum strength for sustained high speed operation. Heavy-duty concentric outer and inner valve springs, and valve spring dampers, also are engineered to allow maximum performance.

NESTLED IN THE vee is the aluminum tandem intake manifold. Branches of the manifold are shaped to provide free flow of the fuel/air charge to all cylinders over a wide range of engine speeds for street and strip flexibility. (The NASCAR version of the Hemi employs a ram manifold, tuned for peak performance in a much less broad engine speed range.) Atop the manifold are two Carter carburetors, an AFB-4324S forward, an AFB-4325S at the rear. Staged throttle linkage permits

CHARGER

much more competitive transmission.

With a 3.23:1 ratio in a limited slip rear axle, the 426/TorqueFlite combination could produce great amounts of smoking, useless wheelspin when the car was called upon to perform for show, not for go. However, judicious application of the foot throttle to maintain a rate of power application just short of wheelspin, and the 6000 rpm manual gear changes, snapped off the 14.16-sec. quarter-mile time for the Charger, though it carried two test crewmen, a crate of test equipment and a full tank of fuel. What would have been Charger's e.t. had there been but one man aboard, had there been little fuel in the tank, and had test equipment remained at the editorial office? Conjecture is that the car would have performed well down in the 13s—and that a set of drag slicks at the rear could have made great additional improvement.

The hefty Hemi engine, the Torque-Flite transmission, the taut Charger unitized body and all else that added up to test weight of 4560 lb. required some husky suspension components— not only to cope with the massive weight of the so-called intermediate sized fastback, but to give it a measure of handling facility.

Forward, in the Hemi/Charger combination, are torsion bars of 0.92-in. diameter, the largest offered in Dodge's Charger/Coronet catalog. These longitudinal torsion bars and associated telescopic shock absorbers offer a ride rate of 118 lb./in. at the wheel, also stiffest in the Charger/Coronet specification book. An anti-roll bar of 0.94-in. diameter is standard on the Hemi-equipped Charger, but is optional on Chargers supplied with engines of lesser piston displacement. At the rear, the Hemi/Charger's longitudinal semi-elliptic leaf springs, measuring 58 x 2.5 in., carry two more leaves than, for example, the rear springs on a 383-cu. in. engine-equipped Charger. These rear springs of the Hemi/Charger give the stiffest-of-all Dodge ride rates, 159 lb./in. at the wheel.

One Dodge Division representative described this stiffest-of-all suspension system: "The handling package, the police package, the trailer towing package, the rally package, it's the same thing, whatever you want to call it, but it's a darn good system."

He proved correct in his statement. The suspension system, though immensely firm, was not harsh and allowed sufficient cushioning to smooth out minor roadway irregularities. The system also provided enough bite for some measure of cornering capability and thoroughly eliminated the tractive instability which plagues some of the more softly sprung Chrysler Corp. cars.

Power-assisted steering, optional on all Chargers, was welcome on this front-heavy Hemi/Charger as it took the effort out of changing the car's direction, yet was quick enough for smart maneuvering.

In some ways, suspension and steering of the Hemi/Charger could be likened to the professional football linebacker. There's not much glory in the job, but the job must be done, surely and well.

Obviously, where there's an offense, there must be a defense to make up a balanced team. Where the Hemi/Charger is concerned, 387.8 sq. in. of braking swept area seems a fairly adequate defense. When *CAR LIFE* testers twice applied the defensive mechanism in all-on stops from 80 mph, the result was smooth deceleration at the rate of 27 ft./sec./sec.— both times. Then the Hemi/Charger did what other, lighter cars haven't been able to do. Test drivers added repeated stops at 27 ft./sec./sec., all accomplished without untoward directional changes, though there was a slight grab here and there, but no extreme rear wheel lockup and only minor vacuum runout on the third and fourth stops.

Generating this outstanding stopping power was a disc-front/drum-

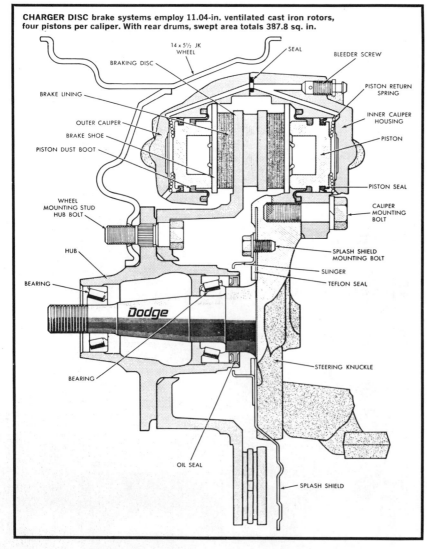

CHARGER DISC brake systems employ 11.04-in. ventilated cast iron rotors, four pistons per caliper. With rear drums, swept area totals 387.8 sq. in.

14 x 5½ JK WHEEL — SEAL — BLEEDER SCREW — BRAKING DISC — BRAKE LINING — OUTER CALIPER — BRAKE SHOE — PISTON DUST BOOT — WHEEL MOUNTING STUD HUB BOLT — HUB — BEARING — BEARING — OIL SEAL — SPLASH SHIELD — PISTON RETURN SPRING — INNER CALIPER HOUSING — PISTON — PISTON SEAL — CALIPER MOUNTING BOLT — SPLASH SHIELD MOUNTING BOLT — SLINGER — TEFLON SEAL — STEERING KNUCKLE — Dodge

rear, 2-circuit, vacuum assisted braking system of the type now universally available as optional, or in some cases standard, equipment on all U.S.-made passenger cars. This sort of brake efficiency was a long time in coming, but is heartily welcomed by car enthusiasts and safety-conscious family men, along with those who would enter automotive competitions. The regrettable part of the entire matter of brakes is that some manufacturers persist in retention of small diameter drum brakes as standard equipment. This pusillanimous braking equipment has time and again proven less effective, less capable of stopping cars than all disc or even disc/drum systems such as that of the Hemi/Charger. Until the latter is made standard equipment, the defensively oriented purchaser must continue to shell out additional cash for the best available defensive team. Those small diameter drums should go the way of the flying wedge.

THE 1967 HEMI/Charger supplied to CAR LIFE showed only minor trim changes from 1966, the Charger's introduction year. Perhaps because 1967 is the second year of production for the Charger, the test car displayed a more finished exterior—more smoothly applied paint and less wide gaps between panels, for examples. Full-width taillights, and the roll-up headlamp eyelids remain as Charger hallmarks. Rear fender panels, smooth in 1966, for 1967 carry notched indentations just rearward of the door pillar. These faintly recall Buck Rogers comic strip rocket ships of the 1930s. The incongruity approaches that of a Green Bay Packer turning up for a ballgame in ballet slippers.

The interior of the Charger also is little changed from 1966. Instruments, including speedometer/odometer, tachometer and gauges are located in four circular pods arrayed across the dash in front of the driver. Numerals and letters, i.e., E-F for fuel, are backlighted cutouts in the circumference

RATED AT 425 bhp, with torque delivery at 490 lb.-ft., the 426-cu. in. hemispherical combustion chamber engine from Chrysler is capable of very strong acceleration, yet is gentle enough for town and freeway.

of the pods. These do not lend themselves well to daylight visibility, but when they are illuminated a fluorescent green for nighttime operation, they prove quite satisfactory. On the console of the test Hemi/Charger, where other manufacturers often locate tachometers, was a clock, its face angled toward the driver. The clock was useful—once the driver became accustomed to its odd location.

Two perennial complaints were noticed within the Hemi/Charger. Carpeting seemed more hacked to size than cut to fit, giving the floor of the car a rag-tag appareance. And, a header molding along the curve of the pillarless expanse of side glass was loose, and hummed and fluttered in the wind

when windows were open. The same condition was noted in the Charger tested earlier (CL, June '66).

One of the advertised selling points of the Charger fastback is the fold-down seating and the flip-down luggage compartment transverse bulkhead which create a seemingly vast expanse of straight-through cargo area behind the driver/passenger compartment. Usefulness of this cargo space, however, is debatable. If an item of cargo—a cooler chest containing 25 lb. of ice, three cartons of soft drinks and lunch, for example—will not fit into the narrow, shallow luggage compartment, it must be placed inside the car, on the folded-down cargo deck. If one isn't a defensive tackle who has

ORNAMENTAL BARS across the Charger's seatbacks were a source of passenger irritation and complaint.

LEG room in abundance is provided for driver and passengers.

MINIMUM TRUNK space and maximum liftover height both are attributable to the Charger's roomy forward, cramped rearward fastback configuration.

chronic complainer about lack of leg room, was satisfied with the Charger accommodations for his frame after a long, looping Sunday circuit.

One gripe stated vehemently by several test crew personnel, their friends, families and other occasional passengers, was with a very hard ornamental bar across all four seat backs. This useless styling fillip was thoughtlessly placed exactly where spines curve and where shoulder blades rest. Fitting purgatory for the stylist who sketched in that little bar would be for him to sit, just sit, in that seat for 1000 miles.

A BIT OF HUMAN engineering also could well have been expended on placement of restraint belts. The manner in which shoulder belts for front seat passengers were installed would be termed, in the vernacular of football, "a busted play." While lap belts were anchored in the conventional fashion, the shoulder belts, some 6 ft. in length, were secured to the body behind the rear seats. This meant that each time cross-chest belts were removed, they were placed on the floor to be kicked and tangled on exit and entry by driver and passengers. The drill was to gather up all the belts, match buckles and tangs, hitch the lap belt, unkink and fasten the shoulder

paid great attention to his isometric exercises, the loading task proves all but impossible. A larger cargo hatch at the rear, perhaps with some of that expanse of glass hinged in some manner, would be welcome to weekend picnickers, campers, fishermen and other haulers of the big and bulky. Perhaps installation of a trailer hitch would solve the cargo problem.

With the rear seats locked in position, cargo space becomes minimal, and rear passenger space absolutely is for no more than two persons—adults or children. The Charger truly is a 2 plus 2 car.

Space for heads, legs, knees, hips and shoulders is more than adequate for four persons within the Charger fastback body. CL's tall tester, the

---

1967 DODGE CHARGER
2-DOOR HARDTOP

DIMENSIONS

Wheelbase, in.	117.0
Track, f/r, in.	59.5/58.5
Overall length, in.	203.6
width	75.3
height	53.8
Front seat hip room, in.	2 x 22.4
shoulder room	58.0
head room	37.7
pedal-seatback, max.	44.9
Rear seat hip room, in.	2 x 19.9
shoulder room	53.4
leg room	34.0
head room	36.5
Door opening width, in.	42.0
Floor to ground height, in.	11.4
Ground clearance, in.	6.1

PRICES

List, fob factory	$3263
Equipped as tested	5289

Options included: Hemi engine; auto. trans.; 3.23 limited slip; radio and heater, power steering, windows and disc brakes; headrests and exterior trim; wheel covers; special handling package; Goodyear HP Power Cushions.

CAPACITIES

No. of passengers	4
Luggage space, cu. ft.	n.a.
Fuel tank, gal.	19.0
Crankcase, qt.	4.0
Transmission/diff., pt.	8.5
Radiator coolant, qt.	18.0

CHASSIS/SUSPENSION

Frame type	unitized

Front suspension type: Independent by s.l.a., ball joints, torsion bars, telescopic shock absorbers.

ride rate at wheel, lb./in.	118
anti-roll bar dia., in.	0.94

Rear suspension type: Live axle, Hotchkiss drive, multi-leaf longitudinal semi-elliptic springs, telescopic shock absorbers.

ride rate at wheel, lb./in.	159

Steering system: Integral power assisted recirculating ball, parallelogram linkage with trailing, parallel Pitman and idler arms.

gear ratio	15.7
overall ratio	19.12
turns, lock to lock	3.5
turning circle, ft. curb-curb	40.9
Curb weight, lb.	4160
Test weight	4560
Weight distribution, % f/r	53.9/46.1

BRAKES

Type: Two-circuit hydraulic, with 4-piston caliper, vented cast iron rotors, front; duo-servo shoes in composite drums, rear.

Front rotor, dia., in.	11.04
Rear drum, dia. x width	10 x 2.5
total swept area, sq. in.	387.8

Power assist: integral vacuum

line psi @ 100 lb. pedal	1510

WHEELS/TIRES

Wheel size	5.5K
optional size available	5.5JK
bolt no./circle dia., in.	5/4.5

Tires: Goodyear HP Power Cushion

size	7.75-14
recommended inflation, psi	24
capacity rating, total lb.	5080

ENGINE

Type, no. cyl.	ohv, 90° V-8
Bore x stroke, in.	4.25 x 3.75
Displacement, cu. in.	425.3696
Compression ratio	10.25
Rated bhp @ rpm	425 @ 5000
equivalent mph	112
Rated torque @ rpm	490 @ 4000
equivalent mph	90
Carburetion	Carter, 2x4
barrel dia., pri./sec.	1.44/1.69

Valve operation: Mechanical lifters, pushrods, overhead rocker arms.

valve dia., int./exh.	2.25/1.94
lift, int./exh.	0.480/0.460
timing, deg.	30-66, 74-22
duration, int./exh.	276/276
opening overlap	52

Exhaust system: Dual reverse-flow mufflers.

pipe dia., exh./tail	2.50/2.25
Lubrication pump type	rotary
normal press. @ rpm	45-65 @ 2000
Electrical supply	alternator
ampere rating	37 @ 12 V.
Battery, plates/amp. rating	78/70

DRIVE-TRAIN

Clutch type	
dia., in.	

Transmission type: Automatic with torque converter and planetary gearbox.

Gear ratio 3rd (1.00) overall	3.23
2nd (1.45)	4.68
1st (2.45)	7.92
1st x t. c. stall (2.00)	15.83
Shift lever location	console

Differential type: Hypoid with torque bias limited-slip.

axle ratio	3.23

strap, in a state of maximum grope, then discover that the driver thus trussed could not release the parking brake, tune a bit of music on the radio or set the clock.

Upholstery was in an ocher shade of vinyl, contrasted with the deep green of the exterior paint, and the black of the nylon carpeting, chromium accented dashboard and vinyl covered dashboard padding. The scheme was sporting, rather than sedate, as is fitting for a car with the ability to "CHARRRRRGE!"

A ND, CHARGING is where the Hemi/- Charger seems most at home. The simple chore of matching freeway speeds from inclined on-ramps allows short unleashings of the 426-cu. in. engine that are purely delightful. Passing slower vehicles on steep, straight upgrades involves the driver in the pleasures of 8-barrel carburetion. The knowledge that the car is king at the stoplight, but making no arrogant display of this monarchy is the oneupsmanship of Hemi/Chargering.

Only once in a great while does the opportunity present itself to CAR LIFE test crewmen to do a little belly-to-the-ground automobile racing. The day CL's test team took the Hemi/-Charger to Carlsbad Raceway, who

BODY LINES of the fastback Charger are little changed for 1967, but panel fit, application of paint and interior finish seem improved.

should appear but the lads from next door, the Road & Track magazine test crew with a 440-cu. in. Magnum-engined Dodge R/T in hand. Solo runs against the electronic timers were the order of the day until, as if by mere chance, the Hemi/Charger and the R/T somehow appeared simultaneously at the staging lights. CL in Hemi/Charger eyed R&T in R/T.

The nods signified mutual agreement. A hand was raised, then dropped.

The R/T holeshot the Hemi/-Charger—but the advantage was short-lived. Beyond 70 mph, the Hemi began to unwind itself and the R/T faded to the rear. Over the rush of wind and roar of induction and exhaust was heard a faint bugle call, "Ta-da-da-dah-da-daaaah!" ∎

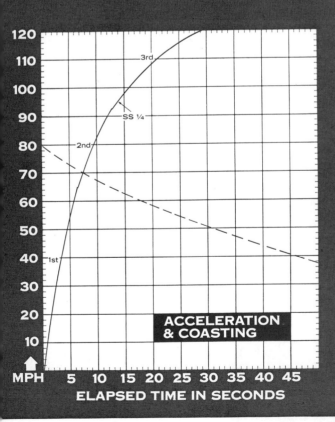

CAR LIFE ROAD TEST

ACCELERATION & COASTING

(Graph: MPH vs. ELAPSED TIME IN SECONDS, showing 1st, 2nd, 3rd gears and SS ¼)

CALCULATED DATA

Lb./bhp (test weight)	10.7
Cu. ft./ton mile	14.5
Mph/1000 rpm (high gear)	22.4
Engine revs/mile (60 mph)	2680
Piston travel, ft./mile	1675
Car Life wear index	43.5
Frontal area, sq. ft.	22.5
Box volume, cu. ft.	475.5

SPEEDOMETER ERROR

30 mph, actual	28.1
40 mph	36.1
50 mph	45.9
60 mph	55.3
70 mph	64.7
80 mph	73.4
90 mph	81.8

MAINTENANCE INTERVALS

Oil change, engine, miles	4000
trans. & differential	24,000
Oil filter change	8000
Air cleaner service, mo.	6
Chassis lubrication	32,000
Wheelbearing re-packing	as req.
Universal joint service	not req.
Coolant change, mo.	12

TUNE-UP DATA

Spark plugs	Champion N-10Y
gap, in.	0.035
Spark setting, deg./idle rpm	0/900
cent. max. adv., deg./rpm	17/2800
vac. max. adv., deg./in. Hg.	19/15
Breaker gap, in.	0.014-0.019
cam dwell angle	27-32/37-42
arm tension, oz.	17-21.5
Tappet clearance, int./exh.	0.028/0.032
Fuel pump pressure, psi	7-8.5
Radiator cap relief press., psi	16

PERFORMANCE

Top speed (6000), mph	134
Shifts (rpm) @ mph—manual	
3rd to 4th ( )	
2nd to 3rd (6000)	93
1st to 2nd (6000)	65

ACCELERATION

0-30 mph, sec.	2.7
0-40 mph	3.8
0-50 mph	5.1
0-60 mph	6.4
0-70 mph	8.0
0-80 mph	10.1
0-90 mph	12.2
0-100 mph	16.4
Standing ¼-mile, sec.	14.16
speed at end, mph	96.15
Passing, 30-70 mph, sec.	5.3

BRAKING

(Maximum deceleration rate achieved from 80 mph)

1st stop, ft./sec./sec.	27
fade evident?	no
2nd stop, ft./sec./sec.	27
fade evident?	no

FUEL CONSUMPTION

Test conditions, mpg	10.1
Est. normal range, mpg	10-13
Cruising range, miles	190-247

GRADABILITY

3rd, % grade @ mph	21 @ 90
2nd	30 @ 75
1st	40 @ 59

DRAG FACTOR

Total drag @ 60 mph, lb.	125

Both the recessed rear window and the raised spoiler at the trailing edge of the boot lid are features borrowed from current sports-racing practice.

New Charger from Dodge

1968 CARS

by Karl Ludvigsen

GENERAL Motors is a tough competitor in the medium-price sector of the U.S. auto market. Ford tried but failed to take on GM's Pontiac, Oldsmobile and Buick models with the Edsel, and is still trying with the Mercury. At Chrysler, the Dodge Division has been the traditional medium-price competitor, and they have fought hard in recent years to build up its share of this profitable market.

Dodge has invested as much money and engineering effort as its pocketbooks would permit in racing. They have been active and successful in stock car racing and drag racing, the two fields in the U.S. that have the most immediate effect on sales. But so far the sales have not risen as much as Dodge would like, presently being at about 5 per cent of the industry total and about one-third of the Chrysler output. They have built a new reputation, one of performance and liveliness

that is more marketable than the old "Dependable Dodge" of over a decade ago, but until now, until the 1968 Charger, it has not quite had the right car to take advantage of that new reputation. In the same way, Ford's emphasis on performance and racing would have been wasted without a Mustang in which the buyer could recognize the results of those efforts.

At Dodge's helm during this adventurous era is Byron N. Nichols, the division's general manager. Responsible for product planning and engineering is Burton H. "Burt" Bouwkamp, who is known as a sound engineer who can drive an automobile well and who knows a good one from a bad one. Under Chrysler's chief stylist, Elwood P. Engle, the studio is run by youthful William M. Brownlie, who gets close to automotive machinery by riding motor-cycles and has a good feel for the functional as well as the handsome in automobile styling.

The same team was in charge five years ago when they first developed the idea of making a car called "Charger". During 1964, Dodge made extensive use of the Charger name, applying it to both its largest and smallest V8 engines and to a team of special factory experimental drag racing sedans that were touring the U.S. Early in 1964, they unveiled an experimental car called Charger II at major automobile shows; this was an extreme fast-back coupe which typified the trend, at that time, to such designs.

In 1964 Plymouth introduced its Barracuda, a two-door model with a true fast back on the compact Valiant chassis. Dodge had been offered a similar model, to embellish with special trim and equipment as it had its Lancer version of the Valiant, but its poor experience with the latter project caused it to rule that out. Instead, Nichols and Bouwkamp decided to create a new car in the $3,500 price range on the longer 117-inch wheelbase of its popular medium-

A fold-down central armrest allows the alternatives of three abreast seating or so-called "bucket" seats.

The grille is a plastic pressure moulding with doors at each end which lift out of the way when the lights are switched on.

Dodge strikes out in a dramatic new styling direction for 1968

size Coronet series.

Bill Brownlie's Dodge stylists successfully married the lower body shape of the 1966 Coronet to the fast-back lines of the Charger II to create the production Charger, which came on the market in February, 1966. It had disappearing headlamps, Chrysler's first since the 1942 DeSoto, and with an elaborate central console it was essentially a four-seater in spite of its relatively large overall size. This did well in the 1966 model year with sales of 28,350, close to the Olds Toronado and Buick Riviera, but in 1967 it tapered off faster than the rest of the industry, failing to reach 10,000 units. To reverse this trend, the 1968 Charger has been given its own exterior sheet metal, entirely different from the new Dodge Coronet, with which it continues to share inner body panels and chassis components. A major change which should broaden its appeal is the use of a rear bench seat, with room for three, and front bucket seats that also permit three-abreast seating when a central armrest is lifted.

Like all Chrysler products, the Charger is of integral body/frame construction. Its front springing is by longitudinal torsion bars, 41 inches long and 0.90 inch in diameter, 0.02 inch smaller than the optional stiffer springing of 1967, but thicker and stiffer than the normal Coronet bar. The front anti-roll bar is a substantial 0.94 inch in diameter. Ratios of the recirculating ball steering gear are 24 to one in the manual version, with 5.3 turns lock to lock, and 15.7 to one with power assist, reducing the turns required to 3.5.

Rear suspension is by live axle placed well forward on the 58-inch leaf springs so that the stiff front portion of each spring serves to control axle wind-up. With the optional large-displacement V8 engines the normal 4½-leaf springs are stiffened, to 6 leaves on the left and 5½ leaves on the right. Tyres are 7.35 x 14 on 6 in. rims with an option of extra-low-profile tyres, F70 x 14, which are

standard on the extra-cost Charger R/T model. There is a choice of brakes, depending on the engine fitted. Lower-powered models have 10-inch drum brakes; 11-inch drums, giving a total swept area of 380 square inches, are provided with the biggest V8 engines. Optional on any model are 11-inch Budd disc brakes, with vented discs, for the front wheels only.

When Dodge introduced the Charger in 1966, it did not offer the famous Chrysler hemispherical-head engine as a regular option. This was rectified in 1967, and the pushrod-o.h.v. Hemi-426 engine remains an option on the 1968 Charger, now with a new camshaft profile giving 284 degrees duration on both intake and exhaust, with 60 degrees of overlap. The other top-rated optional engine is of similar stroke length but of larger bore, providing a displacement of 440 cubic inches with the normal wedge-

type combustion chamber. With a single Carter four-throat carburetter, using vacuum-controlled secondary air valves, this high-torque engine is offered only on the R/T version of the Charger.

The base engine, a 318-cubic-inch V8, is newly equipped with a cast ductile iron crankshaft, the bigger engines still using forged steel cranks. On the next larger engine, of 383 cubic inches, intake ports 10 per cent larger in area have been provided by fitting the head of the 440-cubic-inch V8, which has the same basic block and 4.80-inch centre-to-centre cylinder spacing. Corresponding size increases have been made in the intake manifold and in the carburation, which is Ball and Ball two-throat or Carter four-throat to choice.

Exhaust emission control on the Charger
CONTINUED ON PAGE 124

One of the intermediate powered engines—the 383 cubic inch (6.3 litre) V8 with 4 choke Carter carburetter.

DODGE CHARGER
A Fleet Fastback for Couples or Cargo

"**S**PORTS SEDAN" categorizes Dodge Division's new Charger as well as any other label one might find. Although the Charger embraces a sporting flair with its fastback styling and its performance capabilities, it definitely has a sedan's attributes, too, in that it is designed to carry four passengers and their luggage in elegant comfort.

A latecomer to the specialty car field, the Charger represents Dodge's outlook as to what will sell in that rapidly growing market. Charger joins some distinguished company in the area, namely Ford's pioneering Thunderbird and Oldsmobile's front-wheel-drive Toronado. What that first 4-passenger Thunderbird ('58 model) started has been joined by Corvair Monza (1960), Studebaker Avanti (1963), Buick Riviera (1963), Plymouth Barracuda and Ford Mustang (1964), American Motors Marlin (1965), Toronado and Charger (1966). Although these all fall into the high-

performance 4-seater category, their diversification in cost and mechanical specification spread-eagles the U.S. automotive spectrum.

The Mustang, for example, has a 200-cu. in. 6-cyl. engine as standard power and a conventional drive-train to the rear wheels, and lists for $2398. The DeLuxe Toronado, on the other hand, has a radical but brilliant front-wheel drive arrangement, a hugely powerful V-8 engine and, when equipped with most of the usual accessories, goes out the door at nearly $6500.

The Charger lands at approximately mid-point in this spread with its basic price of $3122, its standard-sized bulk and its conventional V-8 engine and drive-train. With a 117-in. wheelbase and 203.6 in. overall length, it is neither as small as the Mustang, nor as large as the Toronado. If conservative in size and specification, the Charger is at least radical in styling.

Dodge tested the concept with a

showcar prototype, Charger II, in nine major auto shows around the country as much as a year before the car appeared in dealers' showrooms. Nearly all of the showcar's features, from roll-away headlights to 6-in-1, full-width taillight, were retained.

Except that it is done on the next size larger car, the Charger's construction parallels that of the Barracuda. What is basically a 2-door Coronet body is converted with new roof, pillar and deck structures from a conventional notched-back hardtop into a long-sloped fastback hardtop.

A benefit of fastback design is a vent system which allows inner air pressure (whenever windows, fresh air vents, or heater vents are opened, the car's interior is pressurized by the incoming air) to escape out the rear into the low-pressure area following the car. Rubber flaps keep the interior closed off until a slight pressure is created, then swing open to let air out at the decklid/body-joint gap.

The second major departure from normal hardtop configuration is the interior layout. Here, a pair of hinged-back bucket-type rear seats replaces the usual bench seat. These fold forward to form a flat extension of the utility area so that a long, carpeted cargo deck is available. This area is extended when the security door into the trunk is opened, should anyone wish to carry skis, toboggans, surfboards, ladders or other lengthy items. Front seats are more conventional bucket types. Seating capacity is thus limited, overall, to just four people.

Along with its novel lighting arrangement, the Charger has an unusual instrument display. Four large chromed-rim dials confront the driver. The applicable digital information for each dial (left to right: Alternator rate and fuel supply, speedometer and odometer, 6000-rpm tachometer, oil pressure indicator light and coolant temperature gauge) is let into the rim, so that nighttime illumination makes the numbers leap out at the driver. Daytime reading of these dials lacks the immediate clarity of the illuminated condition.

Elsewhere in the interior the Charger utilizes a 1-piece headliner, much in the same manner as the Ambassador DPL (reviewed May *CL*). This single molding of fiberglass is faced with a layer of porous, nonwoven nylon fabric which allows the absorption of noise by the glass fiber backing.

Engines for the Charger are those of the regular Coronet lineup, with a few exceptions. To maintain its performance image, the Charger will have nothing smaller than its 318-cu. in./230-bhp V-8 "standard" engine. Everything Chrysler Corp. makes above that level, except the 440-inchers also is available—361-cu. in., 383 and 426 "Street Hemi"—on order. The customer should have no complaint about a lack of power.

The test Charger's engine was the 383-cu. in./325-bhp V-8 which *CL* has frequently recommended as the "happiest" of all Chrysler products. A look at the performance figures will show why: It is hot enough and big enough to do a sparkling job of moving rapidly a 4000-lb. (curb weight) car, yet it is mild and docile enough for the most old-maidish sort of driving. And, it will return a consistent 13-14 mpg, which seems slightly better than other engines in its size and power category. Although it would be easy to become blasé about this engine, simply because most of *CL*'s Dodge and Plymouth test cars are so-equipped, it never fails to reaffirm test drivers' enthusiasm through its consistently good performance.

These engine specifications are:

disp.	bore x stroke	comp.	carb.	bhp	rpm
318	3.91x3.31	9.0	1x2	230 @ 4400
361	4.12x3.38	9.0	1x2	265 @ 4400
383	4.25x3.38	10.0	1x4	325 @ 4800
426	4.25x3.75	10.25	2x4	425 @ 5000

(A maximum performance 426 hemispherical-head engine also is available on special order.)

Part of the performance credit is due to Chrysler's 3-speed automatic transmission. Since its first appearance in 1957, this transmission has become the standard, in terms of performance, for others to seek. So far, no one has come close to it for responsiveness. General Motors' Turbo Hydra-Matic 3-speed automatics are slightly smoother in shift quality, but at the expense of responsiveness. The Chrysler unit's controllability factor is also high: It can be held in first and second for low-speed or town traffic work, or it can be left in high and, with a light touch on the throttle, provide smooth, fuss-less through-all-three acceleration. *CL*'s testers preferred use of the second gear holding feature for stop-and-go traffic as it gave good engine braking as well as optimum agility. A simple flick of the console-mounted shift lever to the next notch let the transmission shift into high gear as soon as open road was reached.

Because it shares suspension, chassis and all underbody components

CHAN BUSH PHOTOS

CHARGER

with its related Coronet line, the Charger has inherently good handling characteristics. Reasonably firm rate springs, coupled with a front anti-roll bar of 0.84 in. diameter, provide satisfactory lateral stability. Fore-and-aft pitching, a frequent complaint of big-engined, medium-size cars, is non-existent in the Charger. The test car's optional 7.75-14 Goodyear Power Cushion tires on 5.5K rim wheels were helpful to the overall handling, too.

Along with other components from the Coronet, the Charger inherits the 10-in. brake drums. With 2.5-in. wide linings front and rear, these give 314.2 sq. in. of swept area. Although these are doubtlessly adequate for the passive driver, the enthusiast will want to specify the heavy-duty option of 11-in. drums with 3-in. front and 2.5-in. rear linings (swept area 380.1 sq. in.). This option is available on 383 V-8-equipped Dodges and is standard for the hemi-engined cars.

The 12-in. disc front brake and drum rear brake system is not yet

1966 DODGE
CHARGER 2-DOOR HARDTOP

DIMENSIONS

Wheelbase, in.	117.0
Track, f/r, in.	59.5/58.5
Overall length, in.	203.6
width	75.3
height	53.0
Front seat hip room, in.	2 x 22.0
shoulder room	58.0
head room	37.7
pedal-seatback, max.	44.0
Rear seat hip room, in.	2 x 20.0
shoulder roow	58.0
leg room	33.3
head room	36.5
Door opening width, in.	43.0
Floor to ground height, in.	11.0
Ground clearance, in.	7.75

PRICES

List, fob factory	$3122
Equipped as tested	3861

Options included: 383/325 V-8, auto. trans., power steering and brakes, limited slip diff., 7.75-14 tires, tinted glass, radio, Rallye suspension, retractable seat belts, Clean Air pkg., bumper guards, electric clock, undercoating.

CAPACITIES

No. of passengers	4
Luggage space, cu. ft.	n.s.
Fuel tank, gal.	19.0
Crankcase, qt.	4.0
Transmission/diff., pt.	16.0/4.0
Radiator coolant, qt.	21.0

CHASSIS/SUSPENSION

Frame type	unitized

Front suspension type: Independent by s.l.a., ball-joint steering knuckles, torsion bar springs, telescopic shock absorbers.

ride rate at wheel, lb./in.	130
anti-roll bar dia., in.	0.94

Rear suspension type: Live axle, Hotchkiss drive; parallel, longitudinal multi-leaf springs; telescopic shock absorbers.

ride rate at wheel, lb./in.	150

Steering system: Integral power booster, rack and sector gear, trailing parallel idlers with equal length tie rods.

gear ratio	15.7
overall ratio	19.0
turns, lock to lock	3.5
turning circle, ft. curb-curb.	40.9
Curb weight, lb.	3990
Test weight	4330
Weight distribution, % f/r	54/46

BRAKES

Type: Single-line hydraulic, self-adjusting duo-servo shoes in cast-iron drums.

Front drum, dia. x width, in.	10.0 x 2.5
Rear drum, dia. x width	10.0 x 2.5
total swept area, sq. in.	314.2
Power assist	vacuum, integral
line psi @ 100 lb. pedal.	930

WHEELS/TIRES

Wheel size	14 x 5.5K
optional size available	none
bolt no./circle dia., in.	5/4.5

Tires: Goodyear Power Cushion

size	7.75-14
recommended inflation, psi	24
capacity rating, total lb.	4480

ENGINE

Type, no. cyl.	V-8, ohv
Bore x stroke, in.	4.25 x 3.38
Displacement, cu. in.	383
Compression ratio	10.0
Rated bhp @ rpm	325 @ 4800
equivalent mph	112
Rated torque @ rpm	425 @ 2800
equivalent mph	65
Carburetion	Carter; 1x4
barrel dia., pri./sec.	1.44/1.56

Valve operation: Hydraulic lifters, pushrods, rocker arms.

valve dia., int./exh.	2.08/1.60
lift, int./exh.	0.425/0.437
timing, deg.	14-62, 62-18
duration, int./exh.	256/260
opening overlap	32

Exhaust system: Dual reverse flow mufflers & pipes.

pipe dia., exh./tail	2.25/1.88
Lubrication pump type	rotary
normal press. @ rpm	45 @ 2000
Electrical supply	alternator
ampere rating	n.s.
Battery, plates/amp. rating	78/70

DRIVE-TRAIN

Clutch type	
dia., in.	

Transmission type: Automatic with torque converter and planetary gearbox.

Gear ratio 4th ( ) overall	
3rd (1.00)	3.23
2nd (1.45)	4.68
1st (2.45)	7.92
1st x t.c. stall (2.20)	17.4
Shift lever location	console

Differential type: Hypoid with torque-bias limited slip.

axle ratio	3.23

available for Chargers, or Coronets, for that matter, although it can be ordered with larger Dodges and Chryslers. Asked when it might be available for such "enthusiastic" cars as the Charger, the answer is, "We're working on it." General indications point toward a 1967 model announcement for the Coronet-sized disc brakes.

Also befitting its performance-oriented nature, the Charger may be specified with a 4-speed manual transmission. This is the familiar Chrysler-built (New Process Gear Div.) unit with its wide-spaced 2.66-first, 1.91-second and 1.39-third gearset. These are husky, virtually-unbreakable transmissions and have balk-ring synchronizers on all four forward speeds. The standard transmission is a 3-speed manual (3.02-first, 1.76-second) that is synchronized in the two upper gears.

The Dodge Charger should prove satisfying to the auto buyer who wants "something different" but who also wants the proved reliability of an established make and line. The Coronet base gives it just that, and the extensive option list should make it suitable to a wide variety of tastes. ∎

CAR LIFE ROAD TEST

ACCELERATION & COASTING

MPH | 5 10 15 20 25 30 35 40 45
ELAPSED TIME IN SECONDS

CALCULATED DATA

Lb./bhp (test weight)	13.3
Cu. ft./ton mile	131
Mph/1000 rpm (high gear)	23.3
Engine revs/mile (60 mph)	2570
Piston travel, ft./mile	1450
Car Life wear index	37.3
Frontal area, sq. ft.	22.2
Box volume, cu. ft.	470

SPEEDOMETER ERROR

30 mph, actual	29.4
40 mph	39.5
50 mph	49.2
60 mph	58.3
70 mph	68.9
80 mph	78.6
90 mph	88.3

MAINTENANCE INTERVALS

Oil change, engine, miles	4000
trans./dif.	none/36,000
Oil filter change	8000
Air cleaner service, mo.	6
Chassis lubrication	36,000
Wheelbearing re-packing	as req.
Universal joint service	none
Coolant change, mo.	12

TUNE-UP DATA

Spark plugs	MoPar P-3-5P
gap, in.	0.035
Spark setting, deg./idle rpm	12.5/700
cent. max. adv., deg./rpm	35/4800
vac. max. adv., deg./in. Hg.	29/16.5
Breaker gap, in.	0.014-0.019
cam dwell angle	28-32
arm tension, oz.	17-20
Tappet clearance, int./exh.	0/0
Fuel pump pressure, psi	6.0-7.5
Radiator cap relief press., psi	14.0

PERFORMANCE

Top speed (5100), mph	120
Shifts (rpm) @ mph	
3rd to 4th ( )	
2nd to 3rd (4700)	76
1st to 2nd (4900)	47

ACCELERATION

0-30 mph, sec.	3.0
0-40 mph	4.3
0-50 mph	5.6
0-60 mph	7.2
0-70 mph	9.6
0-80 mph	13.2
0-90 mph	16.2
0-100 mph	20.8
Standing ¼-mile, sec.	15.6
speed at end, mph	89
Passing, 30-70 mph, sec.	6.6

BRAKING

(Maximum deceleration rate achieved from 80 mph)

1st stop, ft./sec./sec.	23
fade evident?	none
2nd stop, ft./sec./sec.	24
fade evident?	slight

FUEL CONSUMPTION

Test conditions, mpg	12.7
Normal cond., mpg	13-15
Cruising range, miles	247-285

GRADABILITY

4th, % grade @ mph	
3rd	17 @ 68
2nd	25 @ 58
1st	33 @ 40

DRAG FACTOR

Total drag @ 60 mph, lb.	150

DODGE 426 HEMI CHARGER

HERE'S THE HOT STREET SETUP THAT'LL SHADE MOST ANYTHING THIS SIDE OF A STRIP STOCKER

BY THE CARS STAFF

IN JUST ONE YEAR'S time the Dodge Boys have managed to take an over-stuffed, full-size fastback that was too heavy for drag racing, ill-mannered at high speed and with a seating capacity of only four persons and put it into the supercar Hall of Fame. The car we're referring to is the Charger. Even with the 426 Street Hemi the car was outclassed in the stock ranks. On the NASCAR high-speed ovals the Charger started to go airborne when the stops were pulled out. And on the street Dodge had a rough time selling four-bucket-seat seating in a full-sized car. The public just wasn't ready for that full-length console and wall-to-wall buckets. That was early 1966.

Even with all this on the minus side, we at *CARS Magazine*, recognized it as a potential winner. We backed up our opinion with our Sixth Annual Top Performance Car of the Year Award. Our faith in the product was bolstered when Sam McQuagg proved the Charger on the NASCAR circuit by picking up a national win. Handling problems were solved by the addition of a small aluminum spoiler attached to the area above the fender-to-fender rear lighting. Dodge picked up on the spoiler idea and marketed a duplicate through its dealer network for improved high speed turnpike driving. Chargers also made it big in the funny car-exhibition ranks thanks to Mr. Norm and Al Graeber. Al Graeber was the first with his TICKLE ME PINK pink Charger fuel exhibitionist. After the racing papers and magazines played up the winning Chargers, the street set picked up on Dodge's fastback.

For 1967 the Dodge Boys have made a few changes both in the interest of safety and convenience. At first glance it's almost impossible to tell the difference between a '66 and a '67 model. Fender-mounted directional signal indicators, new bench seating and optional steel mag-type road wheels are the eye-catching '67 changes.

Since we had already checked out the new 440-cube 375-hp street package in a Plymouth GTX shell we chose a 426 Street Hemi version for our test. The Street Hemi engine and component drive line parts feature some re-engineering for 1967. The engine is basically the same

Tester Marty Schorr puts the hemi-honked Charger through its paces on the strip. Stock street hemi is chock full of low end torque and still manages to come on like gangbusters upstairs. Test car was not fitted with new disc brakes. However, drums did a respectable job.

Tester, complete with LBJ-styled "brain bucket" checks out the ultimate street screamer.

Chrome-and-black-crackle-finished 426 really fills the Charger's boiler room. AC is not available.

except for the improved oil pump relief spring. This spring presented a problem on many of the early Street Hemis and was the direct cause of a loss of lube efficiency and lunched engines. The engine is still rated at 425 hp with dual inline quads and tuned cast iron headers. This year, however, Dodge has made available through the factory, chrome vanadium high rpm dual valve springs, bigger quads and a full array of racing rear end ratios for both the large four-speed rear and the smaller automatic version.

Transmission choices this year include the A-833 four speed "rock crusher" with a 2.65-to-1 First and Inland Steel *sloppy* controls and an improved three-speed Torqueflite. Stick flickers should be happy to hear that there's a new HD six-roller pressure plate being used in all 426 four-speed applications. Dial-a-win fans in 1967 will reap the benefits of a special five-disc, paper-type front clutch which enables the Torqueflite to handle additional torque capacity in case the engine is modified for drag racing. Also the number of planet pinions in both the front and rear planetary gearsets has been increased from three to four. This is *the* "hot setup" for street or strip.

Our test Charger was factory fitted (special for us) with 4.10-to-1 Sure Grip gears and came on like a dynamite machine. The combination of Torqueflite, 425 hemi horsepower and respectable gearing made our 4100-pound fastback live up to its name. Most of the Street Hemi machines we have driven were fitted with either 3.23 or 3.55 gears so it was a genuine pleasure to let that "Orange Monster" breathe without having to go over 85 mph. The respectable gearing proved to be a bit too much for highway cruising as the tach rarely ever read less than 3500 rpm. Around town and on the strip the 4.10's really did the job. By going the gear ratio route it enabled us to give up the dial-a-win bit and simply keep the stick in Drive. This combo ushered in an all-new era of drag strip driving. All you have to do is wait for the green and stab and steer. No fancy torque loading or up-shifting from Low. Just stab, steer and get firmly planted in the Charger's contoured bucket!

Having spent so much time with a variety of both street and strip stock Street Hemis we sort of knew what was coming when we ran against the Chrondeks. The best time of the day was a 14.20, 103 mph which we thought was about par for the course for a 4100-pound machine with closed exhausts, power steering and street tires. With cheater slicks and open pipes I'm sure we could have brought the et's down to the high 13's without really trying.

WHAT THE HOT SETUP COSTS

PART	FACTORY NUMBER	PRICE	PART	FACTORY NUMBER	PRICE
CARBS	2836111-112	$75.00 (pair)	4.56-to-1 GEARS (four-speed)	2852580	$73.41
VALVE SPRINGS	2806077	$16.00 (set)	4.56-to-1 SURE-GRIP CASE	1929772	$82.50
HP OIL FILTER	2536186	$ 3.87	3.58-to-1 GEARS (auto)	2070916	$51.63
SCATTERSHIELD	2463235	$73.28	3.91-to-1 GEARS (auto)	2404127	$48.45
SHIELD CLUTCH PAN	2406045	$19.30	4.30-to-1 GEARS (auto)	1738822	$73.41
SHIELD SCREWS	1947953	.60¢ (set)	4.56-to-1 GEARS (auto)	1738823	$73.41
15-inch, 6-inch wide			4.89-to-1 GEARS (auto)	1738824	$73.41
RACING WHEELS	2781585	$42.00 (pair)	RACING PLUGS	N-64Y	$ 1.75 (each)
4.10-to-1 GEARS (four-speed)	2852579	$73.41	RACING PLUG WIRE SET	2525672	$16.61

Our test car was fitted with the standard Street Hemi suspension which is a great deal beefier than the *consumer* HD version. The front sway bar and torsion bars are thicker, the shocks are valved differently and the leaf spring rear is truck-sized. To offset the standard torque reaction when getting off the line, the factory added one extra leaf to the right side spring package. Since the normal reaction consists of the left front wheel raising slightly and the full load thrown on the right rear wheel, the engineers counteracted this by adding the extra leaf. It helps distribute the monster torque put out by the hemi-headed 426 cuber. On the road the heavier duty suspension hinders by transmitting some road noises and shock to the interior, which is less than desirable. It's a stiff, hard-riding package that's not appreciated by the average motorist. And it's just one of the minus features of a *genuine* high-performance supercar. The Street Hemi Charger is not just an image-mobile, it's a red-blooded, muscle-machine!

Completing the fully-integrated total performance package is a super-duty set of brakes which are just the ticket for taming the torquer. Our car was equipped with 11-inch front and rear drum brakes which provide "right now" stopping power. Fade was evident after three or four 75 mph panic stops, which is far more of a torture test than is necessary in a production passenger car. Rarely ever will the average driver have to make repeated panic stops from high, high cruising speeds. For those who are looking for fade insurance there's an optional set of front disc brakes available on the Charger. We were quite satisfied with the drum setup and saw no need for the disc option. The chromed steel wheels on our test machine are optional at extra cost, but the 7.75x14 red line high-performance rubber is standard equipment.

Those who are contemplating buying a Charger in 1967 will be able to take advantage of rear bench seating and imitation bucket front seating with a folding armrest. It's a far more practical setup

Charger is heavier than Coronet and is not recommended for 100-percent strip duty. New rear deck spoiler and road wheels with wide tires update the Charger for '67.

than last year's seating plan and should do a lot for Charger sales. This year's wood wheel is a little beefier and thus more comfortable than last year's tiller. Instrumentation is superb with four round clusters with gauges covering every checkpoint. The speedo goes to 150 which should be good as a status symbol and the built-in tach (sloppy operation) reads to six grand. We didn't particularly care for the power steering at high speeds or when negotiating the quarter as we sort of lost touch with the front end and terra firma. Over 90 mph at full throttle produces a slight wandering effect which gives you the feeling that the front wheels have left the ground. Manual steering is too much around town with the heavy Street Hemi mill, so the frontal wander is something you have to live with.

The noise level of the 426 is higher than *consumer* engines, the idle is a little faster and it does require more maintenance due to the multi carbs and solid lifter camshaft. However, when you check off the Street Hemi box and plunk down $900-plus for the dynamite package, you're getting more than just image trim or flashy engine goodies. The 426 Charger, with or without the new optional steel chromed wheels and vinyl roof, is a total performance vehicle that commands respect. It handles, stops and goes like nothing else in the full-size domestic car market. It's super boss!

1967 DODGE CHARGER

ENGINE

Type	OHV V-8
Displacement	426 cubic inches
Compression Ratio	10.5-to-1
Carburetion	Dual Carter AFB Quads
Camshaft	Solid Lifter, .460/.480 Lift
Horsepower	425 @ 5000 rpm
Torque	490 foot/pounds @ 4000 rpm
Exhaust	Dual headers, dual pipes
Ignition	Dual-point

TRANSMISSION

Make	Torqueflite auto
Control	Floor shift

REAR END

Type	Sure-Grip
Ratio	4.10-to-1

BRAKES

Front	11-inch drums
Rear	11-inch drums

SUSPENSION

Front	Independent, HD torsion bars, shocks, sway bar
Rear	HD leaf springs, shocks
Steering	Power
Overall Ratio	19.4-to-1

GENERAL

List Price	$3200
Price As Tested	$4485
Weight	4100 pounds
Wheelbase	117 inches
Overall Length	203.6 inches
Tire Size	7.75 x 14 Goodyear

PERFORMANCE

0 to 30 mph	3.5 seconds
0 to 60 mph	6.8 seconds
Standing ¼ mile	103 mph
Elapsed Time	14.20 seconds
Top Speed	110 mph
Fuel Consumption	8 mpg

DODGE'S LARGER CHARGER

Unlike toothpaste, which can be purchased in sizes from the tiny travelling tubes to the giant economy versions, the 1968 Dodge Charger comes in but one size. Big.

From 1967 it has been lengthened by 4½ in. to a total of 208 while the wheelbase remained at 117. *Automotive News,* the bible of the industry, lists the Charger among U.S. Specialty cars along with the Mustang, Camaro, Javelin, Toronado and the Thunderbird, et al. The criterion

seems to be wheelbase in some cases and engine size in another. If you find this confusing, you are in good company.

Viewed all by itself, without a reference object for comparison, the Charger appears to belong among the Pony cars. The '68 version has the sporty look associated with the Mustang and its imitators but approaching the car you realize it seems bigger than it was in your first impression. Be not misled, however, for the 208

in. of length and 3925 lb. of weight can be made to *charge* in no uncertain terms.

The Charger for '67 was a very brisk machine, though the buying public was underwhelmed by the long sweep of the ultra fastback. This year's styling, more classic in concept, should have wider appeal.

The basic Charger, equipped with a 230-hp, 318-cu. in. V-8 engine, comes with heavy duty suspension, springs and stabilizers as standard

The 426 Hemi is an object of admiration and curiosity at every fuel stop. One of the most efficient V-8s, the engine delivers almost exactly one horsepower per cubic inch.

Ventilated front disc brakes do an excellent job of bringing the Charger to a halt. Despite front weight bias, car stops in a straight line.

around the tail and heavy duty drum brakes. The *ne plus ultra* comes when you throw your credit rating to the winds and buy the Charger R/T with the 426 Hemi. This tab comes to about $3800 but you'll have 425 hp with which to hurl those two tons of iron down the dragstrip, in elapsed times that will shake up most Corvettes. You also run the risk of gathering an admiring throng of young men at service stations everytime you want your oil checked; they just want to look at all that engine under your hood. With the lid closed they'll still hang around just waiting to hear you fire it up.

There are a number of other things from the option list you'll want and should have. Things like disc brakes ($72.95), tachometer ($51.10) and radio ($60.25). The F70x14 tires, either red or white stripes are standard on the R/T but add $82.40 to the basic Charger price. An oil cooler is also standard, an item usually only seen on all out race cars.

The width of the Charger is 76.6 in. compared to 70.9 in. for a Mustang or 79.9 for a Cadillac Fleetwood. The height is 53.2 in. and again for comparison the Mustang is 51.6 in. tall and the Cadillac 55.6. The lowest roof line of major American cars goes to Firebird, by the way, 50.0 in.; with the tallest being the Chrysler Newport and New Yorker at 56.8.

What all this adds up to is reasonable roominess on the inside. The individual front seats are wide and have a retractable center armrest that permits seating three abreast. There is good hiproom in the rear seat though legroom is only slightly better than that found in the Pony cars. Trunk space is a bit larger but loading remains a problem with the rather high lip at the rear. Removal and replacement of the spare tire is calculated to produce profanity in males and utter helplessness in females.

Getting into and out of the Charger is quite easy with the wide swinging doors which have not one but two stops in the 'door open' attitude. Once seated, one's position is quite comfortable for relaxed reading or

equipment. For this, the kudos of ROAD TEST and, we hope, the beginning of a trend. Also standard are individual front seats, called "buckets," and all the goodies required by the new safety standards. For this the suggested West Coast retail price is $3155.

With this as a beginning the prospective purchaser may start building. The first option up the engine scale is the 383 cu. in. with two-barrel carburetor at an added $73.25. An additional $71.20 will get you the same engine with a four-barrel carburetor and dual exhaust. Neither of these engines are available with the three-speed manual gearbox.

A big jump up the performance ladder comes in ordering the Charger R/T. In standard form the R/T will list at $3621, for which you get the 440-cu. in. Magnum engine rated at 375 hp, an automatic transmission, a limited slip, complete instrumentation, Bumble Bee racing stripes

Heavy duty suspension keeps the Charger reasonably flat under severe cornering. With the 426 Hemi, care must be taken on sand or the wet surfaces least excess power break loose the rear end.

Hard braking produces nose dive but ventilated disc brakes pulled the Charger to straight-line stops.

ever, must be accompanied by over-the-shoulder checking.

The dashboard on the Charger, with its complete instrumentation, is a delight. All the things you need to know are there in well-proportioned round dials to the right of the large speedometer. At the left, also in a good position for easy reading, is either a clock or tachometer. While all the dials are recessed, the insets are not so deep as to prevent easy reading with or without sun glasses.

With the column location, the shift lever is well positioned and quadrant positions easily read. With the console, or four on the floor, the shifter is right where you would order it, given a choice.

On the automatic models the large brake pedal is conveniently located close to the throttle for quick and easy transfer of foot action. On the manual shift cars almost the same relative position is maintained and if one found it expedient he could "heel and toe."

Switches are all rocker toggles and controls for such as dash illumination, radio, etc., are actuated by thumb wheels.

Ventilation and heating are good in the Charger. Air ducts bring either outside fresh air or engine-heated air to the foot wells; the heater is obviously quite capable of dealing with Minnesota winters.

TV watching but for automobile driving not so good. The steering wheel, even for a tall driver, is much too high, and the seats too low. The beltline is almost at shoulder level making the inveterate 'elbow on sill' drivers very uncomfortable. The armrests in the doors do help, but they are a trifle low for best use.

Vision to the front is restricted by the low seating position. Locating the right front fender is a guess-work operation. For the same reason, vision to the rear is limited. The blind rear quarter panels contribute to the general uneasiness about what's going on back there. Reverse, one feels, should only be used after checking on foot to be sure there are no motorcycles, bicycles or Sprites parked behind.

Once under way these problems, except for the wheel position, disappear. Freeway lane changing, how-

Charger dash is well laid out with easy-to-read, aircraft-styled instruments. Switches are rocker types; dash lights and radio are controlled by thumb wheels.

Charger has yet to do away with those noisome quarter windows. The transmission is quiet and so is the engine — most of the time. At idle there is a throaty murmur from the 426 Hemi. Its wilder cam contributes a heady "race car" lope. When the throttle is applied, one can feel the surge as well as hear it; mighty few drivers would want it any other way.

Road wheels are changed by means of the familiar bumper jack. The Charger's jack has a curved section which fits around the bumper, making for a slight improvement in the security of this insecure device.

Because heavy duty suspension is standard (praise Allah!) the Charger's ride is firm without being harsh. On our "rough-as-a-cob" test surface the Dodge behaved admirably without pitch or yaw, and without rattles. The power steering transmitted none of the road shocks to the consultant's arms; in fact, we would have welcomed a bit *more* road feel.

On smoothly paved surfaces the Charger's behavior offered just what good suspension is all about. At no time was there wallowing. Lane changes were made quickly, and without the sensation of being becalmed in a ground swell.

Except in the areas of visibility and steering wheel position, the Charger is a comfortable and convenient package to drive.

On the open highway, or in areas with sweeping bends, one can truly appreciate the things that Dodge has built into the Charger. For the sake of argument here let's assume that everyone can afford the hottest version — power by 426 Hemi and the goodies that go with it; dual exhaust, the wide-tread tires, limited slip and disc brakes. For convenience let's use the three-speed automatic. Weight is going to be 3925 lb. with 2300 lb. of that on the front. Still, the car doesn't feel nose-heavy except on very hard braking. The sound of those 425 horses, just waiting to be unleashed, is music to the ears.

The thing to do, naturally, is take the Charger to the dragstrip. In our case we went to the Orange County International Raceway near Santa Ana, Calif., where we experimented with the automatic gearbox. Our best time with street tires, air cleaner on and in street trim throughout, was 14.06 e.t. and a trap speed of 105 mph. Not bad for a car weighing almost two tons!

On our cornering tests we hurled the Charger through tight hairpins and, while there was some body lean, the chassis stayed flat and maintained a predictable understeer. Our principal complaint was with the power steering which took over too completely right in the center of the steering range where assistance was needed least.

But, the combination of the big Hemi with all its power and the excellent suspension make this a car to be reckoned with in the corners. Against it, of course, is its length. A direct comparison with a close-coupled sports car would be completely unfair. However, comparisons with its peers are in order and we at ROAD TEST will be looking toward the NASCAR series of races in 1968. The Charger which did well in 1967 should gain even more laurels, particularly on the road courses.

Dodge for 1968 has done a tasteful job of incorporating the necessary safety features into the Charger. The matte finish of the dash is glareless and manages to offer a more completed look than some. The aircraft-style instruments add to safety by being easily read. Door handles are well out of the way on the inside though still protruding on the outside. A feature which all the ROAD TESTers admired is the positioning of turn indicator light reminders on the hood as well as on the dash. The hood pair are recessed into otherwise useless scoops toward the front. These reminders are sufficiently bright that they are easily read in sunlight as well as at night.

Brakes on the Charger are among the best we have tested for progressive power assist. There is none of the "stand you on your nose" so often associated with power-assisted brakes. Braking distance was good for a car of this weight, 168.5 ft. In a panic stop there is considerable nosedive but no rear wheel lock-up so that stopping is arrow straight.

The front brakes are of the venti-

Steering wheel position is quite high. Belt retractor on one hip and buckle on the other can cause discomfort.

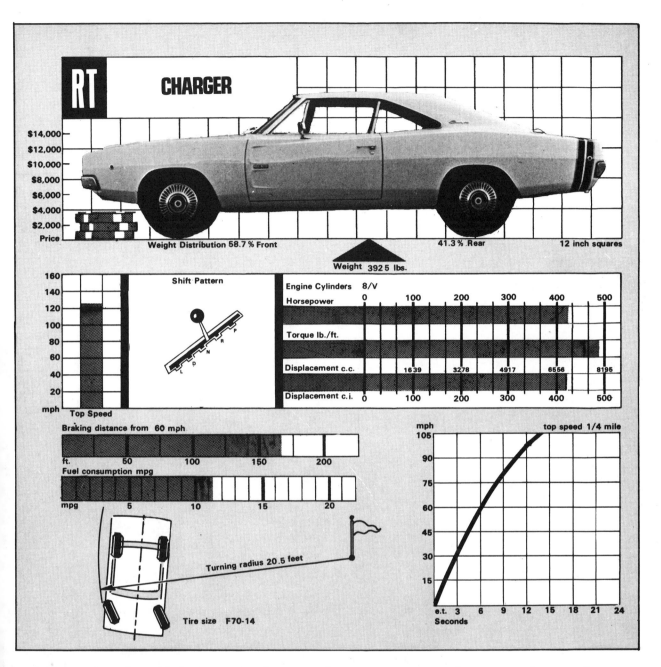

RT CHARGER

Price: $14,000 $12,000 $10,000 $8,000 $6,000 $4,000 $2,000

Weight Distribution 58.7% Front   41.3% Rear   12 inch squares

Weight 3925 lbs.

Shift Pattern

Top Speed (mph): 160 140 120 100 80 60 40 20

Engine Cylinders	8/V					
Horsepower	0	100	200	300	400	500
Torque lb./ft.						
Displacement c.c.	1639	3278	4917	6556	8195	
Displacement c.i.	0	100	200	300	400	500

Braking distance from 60 mph
ft.   50   100   150   200

Fuel consumption mpg
mpg   5   10   15   20

Turning radius 20.5 feet

Tire size F70-14

top speed 1/4 mile
mph: 105 90 75 60 45 30 15
e.t. 3 6 9 12 15 18 21 24
Seconds

lated disc configuration with large calipers. To change pads, the entire caliper assembly is easily removed to provide access.

Still in the area of safety, we found the buckle end of the seat belt to have an annoying habit of dropping between the seats and being difficult to retrieve. This could lead the hasty motorist into a "to hell with it" attitude and failure to use this life-saving device. The position of the retractor over one hip and the buckle over the other also leaves something to be desired.

With the 426 Hemi there is an almost unavoidable urge to show off now and then, like when you are ac-

celerating up a freeway on-ramp. This, of course, raises havoc with fuel economy. Nevertheless, we were pleasantly surprised to find our around-town gas mileage at 11.26 mpg. Using the available power more sparingly, this figure could be improved.

The F70-14 tires give good adhesion on dry pavement but are nowhere in the wet. ROAD TEST recommends the use of wide tread radial ply tires. These will not only give better traction on all surfaces but far greater longevity. This certainly will be a factor for there is bound to be the temptation to participate in the traffic signal grand prix with its re-

sultant wear and tear on tires.

The Charger is not an easy car to classify with a few well chosen words. It has performance to spare, particularly with the 426 Hemi engine. It handles on a par with many of the Pony cars. It isn't as big as a New Yorker nor as small as a Dart so it appears we'll have to go along with the designation of a "specialty" car. And, it's a pleasant specialty car. With the R/T bumble bee stripes the young men who know about such things gather as bees to honey. It is a pleasure to drive too, once a few minor discomforts are overlooked. For 1968 it is larger and, most of all, a Charger. ♠

CHARGER

Totally new styling sports aerodynamic designs. Large emphasis is placed on handling and performance with the Charger R/T added to the model line-up.

For some reason, the sales figures for the Dodge Charger did not meet the expectations of Dodge Management. Nor did a similar designed car produced by American Motors (Marlin), Perhaps the public was not ready for the long fastbacks.

However, racing fraternities found the Charger lines ideal for big circuit racing.

With the belief that Europe's Grand Touring styling lines were setting American trends, the 1968 Charger took on an all new look. It has a totally new body shell which in no way resembles its forerunners. Aerodynamics, however, was the major objective in the new design (this body is used extensively for national circuit racing).

The roofline of the Charger is now a semi-fastback with lines flowing into the rear quarter. The rear quarter is the high point of the styling with its lines

Charger is offered in two models, the standard Charger and Charger R/T. A spoiler is styled into deck lid and flip open gas lid is atop rear quarter panel.

CHARGER

All new instrument panel reflects car's aerodynamic effect by using complete set of gauges. Dodge Coronet R/T models can have same instrument cluster as optional equipment.

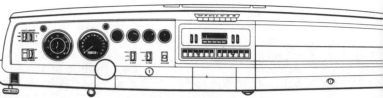

tapering forward toward the front end. This gives the feel of forward motion. At the rear of the body is a spoiler to enhance the competition aspect of the Charger. Furthering the competition concept is a "quick fill" gas cap which is fully exposed on the left rear panel.

For the Charger R/T models there is the optional "bumblebee stripes" running across the rear of the deck lid.

Highlighting the rear of the car are taillights housed in simulated exhaust header pipes. The front end sports a plastic grille with the headlights concealed behind vacuum operated lids.

Inside, the Charger is a mass of instrumentation. Again the theme is aerodynamics, as the dash strongly resembles an aircraft panel. The entire arrangement of engine instrumentation is by gauges. There is also a tachometer and a 150 mph speedometer to carry out the performance theme.

When MOTORCADE drove the Charger, we had the chance to wring out the Charger R/T suspension. R/T suspension includes a sway bar plus high rate springs and shocks. On the corners we felt that the car may be slightly light. However, providing that the road conditions are good, the average driver would never notice this characteristic. On straightaways the car is very stable. Through a one-mile acceleration course, we held a speed of 100 mph with a very impressive smooth ride, which was also virtually wind-noise free. Charger looks good for '68, both sales and performance-wise.

Taillights are inside simulated exhaust exits, a trend from racing. Front grille conceals headlamps. Close up of rear styling shows spoiler formed in rear panel.

CHARGER R/T
The
Clean Machine.

Run with the Dodge Scat Pack

Dodge Charger R/T for '68, most exciting of the super cars. With all this **standard equipment:**

- 440-cubic-inch Magnum V8 engine—biggest standard engine in any super car
- Choice of a rugged four-speed manual or shiftable three-speed automatic box
- Heavy-duty torsion bars, sway bar and shocks
- Heavy-duty (11-inch) brakes
- An extra leaf in the right rear spring to tame the torque
- F70 x 14" Red Line wide tread tires
- Disappearing headlights
- Foam-padded, vinyl-trimmed bucket seats up front
- Full instrumentation (no idiot lights)
- Electric clock
- Bumblebee stripe

Optional: Dodge's formidable Hemi 426 that pours out 425 bhp @ 5000 rpm and 490 lbs.-ft. of torque @ 4000 rpm.

Next step is to see Charger R/T and put it through its paces. The first few feet in Charger R/T will change your idea of cars completely.

 **CHRYSLER** MOTORS CORPORATION

Dodge Charger

It looks like the Chrysler Corporation is flat out
in the automobile business again.

Last year, we applauded Plymouth for building what we thought was the best looking Detroit car of 1967, the Barracuda. A remarkable feat, considering the Chrysler Corporation's odd, unstable styling history which, since the Airflow, has been marked by committee-styled cars which, aside from lacking integrity of design, have oscillated between being far out to the point of vulgarity and being timid to the point of sterility—a seemingly endless series of overcompensations for each preceding year. With this background, we were pleasantly surprised by the '67 Barracuda, but quite prepared to wait years before Chrysler came up with a worthy successor. We conjured a picture of designers and stylists lying about their studios, spent from their Barracuda effort, and barely able to create so much as a new bumper for 1968.

Imagine, therefore, our surprise—again pleasant—when we saw Dodge's new Charger. Working with Chrysler Corporation's 117-in. wheelbase "B" series body/chassis, the designers that we'd imagined were worn out have not only achieved far more than a face-lift, they have easily surpassed the mark of excellence set less than a year ago.

The only 1968 car which comes close to challenging the new Charger for styling accolades is the new Corvette, which is remarkably similar to the Charger, particularly when viewed from the rear quarter. But, we give the honors to the Charger for several reasons. First, the Corvette, being a smaller car in both seating capacity and wheelbase, has a much easier time attaining the desired sporty image. Second, Dodge stylists have shown that they can create a car in the current idiom with originality, combining just the right amount of tasteful conformity with that novelty and freshness which attracts attention. Originality takes guts in Dodge's position as the smaller division of the number three automaker, but the Charger's aerodynamic wedge theme is not only distinctly new but it is very like the new breed of wind-tunnel tested sports/racing cars which are just now making their debut in the 1967 Can-Am series. Third, while the Charger is a vast improvement over its predecessor, the 1968 Corvette is anticlimactic after the Mako Shark show cars which preceded it.

Chrysler Corporation, then, is flat-out in the automobile business again. The Marlin-

Dodge stylists have shown that
they can create a car in the current idiom
with originality, combining just the
right amount of tasteful conformity with
that novelty which attracts attention.

like Charger of the past (really a Coronet with a hastily added fastback roof), and the similarly makeshift Barracuda were grim reminders of the Corporation's close call with financial disaster in the early Sixties. But the belt-tightening policies of Lynn Townsend—Chrysler's chief executive since 1961, and more recently Board Chairman—combined with his intense efforts to improve and increase the Corporation's manufacturing facilities seem to be paying off. The 1967 Barracuda and the new Charger, each with its own distinctive sheet metal now, are evidence of Chrysler's increasing strength and ability to meet both the financial and creative challenge of the specialty car age.

Specialty cars are conceived from a significantly different planning philosophy than that of the bread-and-butter cars which Detroit used to build exclusively. Bread-and-butter cars are built with the primary intention of offending no potential buyer, rendering the cars largely featureless and unexciting. Specialty cars, on the other hand, are built to please specific groups of

customers. We like the more positive philosophy behind the specialty car, and the Charger is chock-full of features with obvious appeal for the performance-minded enthusiast.

The aerodynamic appearance of the Charger (it's as aerodynamically slippery as it looks, according to Chrysler's engineers) is accented by a rear spoiler combined with a truncated rear end for a Kamm effect—a design approach which has become almost mandatory in modern racing cars. The Charger takes on the nose-down appearance common to both NASCAR and NHRA, and the bulging rear fenders should accommodate the racing tires used in both drag and stock car racing with a minimum of rework. The greenhouse, following the sharply curved sideglass, slants steeply towards the center of the car, very reminiscent of Le Mans Ferraris, particularly when viewed from the rear. A tunnel-type backlight is used instead of a pure fastback (a styling feature fast going out of fashion from over-use). The smaller rear window of the tunnel roof also

gives much less distortion to rear vision than a steeply slanted fastback window.

Further visual performance identity is achieved by the use of a racing-style gas filler cap mounted high on the left rear quarter, and quasi fog/driving/parking and turn signal lights mounted low in the front bumper. Matte black paint is used extensively in the grille and around the tail lights. Full wheel cut-outs, fat tires on 6-inch rims, and simulated engine compartment exhaust vents in the hood (which also house turn signal indicator lights, like the Mustang GT) and at the leading edge of the doors complete the Charger's complement of visually "in" features.

The interior of the Charger carries the GT theme further, with bucket seats, map pockets in the doors, and a well-padded dash with a full complement of instruments set in a matte black background. The tachometer and speedometer are directly in front of the driver while the smaller engine instruments are to the right of the driver, but angled towards him.

With all this performance image going for the Charger, we just had to order an engine to go with it—and when you're talking a Chrysler product, the performance engine is the Hemi. There just isn't more honest horsepower available off the showroom floor than you get from this bright orange monster. While there are larger displacement engines to be had (Dodge offers a 440 cu. in. V-8 option for the Charger for less money than the 426 cu. in. Hemi), none of them can be had with two 4-barrel carburetion.

The Hemi, despite its high performance carburetion, comes very close to meeting smog control regulations without any modifications, hence, has had only minor alterations to the carburetor and distributor calibrations to meet the new laws. The carburetors feed the hemispherical combustion chambers through huge ports and 2.25-in. intake valves with thin (.309-in.) stems, all calculated to put as much fuel/air mixture in the Hemi as possible. The exhaust system is as efficient, with 1.94-in. valves, thin stems, and cast headers leading to a 2.5-in. dual exhaust system.

The rest of the Hemi is just as tough, with cross-bolted caps for three of its five main bearings; a specially heat-treated, forged steel crankshaft; big, husky connecting rods; forged domed pistons; solid lifters and heavy duty pushrods; and a dual-breaker distributor—in short, a racing engine. And that's what it was originally designed for.

The only 1968 car which comes close to challenging the new Charger for styling accolades is the new Corvette, itself remarkably similar to the Charger, particularly when viewed from the rear.

When Chrysler decided to sell the Hemi as an option, they found it was cheaper to carry over the racing parts into production, in most cases, than to tool up for cheaper, street parts. For all-out competition, about all you need is the high compression pistons (same basic design, but more pop-up), a longer duration camshaft, and a set of tubular headers. For stock car racing, there is a very special "ram-tuned" intake manifold and a giant Holley 4-bbl. carb.

Our "street" Hemi was more than powerful enough for any use an ordinary citizen might find. Rated conservatively at 425 hp and 490 lbs./ft. of torque, the Hemi propelled the Charger through the quarter-mile traps at just over 105 mph, covering the distance in 13.5 seconds—not bad for 4346 lbs. test weight and a "cooking" engine. The drag racers buy a 500-lb. lighter 2-door sedan, and do some of the tuning we mentioned above, to go through the traps at close to 130 mph—just in case you had any doubts about our engine being in street tune.

Some of you may have had a Hemi before, and may have experienced some problems with it, particularly in the area of oil consumption. For 1968 the Hemi has undergone some changes to fix this problem and to insure against some others. New valve stem oil seals have cured the oil consumption problem, an oil pan windage tray has permitted the addition of an extra quart of oil to the sump to make sure that the oil pick-up never sucks air, and a fuel vapor separator has been added to the fuel line to prevent vapor lock (which can make hot starts difficult). A slightly longer duration camshaft is also new. Although the peak rating hasn't changed since 1967, the new cam improves the shape of the power curves. We suspect, however, that the camshaft and the windage tray are responsible for the Charger's extra one mph at the end of the quarter-mile, compared to the Plymouth Hemi Satellite we tested in April, 1966.

The Satellite we tested was a 4-speed manual, and we remarked at the time that we'd rather have had an automatic, so we ordered our Charger with one. We were right; the automatic is the plan. Driving through the special high-stall-speed torque convertor which comes with the Hemi, you can either shift manually, winding the Hemi right out to 6500 rpm, or leave it in Drive, where the TorqueFlite shifts for you at

DODGE CHARGER

Manufacturer: Dodge Division
Chrysler Corporation
7900 Joseph Campau
Detroit, Michigan

Number of dealers in U.S.: 3128

Vehicle type: Front-engine, rear-wheel-drive, 4-passenger sports sedan with all-steel integral body/chassis

Price as tested: NA
(Prices for the 1968 models had not been released by the manufacturer at press time)

Options on test car: Hemi engine, automatic transmission, power steering, power disc brakes, HD suspension, limited-slip differential, 15-in wheels and tires, sports console, floor-mounted gearshift, AM radio, vinyl roof, rear window de-fogger, special paint

ENGINE

Type: Water-cooled V-8, cast-iron block and heads, 5 main bearings
Bore x stroke..4.25 x 3.75 in, 108.2 x 95.2mm
Displacement..............426 cu in, 6981 cc
Compression ratio..............10.25 to one
Carburetion...............2 x 4-bbl Carter
Valve gear........Pushrod-operated overhead valves, mechanical lifters
Power (SAE)..........425 bhp @ 5000 rpm
Torque (SAE)........490 lbs/ft @ 4000 rpm
Specific power output....0.99 bhp/cu in, 61.1 bhp/liter
Max. recommended engine speed...6500 rpm

DRIVE TRAIN

Transmission...............3-speed automatic
Max. torque converter ratio........2.1 to one
Final drive ratio...................3.23 to one

Gear	Ratio	Mph/1000 rpm	Max. test speed
I	2.45	9.7	63 mph (6500 rpm)
II	1.45	16.5	107 mph (6500 rpm)
III	1.00	24.0	139 mph (5800 rpm)

DIMENSIONS AND CAPACITIES

Wheelbase........................117.0 in
Track............F: 59.5 in, R: 59.2 in
Length..........................208.0 in
Width............................76.6 in
Height...........................53.2 in
Ground clearance...................5.7 in
Curb weight.....................4035 lbs
Test weight.....................4346 lbs
Weight distribution, F/R......55.5/44.5%
Lbs/bhp (test weight)..............10.2
Battery capacity....12 volts, 78 amp/hr
Alternator capacity................445 watts
Fuel capacity....................19.0 gal
Oil capacity......................6.0 qts
Water capacity..................18.0 qts

SUSPENSION

F: Ind., unequal-length wishbones, torsion bars, anti-sway bar
R: Rigid axle, semi-elliptic leaf springs

STEERING

Type........Power-assisted recirculating ball
Turns lock-to-lock.........................5.3
Turning circle..........................41 ft

BRAKES

F.......................11.0-in vented disc
R............10.0 x 2.5-in cast iron drum
Swept area.......................387.8 sq in

WHEELS AND TIRES

Wheel size and type...6.0JK x 15-in, stamped steel wheel, 5-bolt
Tire make, size and type....Goodyear F70-15, 2-ply nylon, tubeless
Test inflation pressures...F: 30 psi, R: 30 psi
Tire load rating.....1280 lbs per tire @ 24 psi

PERFORMANCE

Zero to	Seconds
30 mph	1.7
40 mph	2.5
50 mph	3.5
60 mph	4.8
70 mph	6.0
80 mph	8.5
90 mph	10.0
100 mph	12.5

Standing ¼-mile.........13.5 sec @ 105 mph
80-0 mph panic stop.........274 ft (0.78 G)
Fuel mileage......9-12 mpg on premium fuel
Cruising range...................171–228 mi

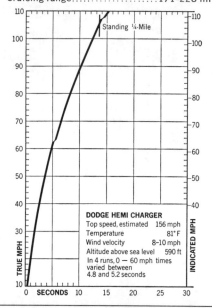

Standing ¼-Mile

DODGE HEMI CHARGER
Top speed, estimated   156 mph
Temperature   81°F
Wind velocity   8-10 mph
Altitude above sea level   590 ft
In 4 runs, 0 — 60 mph times varied between 4.8 and 5.2 seconds

TRUE MPH / INDICATED MPH / SECONDS

CHECK LIST

ENGINE
Starting.................................Fair
Response..........................Very Good
Vibration...............................Good
Noise..................................Fair

DRIVE TRAIN
Shift linkage...........................Poor
Shift smoothness.......................Good
Drive train noise................Very Good

STEERING
Effort............................Excellent
Response..........................Very Good
Road feel..............................Poor
Kickback...........................Excellent

SUSPENSION
Ride comfort...........................Good
Roll resistance...................Very Good
Pitch control.....................Very Good
Harshness control......................Fair

HANDLING
Directional control...............Very Good
Predictability....................Very Good
Evasive maneuverability..........Very Good
Resistance to sidewinds..........Very Good

BRAKES
Pedal pressure....................Very Good
Response...............................Good
Fade resistance...................Very Good
Directional stability..................Good

CONTROLS
Wheel position.........................Good
Pedal position....................Very Good
Gearshift position................Very Good
Relationship......................Very Good
Small controls....................Very Good

INTERIOR
Ease of entry/exit................Very Good
Noise level (cruising)..................Good
Front seating comfort..................Poor
Front leg room....................Very Good
Front head room...................Excellent
Front hip/shoulder room..........Very Good
Rear seating comfort...................Good
Rear leg room..........................Good
Rear head room....................Very Good
Rear hip/shoulder room...........Very Good
Instrument comprehensiveness....Excellent
Instrument legibility...............Excellent

VISION
Forward...........................Very Good
Front quarter..........................Good
Side..............................Excellent
Rear quarter...........................Fair
Rear...................................Good

WEATHER PROTECTION
Heater/defroster..................Excellent
Ventilation.......................Excellent
Air conditioner.........................—
Weather sealing...................Excellent

CONSTRUCTION QUALITY
Sheet metal.......................Very Good
Paint.............................Very Good
Chrome............................Very Good
Upholstery........................Very Good
Padding...........................Very Good
Hardware..........................Very Good

GENERAL
Headlight illumination............Excellent
Parking and signal lights.........Excellent
Wiper effectiveness...............Excellent
Service accessibility..................Fair
Trunk space.......................Very Good
Interior storage space............Excellent
Bumper protection.................Very Good

about 5500 rpm. If you keep your foot in it that long, the 2-3 shift has you doing well over 90 mph. If you cool it, the automatic lets you drive the Hemi like the 230-hp, 318 cu. in. (standard equipment for the Charger). It would take a fairly sharp mother-in-law to suspect that you had anything but the most docile of powerplants underneath the hood.

We were prepared to not like the brakes on our Charger, as the brakes on Chrysler's "B" body cars have previously fallen short of our standards, but things have changed. We ordered the disc brake option, wanting all the stopping power we could get to go with the Hemi's go power, and found the brakes to be very satisfactory. Directional stability was good, and our stopping distances were right around 274 ft. (.78 G), a perfectly acceptable figure, considering the mass of the car. We did encounter fade once, early in our braking tests, which we attributed to "green fade," a phenomenon that new brake pads go through once before they settle down. Afterwards, we experienced no fade in five successive panic stops from 80 mph.

Handling was dominated by the Charger's inherent understeer characteristics, a function of both the massive Hemi engine in the front of the car and the large front anti-sway bar. The understeer tendency was strong enough that once the limit of adhesion was reached and the front end began to plow, only instant full throttle in the lower gears would get the rear end out. A gentle increase in throttle would only increase the amount of understeer. By anticipating breakaway, we could coax the Charger into a 4-wheel slide with a flick of the wheel and a simultaneous increase in throttle. This induced power-slide was fairly easy to control, but it took up a lot of the road. Generally, the Goodyear F70-15 tires gave good performance and allowed fairly fast cornering without breaking traction—the only way to go, on the street; other maneuvers we restricted to the test track. The Charger assumes a fair amount of body lean when cornering, despite the giant anti-sway bar, stiff springs, and heavy-duty shock absorbers—all of which come with the Hemi.

The Hemi Charger's ride, while harsh by most standards, will be called appropriately firm by most enthusiasts. There will be those who will argue that a Pontiac GTO or an Olds 4-4-2 handles as well without the attendant harshness. But both of these cars suffer from a certain amount of axle hop under hard braking and acceleration, something we didn't encounter with the Charger. It's all a question of how hard the rubber bushings are, and, in the case of the Charger, how many leaves the rear springs have. We'd rather suffer a harshness than axle hop, if a common solution to both problems can't be found. Much of the harshness we felt resulted from the 30 psi tire pressures that are recommended

with the Hemi.

While we are discussing handling, we ought to point out that unless your Hemi Charger is going to be used strictly on the drag strip, power steering is a must, not only for it's ease of operation—you've got to be a weight lifter to park a manual steering Hemi—but also because of the faster steering ratio in the power unit. The manual steering has an overall ratio of 28.8-to-one while the power gear is 18.8-to-one—almost twice as fast.

Our main objections to the Charger were on the inside. The seats are terrible—they just don't do anything right. Our unhappiness concerned not so much the seat cushions themselves, but the position of the seat in the car and the angle between the seat proper and the seat back. The seat is very low, relative to the steering wheel, and the seat back—not adjustable—seems to be almost perpendicular to the seat cushion, forcing us to sit bolt-upright. The guys who design seats should have to sit in them while they work at their drawing boards.

We also didn't like the shift lever in the optional console we ordered. Not only is it ugly and out of place in the context of the rest of the Charger's interior, but the detent button is directly on top, making for an unnatural motion when shifting manually. Of the levers we've seen, the T-handle with the button on the side, like the Cougar and the Mustang, or the "goal-post" shifter used by Buick and Oldsmobile, where one squeezes the crossbar to release the detent, are both excellent. We'd settle for either in place of the Charger's (which is shared by all Chrysler console shifters).

With the exception of the rear quarters, vision from within the Charger is good, and we aren't prepared to sacrifice the attractive tunnel-roof wings for visibility. We do, however, recommend a right-hand outside mirror to compensate.

We don't care for (and didn't order) optional belt-like stripes around the rear quarters that Dodge is emphasizing this year. Stripes—like fastbacks—are out in any form; matte black anti-glare paint on the hood is in now, and a good design could be worked into the Charger's hood vent sculpturing.

The Chrysler Corporation is opposed to ventless door windows, on the grounds that there really isn't a practical flow-through ventilation system. So the Charger still has vent windows, and we suspect that Chrysler might just be right. Time will tell. We were glad to have them on our Charger, because air-conditioning is not available with the Hemi engine—it just won't fit.

To add frosting to the cake, the new Charger is 165 lbs. lighter than the old one, and while at this writing prices were as unavailable as peace in Vietnam, we suspect the new Charger will be cheaper than the old one. These days, when you get something better for less, snap it up. ●

A PAIR OF "DANDY'S"

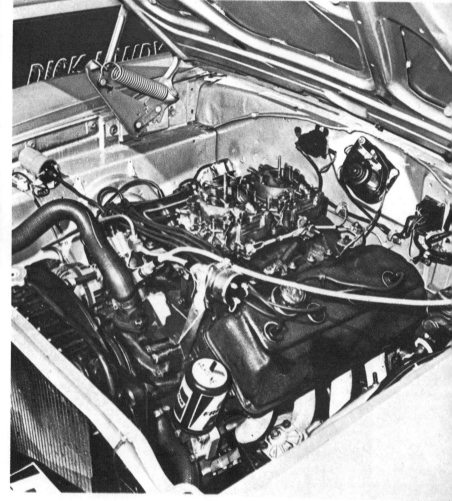

Anybody can become President, right? Well, almost anybody. Dick Landy's got more than his share of the necessary credentials; comes from a large family, plays touch football, is kind of a folk hero, even builds neat cars. For the '68 campaign he's in the running — not for the top office in the land — but Top Stock, which is nearly as good. And his brother Mike will be in there stumping — hitting the primaries — and secondaries, too — on a street-type 440 Coronet R/T. "Dandy Dick" himself, as he used to be known in the good old match-race days, handles the 426 hemi Charger.

*"Dandy Dick" Landy is ready to hit the trail for
another year of Performance Clinics and drag
racing. His classroom is this pair of '68 Dodges*

Eric Dahlquist

photography: Eric Rickman

Set your watch ahead; you've just passed through a time zone. Back on the other side are the good old days of the amateur automobile sportsman, unsophisticated backyard engineering, disorganized drag races (that the remembering seem better than they were) and the expenditure of thousands of hours of enthusiastic labor, all in the name of the sport. Today, some of that heady, idealistic atmosphere is still around but the whole complexion of drag racing has changed — it has fragmented into two separate worlds.

Dick Landy is one of the new men — professional drag racer. Five years ago, a professional was kind of a non-person. With the exception of Don Garlits, Chris Karamesines and maybe a few others, individuals deriving all their income from drag racing didn't exist. Now it's a different world, populated by the Landys, Nicholsons, Schartmans, Jenkinses, Hubert Platts and still, you know it, Don Garlitses; stars of a lesser magnitude to be sure, but not very much different from Mario Andretti or A.J. Foyt. Probably the most significant aspect of this year's NHRA Nationals (overlooked by most of the nation's tradition-oriented drag racing press) was the behavior of the fans, thousands of them, swarming out of the stands after the last round of Top Fuel to canonize their hero — Don Garlits. It had never happened before.

Dick Landy got his race cars early this year and even drove the Dodge Charger home from Detroit in September. That would have been completely out of the question two years ago when he herded a factory fuel funny car, but Chrysler has redirected their interest to something closer to what they sell. If you stand on the back straightaway at Riverside and watch Bruce McLaren's world-beating Can-Am Group 7 cars — machines that are aerodynamically correct and properly spoilered — zip past at 200 mph, always on the verge of becoming airborne, you know another reason why the factory became leery of funnies twice the size, unstreamlined and perilously tall.

No, they've found it far more rewarding to initiate the now-famous Dodge Performance Clinics, where Dick can tell you the right way to use the right parts and how to get them. And, of course, you don't have to run Dick's cars except at the Nationals because that would be like asking your local high school team to play the L.A. Rams. He participates only against other pros but you can learn something if you pay attention; that's the whole idea. ■ ■

Chart on following page

ABOVE — Inside the boss's machine there is a Motorola-Jones Tel-Tale tach and super-stout shifter, the Hurst Competition Plus. TOP — When Landy says he has a deep-sump oil pan, he means d-e-e-e-p, like 8 quarts, maybe. Ideally, oil float-level should be 5 inches below block. BELOW — And, of course, the "good guys," members of the Scat Pack, Dick Landy (right) and brother Mike. The absolute latest scoop is that Dick's hemi Charger is being set up to run AHRA's new 3400-pound super stock class, where weight will be standardized and 13.5:1 pistons are legal. Given the incentive of heads-up competition and pieces hemi loves, action should be frantic!

	Dandy Dick's 426 Dodge Charger	Brother Mike's 440 Dodge R/T
Bore & Stroke:	4.25 x 3.750 inches	4.320 x 3.750 inches
Overbore:	.005-inch	Std.
Pistons:	Stock 12.5:1. (Note: NHRA rules change allows use of any piston shape providing max. dome cc is 88.3.) Valve clearance may require some milling on piston top. Clearance .008. Right piston, 2836164; left, 2836163	Forgedtrue 12.5:1 with .070-inch valve relief. Running clearance .008
Piston pin:	1.030-inch	1.094-inch
Rings:	Dykes-type, two compression (end gap .016-in.), one oil (.020-.030-in.) PN 2808423. (These are .005 rings.)	Same
Deck height:	See "pistons" above.	.027-inch below block
Connecting rods and crankshaft:	Stock. (Note: Crankshafts are Tufftrided for long wear and should not be polished for extra clearance.) Connecting rod side clearance should be .012-.018-inch.	Same
Main bearings and connecting rod bearings:	Clevite .0015 to .003	Same
Camshaft:	Isky 590, 318°, .590-inch lift, 104° intake lobe center. (See HRM Oct. '66.) Valve lash is .028-.032-inch cold.	Isky 1012B. 104° intake lobe center. Valve lash is .028-.032-inch cold. 323°, .520-inch lift
Rocker arms:	Stock	Adjustable rocker arms and pushrods from Stage III. PN 2463242, right; 2463243, left; pushrods 2402326
Valve Springs:	Isky 4105 outer, 906 RH inner (PN 2836104) installed at 1.86-inch cold	Isky 4105 outer, 906 RH inner (PN 2836104) installed at 1.86-inch
Heads:	Stock with exhaust valve face cut to 58° for clearance with Isky cam. Volume equals 167.7cc.	Stock. Volume equals 79.5cc.
Intake manifold:	Stock with all sharp edges removed and dividers milled down. #2531943	Edelbrock high-rise 4-bbl
Oil pan:	Modified for deep sump. (See HRM February '66.) K-member must be notched slightly for clearance and then reboxed with identical-thickness steel. Milodon oil pickup system is used.	Same
Ignition:	Prestolite 250 transistor with hemi distributor (PN 2444333). Mechanical tach drive uses S-W "T" adapter (PN 669 X K5) to operate Motorola-Jones Tel-Tale tach and Synchro-Start over-speed governor (PN GHA 5A430A-U). Over-speed governor is used to limit rpm to 8000 in case of missed shift. Total distributor advance 34-38°, full advance at 800-1000 rpm (with vacuum line disconnected).	Prestolite 250 transistor with hemi distributor (PN 2444333). Automatic transmission-equipped cars do not require over-speed governor.
Fuel system:	Std. Carter dual AFB's updated with jet kit (PN 2836137). Stock fuel pump is used with two Bendix Blue Top electric pumps at rear. Gasoline is routed through Milodon "Cool Can" and 3/8 Carter filter before carburetor.	Std. Carter AVS (Air Valve Secondary) richened 2%. Remainder of system identical to hemi.
Lubrication:	30W Valvoline Racing Motor Oil with Fram high-capacity racing oil filter. Dick recommends that this oil be used in all high-performance engines because of its excellent antifoam properties.	Same
Transmission:	Heavy-duty 4-speed all synchromesh modified to slick-shift configuration (HRM Mar. '66). Hurst Competition Plus shifter is used with Hurst Line-Loc on front brakes only. Hurst reverse lock-out has been added. For racing applications only, automatic transmission fluid can replace normal lubricant to lessen drag.	TorqueFlite modified by B&M Automotive incorporates manual shift plate (HRM Sept. '67) and quicker 2-3 shift. Street hemi torque-converter has been adapted to 440 wedge automatic by using special flex-plate (PN 2466326). Hurst Dual Pattern shifter is used.
Clutch-pressure plate assembly:	Clutch 2800845, plate 2800846. Stock with Schiefer 40-pound forged steel flywheel that will not explode. RC scattershield/bellhousing used.	None
Differential:	Stock heavy-duty 9¾-inch Sure-Grip-equipped unit with 4.88 final drive	Identical except for 8¾-inch pinion and 4.56 final drive
Wheels & Tires:	Front, 4 x 15-in. Cragar wheels fitted with Goodyear 7.75 x 15. Rear, 6 x 15-in. Cragar rims with Goodyear 10.50 x 15 slicks. Recommended air pressure 50 psi front, 10-16 rear. (Note: In an effort to prevent tires from spinning on rims, some racers use very light inner tubes but these do not push against the tire with sufficient force at lower pressure. Standard dragster inner liners seem to work best.)	440 uses same wheels and front tires as hemi, but rears are 8.90 x 15, inflated to 12-15 psi.
Suspension:	Front stock 6 cyl. torsion bar, rear Factory Experimental leaf springs, (PN 2836128, right; 2836129, left). Shocks are std. production front with about 10,000 miles wear and dust shields removed for lightness. Rear shocks are heavy-duty and pinion snubber is shimmed to within one inch of floor.	Same
Headers:	30-inch x 2-inch tubing to 3-inch x 12-inch cloverleaf collectors by Doug's Headers.	38-inch x 1⅞-inch tubing to 2¾-inch x 12-inch cloverleaf collectors by Doug's Headers
Total weight:	3650 pounds with 5 gallons of gas	3550 pounds with fuel tank half full
Performance:	10.86-127.10	11.99-118.10

WE'VE GOT YOU CORNERED
CHARGER R/T

We'd like to hand you a line. Right through the esses. And suddenly "sport sedan" takes on an all-new meaning. Wide-treads, heavy-duty springs, shocks, brakes, sway bar. We wouldn't sell a car like this without them. Magnum 440 or optional Hemi. Dodge will see you around.

STANDARD CHARGER R/T EQUIPMENT
- 440-cid Magnum (4-bbl.) V8, 375 hp
- Choice of 3-speed automatic or Hurst 4-speed manual • Dual exhausts
- HD suspension • HD shocks • HD brakes
- Dodge Charger Rallye instrument panel • F70x14 wide-treads

OPTIONAL
- 426 Hemi

DON'T BE CAUGHT DEAD WRONG—DRIVE SAFELY.

 CHRYSLER MOTORS CORPORATION

Dodge Scat Pack ... the cars with the Bumblebee stripes

We were a bit early (two months) for the Riverside-Motor Trend 500, but it worked out better that way. Good-handling street runner can use help before serious racing.

Twin Carter-carbed 426 cu. in. hemi is surprisingly docile on the street circuit. Comes on hard in racing, with proper refinements. Stock equipment includes anti-smog hardware, though not pump. Fuel fill, right, is snap-open "racing" type. It's too handy here and should be fitted with a lock.

SHOWROOM RACE

BY STEVE KELLY ■ It's doubtful that I'd ever want a hemi-engined Dodge Charger 500 for my street machine, but if I did, it would be an assembly-line copy of the kind of car used in 17.4 NASCAR action. If it was a tunnel-port 427 Torino that interested me, I'd still be searching for one. You've got to hand it to the Chrysler guys; if they race it, they also sell it. That really doesn't make them heroes, but it does help promote the image of stock car racing. When you can buy your race car, or at least the basics of one, through a dealership, you're a lot closer to racing *real* stock cars.

Charger 500's are specially outfitted models of Charger R/T's. The differences lie in the same body revisions that contribute to better aerodynamics, primarily to give the stock car racers a better break. This is a limited-edition car right now, since five hundred or so must be built in order to comply with the F.I.A. description of "stock." But if they catch on with the buying public, that's fine, and more will be built.

The grille, normally inset, is moved forward, flush with the leading edge of the frontal sheet metal. This eliminates the air trap of regular Chargers. In back, the rear window is angled sharply and set in new metal stretched between the sailfins. Standard production Chargers have a near-vertical rear glass, set almost even with the rear seat back. With the 500 config-

uration, there's a lot more room for a package tray, but almost none for a deck-lid. There is one, but it's about as big as a glovebox door. As much grain as you'd care to pour into the trunk can be carried, but suitcase size is restricted to ultra-slim designs. With a little jockeying, though, you can fit a lot in there, but nonetheless it's not an easy job. Okay, it may be a gripe, but Buddy Baker, Charlie Glotzbach, or Bobby Isaac will probably never care about it, or how handy the map pockets are in the doors. They travel light, and always on the same road.

In essence, that is what this car is designed to do. It just happens that you can also buy it. Part of the reason is that although Chrysler Divisions may be making money, they're not exactly floating in the green stuff. If they can sell a few of their race car-type machines, it helps cover designing costs. In most instances, Chrysler has had to work the reverse by racing facsimiles of production cars. Now they've followed the competition by building "special edition" hardware and furthered this by putting them up for retail purchase. We'll find out later how this marketing philosophy works.

Charger 500 power is by either a 440 cubic inch "wedge" developing 375 horsepower, or by the optional 425-hp, dual-four-carbureted hemi. In both instances, the transmission choice is between a four-speed manual and a TorqueFlite three-speed automatic. Rear gearing is 3.23:1, standard for the automatic,

FAR LEFT — Dash is a bit of all right. Gauges are well-placed, easy to view, and angled toward driver. Excellent interior comfort and room is part of the bargain.
NEAR LEFT — Hemi-engined MoPars with automatics have trans coolers in standard form.

Body shape is a real wind-cheater. Air-traps have been designed out. Wait till a 500 gets on a super-speedway: half-a-foot lower and half-a-light-year faster.

photography:
Eric Rickman

You don't have to wear a driving suit, crash helmet, or goggles in this Dodge á la NASCAR stocker — but if it makes you feel better, go ahead

and 3.54:1, standard with four-speed. Lower ratios (higher numbers) can be had through dealers' parts counters and are absolutely necessary for anything but street operation. Let's face it: If you've got a hemi in *anything,* it's going to be for more than street use.

Each 500 in use for this test was hemi-equipped. Three of them were readied for us, but we used only two. One of them, the first four-speed car, was "borrowed" (by person or persons as yet not convicted) and most of the parts liberated. Due to this unexpected car loan (that's not what the police termed it), we spent most of our time with the automatic car. Given the choice, that's the way I'd have it, anyway. Four-speeds are nice, and generally a little quicker; but the TorqueFlite's the way to go on the street, and it's certainly no slouch on the track unless the track has bends in it, and then there's no way an automatic will work there).

Driving ranged from in-town, bumper-to-bumper conditions to high-speed (well, not real high) runs across the desert. We covered a good bit of the Southwest, including Riverside International Raceway and Orange County International Raceway. This is the kind of car you make excuses to drive. Other than its altered roof and grille, it is a Charger, and everything said here applies to "production" Chargers too.

Equipped as it was, the automatic car is easily one of the best high-speed stockers we've sampled, and quite a few of them have been put in our hands too. We get irritated at cars that are too quiet, and that sometimes diminish handling for the sake of comfort — or cars that are extremely noisy, handle well, but give you an earache within an hour. Handling without earaches is an apt summation of the Charger. One other thing: The wind glides around this car so smoothly it hardly makes a sound. Keeping a vent window open at 70 or thereabouts is rough, but it proves that a good amount of wind is directed alongside the car, the correct path for it to assist stability.

Steering and braking are good at all speeds. Both cars had power steering and power-assisted front disc brakes, all of which are optional. Low-speed maneuvers produced predictable wheel directing, though washout (or front-tire roll-under, if you prefer) is easy to get if you push the car hard 'round a tight bend. On top end, there's no absence of road feel. Earlier MoPar power steering tended to relieve the driver of contact with the front wheels, but that's all been remedied. Standard brakes are drum-type, and of fairly good size for hemi cars, but we wouldn't have one without front discs for street driving; that's a lot of weight out in front. Discs are mandatory. They worked repeatedly in 100-plus mph to zero stops, without complaint or loss of stopping power.

SHOWROOM RACER

Interior dimensions satisfy the requirements of a six-footer, and that's getting harder to accomplish on intermediate-size cars each year. Rear leg and head room is generous, and this is one of the few cars we've tested lately with more seat adjustment than we could use. A neat item for the '69 Dodge is a manual bucket-seat adjuster, which costs just under $40 and allows both vertical and tilt adjustment. There're six variations of it, plus the ten positions of the regular fore-and-aft adjuster. Since Chargers aren't available with tilting wheels, this item makes comfortable seating possible for drivers of all sizes.

Beginning this year, stock car racing under F.I.A. sanction prohibits use of more than one carburetor, which means Chrysler will be dragging out all their old non-stock, single-four intake manifolds for hemis. They've been using these ever since a ruling forced the removal of the stock dual-four intake and replacing it with the singles. Sometimes it doesn't pay to be too fast. However, drag racers will make out okay, since the two-fours are still stock and therefore legal.

But it takes more than a pair of four-throat Carters to make a hemi work right. Getting one in the 13's for a quarter-mile, in stock clothing, is about all one can ask for. Well, we got it that far, but we had to revert to open headers in order to do so. An open-header 426 ought to catch high 12's, but this was the 3.23-geared automatic, with street plugs (N-10Y Champions), no carb rejetting, ignition at 12 degrees Before Top Dead Center on the crank, and total advance not cutting in until past 3000. With an automatic having a sub-2000-rpm stall speed, this is like running with one flat tire. The mere fact that it bested 100 mph in this form calls for a Purple Heart. A top e.t. of 13.80 seconds and a speed of 105.01 mph was the result of this mediocre effort.

We got down to cases with the four-speed. Norm Thatcher put in time here, slipping in a 4.10:1 limited-slip rear gear set and recalibrating the distributor to

49° total, all of which were at work by 2500 rpm. In short, it was prepared for quarter-miling. Orange County International Raceway management consented to let us burn off some more tire rubber, and we did a good job of it.

With the automatic car, we moved the lever as the tach needle passed 5500 rpm. Stock TorqueFlites have a slight delay, so the actual shift took place at 5700-5800 rpm. We buzzed the stick car to six grand for each shift. The 4.10 gear brought us through the traps in high gear at 5200 rpm, using a 29-inch-diameter tire. A lower gear would certainly help, but the 4.10 is just about the steepest you can use and still get decent street operation. Best time with the stick-shift machine was 13.48, and 109 mph. As we said, a hemi will go in the 12's with external touching-up, but a really good teardown — and money — will put a hemi-stocker at the 11-second break-even mark.

A Borg & Beck dry-plate, 11- by 7-inch disc clutch assembly is used for both 426 and 440 powerplants. It does a better-than-average job too, producing longer-than-expected service before needing a rest. Any clutch that'll continue to stick after 10 or 12 successive runs while a 490-lbs-ft engine is thrashing against it can't be all bad. The Hurst linkage used here is a welcome addition to ease the shifting task.

If the photos suggest a rather high ground clearance here, it's due to the 15-inch wheels and F70 tires supplied with hemi-equipped Dodges. We also had a little trouble getting used to their appearance, but a good tire is worth a lot more than low riding height. Dropping the car is comparatively easy. Large-diameter front tires are no longer a drag racing speed secret, so they're worth having.

More than 2500 miles of driving went by during our Charger time. Didn't mind a bit of it, either. So what about the trunk? It'll still hold a lot of wheat, right? Just pour it in. We may not be planning to buy a Charger 500, but it won't be because we don't like them. It has more to do with practicality. The older you get, the more practical you're *supposed* to be. Right now, we're busy makin' everybody see how practical we are. Soon as we've done that, then we can go buy a hemi-engined something-or-other.

■ ■

VEHICLE
Charger 500 coupe

PRICE
Base ....(440 engine, std.) $3591.00
As Tested
  (Hemi: $648.20, extra) $5261.00

ENGINE
Type ....OHV V8
Cylinders 8
Bore and stroke ....4.25 x 3.75 in.
Displacement ....426 cu. in.
Compression ratio 10.25:1
Horsepower ....425 @ 5000 rpm
Torque ....490 lbs.-ft. @ 4000 rpm
Valves: Intake ....2.25-in. dia.
        Exhaust ....1.94-in. dia.
Camshaft:
  Lift ...490-in. intake; .480-in. exhaust
  Duration ....284° intake and exhaust
Tappets ....Mechanical, .028 lash
Carburetion ....Dual Carter AFB
                       series 4-bbl
Exhaust ....Dual, low restriction

TRANSMISSION
Type ....Manual: Floor-mounted shift,
             synchro all forward gears
         Auto: Torque converter with
       automatically operated planetary
                   gear transmission

Ratios:	Automatic	4-speed
1st	2.45:1	2.65:1
2nd	1.45:1	1.93:1
3rd	1.00:1	1.39:1
4th		1.00:1

Clutch ....11-inch diameter, dry-plate
        Borg and Beck. 2523-lb. total
                         spring load

DIFFERENTIAL
Type ....Separable type unit,
        friction-bias limited slip with
          8.75-in.-dia. ring gear, on
          automatic. Unitized housing
             and 9.75-in.-dia ring
               gear, 4-speed
Final drive ratio.....3.23:1, TorqueFlite
                       4.10:1, 4-speed

BRAKES
Type ....Front disc/rear drum with
        power assist. Floating-caliper
                         design
Dimensions:
          Front ...Disc, 11.04-in. dia.
          Rear .....Drum, 10-in. dia.
Total effective area .....131.6 sq. in.
Percent brake effectiveness,
  front 60%

SUSPENSION
Front ....Independent, lateral,
             nonparallel control arms
                  with torsion bars
Rear ....Parallel, 58 in. x 2.5 in.,
           longitudinal semi-elliptic
           rear springs. One piece-type
                  axle housing
Shocks ....Tubular, double-acting,
             1.0-in. piston dia.
Stabilizer ......Front only, .094-in.-dia.
Tires .....F70 x 15, 4-ply rated, belted
Wheel rim width ....6.0 in.
Steering:
  Type .....Chrysler. Recirculating ball
           with integral power assist
  Gear ratio 15.7:1
  Overall ratio 18.8:1
  Turning circle ...40.9 ft., curb to curb
  Wheel diameter ....16.0 in.
  Turns lock to lock 3.5

PERFORMANCE
Standing-start quarter-mile
  (Automatic) . .13.80 sec., 105.01 mph
  (4-speed): ....13.48 sec., 109.00 mph

FUEL CONSUMPTION
(TorqueFlite-equipped car only)
Best reading ....14.51 mpg
Poorest ....7.3 mpg
Average ....11.05 mpg
Recommended fuel ....Premium

DIMENSIONS
Wheelbase ....117.0 in.
Front track ....59.5 in.
Rear track ....58.5 in.
Overall height ....54.2 in.
Overall width ....76.7 in.
Overall length ....206.6 in.
Shipping weight ....3305 lb.
Test weight ....3740 lb.
Body/frame construction ......Unit
Fuel tank capacity ....19 gal.

THE CROWN COMES BACK

A four-speed Dodge Hemi Charger 500 takes the title of quickest test car. The automatic version wasn't far behind.

CAR LIFE ROAD TEST

THE NEW CHAMP had a score to settle, not only with the previous holder of CAR LIFE's quickest test car title, but with the magazine. The new champ is a Dodge, a Charger 500 with Hemi and four-speed. Last year's Dodge Hemi wasn't close to the championship, didn't even a get a good conduct medal, and we said so.

This year, things were different. Dodge sent a team—two Charger 500s, both Hemi-powered. One had a stick shift and the other an automatic.

The four-speed car, showroom stock right down to its tires and 3.55:1 axle ratio, turned an E.T. of 13.68 sec. The automatic—and mind, this is a car Mom could drive to bingo games— clocked a 13.92 sec. E.T.

The Chargers were more than just dragstrip terrors. On the handling course, they slammed through turns like the disguised NASCAR racers they really are, both drivers secure in the knowledge that they could run in close company because the cars would cover for human mistakes. In town, they responded to command, stuck to the road through rain and mud, and came through an hour-long freeway snarl without so much as a fouled spark-plug.

One has to be a student of Charger styling to notice what's different between everyday Chargers and Charger 500s. First, there's the modified fast-back with its flush rear window to replace the buttress-back on the rest of

the line. The flush grille takes a little longer (it's not recessed or divided), while the fixed headlights look completely ordinary. And, the characteristic Scat Pack bustle stripe is there. The overall effect, though, seemed to be a leaner, subtler package. It should be. Dodge expects an extra 5 mph or so from the shape at the NASCAR Super-speedways. NASCAR rules say Dodge must build at least 500 500s. Hence the name.

The special body modifications are not done at the factory. Instead, the required parts are shipped off to a builder where the rework is performed mostly in the area of the C-pillar and rear deck. Any body flaws the 500 has, it probably picks up there. The finished product still shows the old rear window mounting spot, and the trunk lid fit on our test car allowed water leaks.

Playing the option game is the usual way to get a high performance car,

CHARGER 500s

but the Charger 500 starts out impressive. The only significant performance option our matched pair of test cars had over and above the standard package was the Hemi engine. The 440 Magnum is standard in a Charger 500, along with the H.D. TorqueFlite, but the four-speed is no extra cost. Either transmission comes with its respective axle group and handling package (Track-Pack in Chrysler Corp. jargon).

Front disc brakes with power are a delete option, as are myriad other small touches like tach, rally-pack-type instrument panel, Hurst shifter. As a whole it makes up a good performance automobile.

We expected a great deal of difference between the automatic with the 3.23:1 rear axle ratio and the four-speed with a 3.55:1. There was little. The manual was slightly quicker in the last half of the quarter, by virtue of the lower axle ratio and a slightly sharper engine tune. But while the automatic could click off 13.9 sec. quarter elapsed times all day, the manual had to be worked hard to get its quicker times. Because of its lower

starting gear (9.40:1 vs. 7.92:1 overall for the automatic) it was hard to get a good bite out of the hole. Once underway, the next challenge was making a clean, smooth shift. That was no easy task with the stiff, balky four-speed. If the driver concentrated too long on getting a gear cleanly, the lag would often cause enough interruption in the power flow to break the tires loose again. Snap shifting cured this, but after missing a couple and watching the tach needle swing past seven, we became a little cautious. Finally, after a bit of practice and some brute-force shifter antics, times started to drop. On the last run, as dusk descended, the four-speed Charger recorded a

IMPRESSIVE HEMI engines had intelligent camming. Tire-smoking torque was taken from low end and added to top of the rev range, making Chargers fast without ferocious street manners.

TUNNEL PORT trunk is penalty of aerodynamic flush rear window, causing shortened trunk lid and inaccessible spare. Penalty: One muddied suit.

13.68, thus retrieving the honor of fastest production, full size CAR LIFE test car from the Mustang Mach I. (See March, "The First Great Mustang," page 64.)

The power and speed were spectacular, as expected; but most impressive was the integration of the overall performance package. Our two 500s seemed to do everything—go, stop, handle—smoothly and better than most other test cars. Brakes, chassis, and engine all seemed to complement each other. The key word here is chassis, since it was the superior suspension control that allowed the exceptional braking and power to be alloyed into the handling of the cars.

On the Orange County International Raceway handling course, they quickly displayed the predictable neutral handling that has become characteristic of performance MoPars. But there was something more. Testers soon found they were able to break deeper and deeper into the corners, even after turning the wheel. With practice it was possible to set up the drift angle, delicately balancing braking against steering—a technique known as "pitching" in racing, allowing phenomenal corner approach speeds. Coming out, it was the same except vice versa. Maintaining the drift with the throttle, at the proper moment the driver could correct with the wheel and immediately

blast full bore out of the corner and down the straight. That violent torque exhibited on the strip was quickly put to use accelerating instead of generating useless rear side-slip. These are all characteristics a race car builder shoots for and has to work hard to get. On a street machine they are a rare pleasure.

Reflecting, it is hard to say just what fundamental handling trait prevailed: understeer, oversteer or neutral. Mostly it was a matter of doing anything the testers liked, but specifically they displayed neutral steering with a slight initial understeer.

Handling integration was helped by both the brakes and engine. Brake

INTEGRATED PERFORMANCE Package is best description for Charger's handling. Superlative suspension allowed late braking and early acceleration in corners and extremely predictable neutral handling gave drivers a wide latitude of cornering maneuvers. Driver on the right won.

VERY thorough instrument panel complemented "all business" aura of the Chargers. Clock-shrouded tachometer was the only annoyance.

FINE interiors added comfort, good looks and definitely took Charger 500s out of the budget Supercar field. Buckets are too flat.

CHARGER 500s
continued

modulation, for instance, was definitely superior to a lot of power assisted disc/drum systems we've tested in the past. Rear wheel lock was there, if the driver tried hard enough, but it came much later than usual, allowing better utilization of the front disc. Our standard eight-stop test produced initial deceleration rates of 27 ft./sec./sec., certainly well above average. But stopping two tons of 80-mph automobile requires a lot of energy absorption, and predictably they began to fade, registering a couple of stops at 24 ft./sec./sec. Then, with smoke pouring off the front disc and the pungent odor of hot linings filling the car, the rate climbed back up to 28 ft./sec./sec. and stayed there for the duration of the test. We suspect a super-hard lining material was installed, and the first hard stops had glazed them. Then as they got extremely hot, the glaze wore off, and the pads got stickier.

It was the predictable *feel* of the pedal, however, that allowed the race-car-like braking in turns. The driver simply knew where he was in the braking spectrum—a trait seldom forthcoming in most power disc systems.

A surprising aspect of the Chargers' "integrated performance system" came from, of all places, the Hemis' power curve. We first noted in in street driving, then in exiting from corners fast. Low speed torque was *not* excessive. Moving smartly away from a stop or blasting out of a corner seldom provoked uncontrolled wheelspin. Rather, the engine was cammed to spread its massive torque over its entire rev range. Unlike so many Supercars that have tire-burning power at low speeds and then run out of breath early, the Hemis seemed to feed the power to the ground in precisely the right amounts, all the way to 6000 rpm. This was further emphasized during one of the worst rain storms in recent California history. At first, we were leery about driving Hemis in such a deluge because they delivered such power so willingly, but we soon found that they were little different in the rain than a less powerful car. The driver would have had to *try* to break the drive tires loose, so we motored past many a worried sports car on the rain swept roads. No small credit must go to the Goodyear Polyglas tires, whose wet weather performance is very good, and close to that of radials.

Inside, upholstery, seating and instrument panel emulated the performance aspect, yet instilled the right touch of luxury and quality. The dash panel was a duplicate of the Super Bee (February CAR LIFE, page 48) with full instrumentation using real dials with real numbers. The clock-hidden tach-

---

HEMI CHARGER 500
'69 DODGE 4-SPEED* & AUTOMATIC

DIMENSIONS

Wheelbase, in.	117
Track, f/r, in.	60/59
Overall length, in.	208
width	77
height	53
Front seat hip room, in.	22.5 x 2
shoulder room	58
head room	37.4
pedal-seatback, max.	43
Rear seat hip room, in.	59.5
shoulder room	58.1
leg room	34.1
head room	36.4
Door opening width, in.	42.5
Trunk liftover height, in.	34

PRICES

List, FOB factory	$3591
Equipped as tested	$5026 ($5261)

Options included: Hemi engine, $673; 4-speed and H.D. Torque-Flite, N.C.; Track Pack $110; power disc brakes, $91; tachometer, $50.

CAPACITIES

No. of passengers	5
Luggage space, cu. ft.	17.4
Fuel tank, gal.	19
Crankcase, qt.	5
Transmission/dif. pt.	16/4 (8/5.5)
Radiator coolant, qt.	18

*Four-speed data in brackets when differing from automatic.

CHASSIS/SUSPENSION

Frame type: Unitized.
Front suspension type: Independent by s.l.a., torsion bars.

ride rate at wheel, lb./in.	118
antiroll bar dia., in.	0.94

Rear suspension type: Hotchkiss live axle, multileaf springs.

ride rate at wheel, lb./in.	150

Steering system: Integral assist, recirculating ball gear.

overall ratio	18.8:1
turns, lock to lock	3.5
turning circle, ft. curb-curb.	40.9
Curb weight, lb.	3950 (4025)
Test weight, lb.	4135 (4245)

Distribution (driver),

% f/r	57.4/42.6 (57.1/42.9)

BRAKES

Type: Power assisted disc front, drum rear.

Front rotor, dia. in.	11.04
Rear drum, dia. x width	11.0 x 2.5
total swept area, sq. in.	387.8

Power assist: Integral.

line psi at 100 lb. pedal	1100

WHEELS/TIRES

Wheel rim size	15 x 6.0JJ
optional size	n.a.
bolt no./circle dia. in.	5/4.5

Tires: Goodyear Polyglas.

size	F70-15
normal inflation, psi f/r	28/28

ENGINE

Type, no. of cyl.	V-8
Bore x stroke, in.	4.25 x 3.75
Displacement cu. in.	426
Compression ratio	10.25:1
Fuel required	premium
Rated bhp @ rpm	425 @ 5000
equivalent mph	119 (109)
Rated torque @ rpm	490 @ 4000
equivalent mph	95 (87)

Carburetion: Carter AFB 2x4.

throttle dia., pri./sec.	1.44/1.69

Valve train: Mechanical lifters, pushrods and overhead rocker arms.
cam timing

deg., int./exh.	36/68/80-24
duration, int./exh.	284/284

Exhaust system: Dual, balance pipe, reverse-flow mufflers.

pipe dia., exh./tail	2.5/2.25
Normal oil press. @ rpm	55 @ 2000
Electrical supply, V./amp.	12/37
Battery, plates/amp. hr.	78/70

DRIVE TRAIN

Transmission type: 4-speed manual.
Gear ratio 4th (1.00:1) overall (3.55:1)

3rd (1.39:1)	(4.94:1)
2nd (1.93:1)	(6.86:1)
1st (2.65:1)	(9.40:1)

Clutch type: Single dry plate Borg & Beck.

dia., in.	11

Transmission type: 3-speed automatic with torque converter "Torque-Flite."
Gear ratio 3rd (1.00:1) overall 3.23:1

2nd (1.45:1)	4.68:1
1st (2.45:1)	7.92:1

Shift lever location: Console.
Differential type: Hypoid, limited slip.

axle ratio	3.23:1 (3.55:1)

AUTOMATIC Charger had more bite off the line, holding the edge until four-speed nipped ahead half-way down the dragstrip.

EXCLUSIVE STYLING features of Charger 500 are functional. NASCAR rules stipulate at least 500 cars must be built to qualify as a stock car. Dodge found that flush grille and semi-fastback rear window lowered drag at the Super/speedway speeds, had 500 examples built.

ometer takes some getting used to, though. Only after thorough familiarization can the driver associate the needle position for the numbers he can't see. (Order yours without the clock and buy a wristwatch.) The bucket seats were comfortable, but like many others, were sat on and not in. The two undersized testers at first complained about the steering wheel positions' being too high relative to the seat. That was soon rectified, however, by a quick adjustment to the optional six-way seat in the automatic car, and a simple nut and bolt adjustment to the tracks in the standard. Nice touch.

For a car with so much performance, we were expecting a few glaring compromises. Only by chance did we find one—more accurately a non-compromise in performance terms. The trunk lid had to be shortened. It's a tunnel and you literally have to dive in head first to retrieve something in the forward section. What price performance? One muddied suit. That's $1.75. Well worth it. ∎

CAR LIFE ROAD TEST

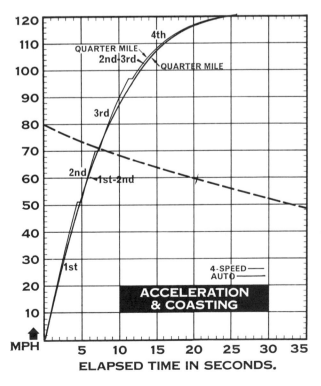

ACCELERATION & COASTING

ELAPSED TIME IN SECONDS.

4-SPEED ——
AUTO ——

CALCULATED DATA

Lb./bhp (test weight).....10.0 (10.3)
Cu. ft./ton mile........145.5 (156.1)
Mph/1000 rpm (high gear)23.9 (21.8)
Engine revs/mile
  (60 mph).............2500 (2755)
Piston travel, ft./mile....1562 (1720)
CAR LIFE wear index....39.1 (47.3)
Frontal area, sq. ft.............22.6

SPEEDOMETER ERROR

Indicated	Actual
30 mph	28.6 (30.7)
40 mph	39.2 (40.4)
50 mph	49.6 (50.1)
60 mph	59.4 (60.0)
70 mph	69.3 (69.6)
80 mph	79.0 (79.1)
90 mph	88.4 (88.4)

MAINTENANCE

Engine oil, miles/days.....4000/90
  oil filter, miles/days.....8000/180
Chassis lubrication, miles.....36,000
Antismog servicing, type/miles.....
  tuneup check/12,000; replace PCV
  valve/12000
Air cleaner, miles.....replace/24,000
Spark plugs: Champion N-10Y.
  gap, (in.).................0.035
Basic timing, deg./rpm....TDC/700
  max. cent. adv., deg./rpm.30/3100
  max. vac. adv., deg./in. Hg 19/15.0
Ignition point gap, in.....0.014-0.019
  cam dwell angle, deg..........37
  arm tension, oz...........17-21.5
Tappet clearance,
  int./exh..........0.028/0.028
Fuel pressure at idle, psi.......7-8.5
Radiator cap relief press., psi.....16

PERFORMANCE

Top speed (5700),
  mph............136 (134 @ 6100)
Test shift points (rpm) @ mph
  3rd to 4th (6200).............(97)
  2nd to 3rd (6200)........102 (70)
  1st to 2nd (6200).........60 (51)

ACCELERATION

0-40 mph.................3.3 (3.3)
0-50 mph.................4.4 (4.4)
0-60 mph.................5.7 (5.7)
0-70 mph.................7.1 (6.8)
0-80 mph.................8.8 (8.4)
0-90 mph..............10.6 (10.0)
0-100 mph.............12.8 (12.3)
Standing ¼-mile, sec....13.92 (13.68)
  speed at end, mph....104.5 (104.8)
Passing, 30-70 mph, sec.....4.8 (4.4)

BRAKING

Max. deceleration rate from 80 mph
  ft./sec./sec...............28 (28)
No. of stops from 80 mph (60-sec.
  intervals) before 20% loss in deceleration rate........8 (8) no loss
Control loss? Slight.
Overall brake performance.very good

FUEL CONSUMPTION

Test conditions, mpg........6.0 (8.5)
Normal cond., mpg...12-14 (13-14.5)
Cruising range, miles........230-280

the incredible dodge daytona!

***Don't laugh, baby—
they're serious about
selling this car in the
good ol' U.S.A. Story,
photos: Karl Ludvigsen***

HAVE you found your daily transportation to be too dull, too ordinary? Do the kids on the corner look the other way when you and your car cruise by? The Dodge division of Chrysler (US) has the key to your dilemma. It's the Charger Daytona, an automobile that's anything but routine. In fact, even after seeing one it's hard to believe that it really exists.

There has to be a reason to build a car like the Daytona. It's US stock car racing. Dodge is tired of taking a licking from Ford in the big NASCAR events that spell sales success — or failure — in the south-eastern United States. To beat the Fords it decided to design a new version of its Charger coupe with the lowest possible aerodynamic drag, one that would slip through the air with speed and stability. The Daytona is the startling result.

Though it's made for racing, the Charger Daytona can't yet be raced. To meet a NASCAR requirement it was introduced on April 10. To race the Daytona at Bill France's new track at Talladega, Alabama, on September 14, Dodge must build and sell 500 of them.

Since there aren't 500 racers out there who want these cars, they're being offered for street use at $3993 apiece, with a 440 cu. in. V8 engine developing 375 bhp.

I haven't seen one coming down the highway yet, but they're out there somewhere, scaring motorists and pedestrians alike.

The scientific rationale behind the Daytona is faultless. For 14 weeks Chrysler Corporation aerodynamicists slaved over full-size and 3/8-scale Daytonas in wind tunnels and on the test tracks.

Two different aluminium noses were tried on a test car — one even longer than the final design, believe it or not! The peak line of the nose had to be kept high so the fibreglass front end could qualify as a bumper on the cars used on the street.

Drag was drastically cut by the new shape, so much that Dodge claims a 10 to 15 percent improvement in fuel mileage at 70 mph. But handling and stability were terrible, certainly not tolerable at the 180 mph lap speeds being turned at the fastest NASCAR tracks. To the rescue: a spoiler under the nose, air relief vents above the front wheels, and a soaring wing at the rear.

When wings on racing cars were banned in Europe — and Australia —

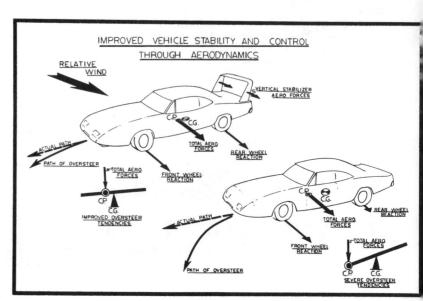

one of the excuses was that they'd never be used on production cars. Meanwhile, Dodge was putting the lie to that. Many different shapes and heights were tried before the final wing section, a modified design of inverted Clark Y-type, was adopted. It's adjustable for angle within a five-degree range.

Most technical was the determination of the wing's height. It was raised just high enough to allow the boot lid to be opened! The pylons supporting the wing are important too, as vertical stabilisers. NACA 0012 airfoils in section, they put larger feathers on the Charger Daytona arrow.

Is all this hardware likely to fall off the charging Daytona? Not with the four bolts that hold each pylon to a steel plate inside each rear fender.

And the pylons and wings are **very tough solid aluminium castings. The** wing's strong enough to sit on, **as** a Chrysler executive proudly — **and** uncomfortably — demonstrated.

Does the Charger Daytona **really** work? After the 500-mile inaugural **race** at Talladega we'll know if it can **do** the job for which it was designed. **As** a car for the street, it's incredible. I have to admit that at over 100 mph on an expressway it certainly **does** feel stable.

I had little opportunity to check **its** cornering, which was acceptable **by** current standards, as were its ride and performance with the 375 **bhp** engine and automatic transmission.

Painted fire-truck orange-red, the Charger Daytona is the most attention-getting automobile I've ever driven.

Parking it was a near-impossibility, with several feet of nose swooping down below my field of view. Looking back, the wing and pylons are blocked from sight by the roof and rear quarters. But bystanders can see them all right, painted a contrasting black, and fall down in prayerful attitudes when a Daytona passes by.

A spectacular car the Daytona certainly is. An attractive one it emphatically is not. But in stock car racing, beauty is as beauty does. After September 14 at Talladega the Charger Daytona may look just wonderful to everybody at Dodge. If it doesn't, they'll have built 500 ugly cars for nothing. ●

ABOVE: With lights down, that monstrous front cuts drag, but destroys handling.

LEFT: Diagram shows vertical fins at rear improve the Daytona's stability.

RIGHT: Rear foil is set high — so that the boot can be opened.

Don White, Dodge Charger race driver, USAC stock car champ, 1963 and 1967, all-time (39 races) stock car winner in USAC history.

"You know Charger. Every race fan's idea of a real automobile. One that looks good, and seemingly drives itself at any speed, and has a feeling of complete control. That's Charger R/T for 1970. As a Midwestern driver, the thing I go for along with blazing power is the optional mechanically adjustable six-way driver's seat. It works just as good as most power adjustables, and makes those long trips between race tracks a whole lot easier.

"Charger R/T is my kind of car. Soft suspension and plenty of back seat room for the crew. I don't do too much drag racing, but at the sanctioned drag strip I topped 100 in the quarter with my street Charger R/T. It was equipped with a 440 Magnum V8 coupled with the TorqueFlite automatic gear changer. Replace that with an optional 440 V8 SixPack—three big Holleys on high rise manifold—or the Hemi 426, and you'll do even better.

There's a four-speed manual Hurst selector available also . . . the kind I use on my USAC stocker.

"Incidentally, Charger R/T's Torque-Flite this year has a new stickshift gate that's as fast and sure and crisp as any manual shifter, but quicker.

"All in all, Charger R/T is one of the greatest buys a true performance-minded guy could find anywhere.

"As I said, Super Bee may out-drag it, but what other cars can offer Charger R/T's features? If you gotta go (quick)—go Charger R/T—but remember, do it at the strip!"

1970 Dodge Charger R/T
DIMENSIONS

WIDTH
Track, front 5
Track, rear 5
Maximum overall car width 7

LENGTH
Wheelbase 11
Overall car length 20

HEIGHT
Overall height 5

FRONT COMPARTMENT
Effective headroom 3
Maximum eff. legroom, accelerator..... 4
Shoulder room 5
Hiproom 6

REAR COMPARTMENT
Effective headroom 3
Minimum eff. legroom 3
Rear comp. room 2
Shoulder room 5
Hiproom 6

CAPACITIES
No. of passengers ....
Fuel tank, gal. ....
Crankcase, qt...4 (5 when replacing oil fil

CHASSIS/SUSPENSION
Body/frame type ....unitia
Front suspension ....torsion b
Rear suspension ..asymmetrical leaf spri
Steering system ......recirculation ball g

BRAKES—DRUM
Heavy-duty brakes, standard,
(automatic adjusting)
Front ....11 x
Rear ....11 x

WHEELS/TIRES
Wheels ....14 x 6.
Tires ....F70 x 14 whitew

ENGINE
Type and no. of cyls. ....
Bore and stroke ....4.32 x 3
Displacement, cu.-in. ....
Compression ratio ....9.
Fuel req. ....premi
Rated BHP @ RPM ....375 @ 4
Rated torque (lbs./ft. RPM) ......480 @ 3
Carburetion ....Carter 4-B
Valve train ....Hydraulic lifters, pushro
                and overhead rocker ar
Cam timing
  Intake duration 2
  Exhaust duration 28
Exhaust system ....d

DRIVE TRAIN
Transmission type ......3-speed TorqueF
                            automa
Gear ratios 1st 2.4
2nd 1.4
3rd 1.0
Rev. 2.2

Additional optional equipment on Don Whit
Charger R/T test car consisted of these iten
road wheels, vinyl roof, center console, sin
lated walnut steering wheel, and raised-wh
letter tires.

Dodge's Flying Machine

Dodge's Daytona Charger wasn't designed for the street, but it has got to be the ultimate boulevard mind-boggler of all times!

BY THE CARS STAFF

BEFORE GOING into the how and why of the Daytona Charger, we would like to clear up some misconceptions which can be directly attributed to the styling of the Daytona. First off, Dodge *is not* going out of the auto business and into airplane manufacturing. And secondly, Dodge *is* serious about mass producing the Daytona and anyone with the guts can order one from their local dealer.

Now that that's cleared up we can get into the Daytona. It's unquestionably the mind-bendingest car we have ever road tested (narrowly edging out the Ramchargers' Candy striped A/FX Stage III wedge we street tested in '64) and certainly the most outrageous machine ever to come out of Motown. To some it's beautiful and to others it's downright ugly. It's the kind of car that you either like or hate. It's not a middle-of-the-road compromise machine. We spent two weeks with it in and around New York City and really had a time with it. To give you an idea of what people thought of it, here's a cross section of comments:
1. "If Dodge tries to sell that thing, they'll be laughed out of business!"
2. "I got gypped! My R/T is loaded with every available option and I didn't get the nose and wing."
3. "Hey Batman, does it fly?"

4. "Wow. It's the grooviest—like a beautiful trip. I must have one."
5. "They gotta be kidding. Who would buy such an ugly boat with a clothes dryer on the back?"
6. "Boss, man. You really know where it's at!"

We found it to be a straight 50/50 deal after parking it in front of a major speed shop in the area and having the counterman take a popularity poll.

The Daytona we tested was one of the first hand-built prototypes manufactured. Finished off in Hemi Orange with black trim, it didn't stand a chance of not turning a head on any street. If the nose and paint didn't get

"If Dodge tries to sell that thing, they'll be laughed out of business"

Daytona looks more like a UFO than a production passenger car, especially when surrounded by conventional traffic on a main street.

'em, the tail treatment did. We had a ball with this one.

Basically, the Daytona is a straight stock Charger with the old 500 roofline (full fastback, shortened deck lid) with a bolt-on nose and rear wing. It replaces the 500 as the factory nascar car and is available as a street machine with either 440 wedge or 426 Street Hemi power. It is the most streamlined, most advanced factory (stock) race car on the high speed ovals and is unquestionably an advance warning of things to come in the future. This goes for race machines as well as street and high speed road cars.

The beauty part of the Daytona Charger is that the front and rear end treatments are 100 percent functional, which sets it off from the common garden variety members of the spoiler and wing set (Boss Mustangs, GTO Judge, Firebird Trans-Am, Hurst Olds, etc). It was designed as a super-efficient race car and then carried over as a street model. It was not built to sell more cars or to appeal to a broader market. In fact, Dodge originally planned to market only the legal minimum needed to meet nascar specifications. They created a monster, however, and to date orders have totaled more than four times the nascar legal minimum. The orders were placed by dealers who saw only pictures. And, you know, they don't particularly care whether they sell them or not. Who could ask for a more magnetic drawing card than a brightly-painted Daytona sitting in the display window?

Our Daytona, finished in Hemi

Good friend and brave soul Joe Kocheck parked in front of Nathan's world famous eatery to check out reaction to '70 Daytona. Most passersby couldn't believe it was for real.

Small mesh grille and custom duct work keep the mill at normal running temperature. Hood is actually secured only by chromed NASCAR hood pins. Flush key locks are recommended.

Charger 500 fastback roof and extended wedge front account for a 15 percent fuel economy increase at 70 mph over conventional Charger.

Orange with black trim, sported 440-cube/375 hp wedge power backed up by a three-speed auto and 3.54 Sure Grip gears. The combination proved to be perfect for cruising at highway speeds as well as for around town jaunts. The optional 3.91 cog is a far better choice for "getting it on." At first we thought the Daytona would be rough getting used to, between the gaping stares and the 10 inches or so of sheet metal that extends forward of the stock bumper location. You see, line of sight drops off at the bumper line and you have to do some fancy judging or else you're in trouble.

And, we really sweated the small chicken wire mesh grille opening which looks like it has the cooling area to handle a lawn mower engine and certainly not a monster wedge with a high temperature (smog control standards) thermostat. And, then there's that big black wing that follows you whereever you go!

All it took was a couple of spins around town to get used to the bolt-ons. The cooling problem we had anticipated never arose. While the mesh setup represents less than 70 percent of the original stock Charger cooling area, the results are fantastic. With this sutup 100 percent of all available air flow is directed to the radiator via the mesh opening and ducts under the nose. A Trailer Towing radiator is standard and the unit is well shrouded for maximum efficiency. And, the reverse scoops on the fenders actually vent out the engine compartment and help complete a full cycle cooling pattern. We encountered absolutely no problems in the worst NYC rush hour traffic.

The reason behind the nose and tail treatments is to stabilize the car on the straightaways where speeds are now aproaching the 200 mph mark and to improve cornering traction at high tract speeds. Under 70

mph on the open road it's almost impossible to detect any difference in the car's stability. Once we were up around the century mark we found the car amazingly stable under high crosswind conditions and it seemed to develop a super sure-footedness condition. We also noticed this to some degree when corning at super high speeds. It felt as though the Daytona was losing some of its understeer characteristics, especially under high side force crosswind conditions. Under normal driving conditions, the modifications seemed to offer no more than unreal head turning power.

Basically, a stock car tends to pivot at the rear as speed increases, adversely affecting the steering. The spoiler acts to control lift as speed increases, making the car more stable. The high negative force created by the adjustable (for various angles of attack) rear wing helps keep the car on the road. The rear wing and front "plow" act to reduce oversteer when corning at high speeds in a heavy crosswind situation.

To make sure the Daytona was aerodynamically correct, various wind tunnel complexes were used to test 3/8-scale and full-size models. And then the finalized product was tested on the high speed track. It's extremely interesting that while there's an additional 10 inches up front which accounts for a 10-percent gain in cross sectional area, there's no major change in the Daytona's center of gravity.

There's also an economy factor to consider, even though not too many economy-minded car buyers will even consider the Daytona. At 70 mph, the Daytona Charger gets 15 percent more fuel economy than a comparably powered and set up conventional Charger. The tapered nose and fastback 500 roofline get the

CONTINUED ON PAGE 92

Note similarity between Daytona and Sting Ray frontal styling. Dig the headlight doors.

Race car driver Charlie Brownstein and friend couldn't quite get over the rear wing. They wanted to put one on Charlie's Camaro. Steel nose piece bolts up to stock Charger body. Note sloppy rubber moldings. Reverse fender scoops help cool the engine compartment.

THE CHARGERS OF

By A.B. Shuman

Around Hamtramk and Highland Park they're calling 1970 "the year of the compact," and luckily (meaning through no insight on the part of Chrysler's traditionally myopic product planners) Dodge had Dart, the right car for which the right time had finally come, in its corner. But, while sales were booming with the small cars, the intermediates were taking a beating. Luckily, again, Dodge had already planned to consolidate, trim, and revitalize Coronet and Charger for '71. The decision had nothing to do with the 1970 sales figures, though they did indicate its validity, as it was made some time ago. There were several aspects involved. First, the multiplicity of Coronet and Charger models, with all the various options, complicated production line scheduling. In effect, with all the permutations of paint, engines, and accessories, it's conceivable that the "same" car could never be built twice. Then, too, this proliferation produced situations where two different models were in sales competition with each other, as in the case of a Coronet Super Bee versus a Charger Super Bee.

If one or the other had to go then, the only thing to decide was which one. Coronet's strongest years had been 1965 and '66, immediately following its reintroduction by Dodge when it accounted for about half of the division's total sales. Charger, on the other hand, while still not approaching the volume of Coronet sales, had been debutted as a semi-limited production speciality car but really caught on. And, as it progressed from its initial angular, teardrop-flatback configuration to the more

pleasing Coke bottle-tunneled backlight shape, its popularity skyrocketed, reaching a high in 1969, with production of just over 70,000 units (100,000 less than Coronet). So, while Charger's star was still rising, Coronet's at the very least was remaining fixed in the sales heavens. Yet, it still had a substantial lead on Charger. Obviously, it wasn't ready to be done away with.

Examining the situation from another aspect, a check into what percentage of Coronets were hardtops and what percentage sedans, along with a new wave of realization that the reasons people chose one body style over another were quite definite, eventually led to the concept of designing two totally different cars to fulfill the two divergent needs. This became Dodge's one-two punch in the intermediate line: Charger and Coronet would both continue, but as two distinctive entities. The Coronets, built on a 118-inch wheelbase, would serve the needs of the four-door contingent, while Charger, on a 115-inch wheelbase, had blossomed from a single special two-door hardtop to a whole line of cars: six different models fitting into three series. The plan was not completely unique, as GM introduced the two-wheelbase-length plan for their intermediates (112 inches and 116) in 1968. The elimination of the sedan-hardtop split personality through the use of two different wheelbases and two different floor pans (the common denominator when everything is built on the same chassis) freed the stylists and engineers to develop packages which more closely approached what the two market factions wanted. Now Charger, like the Ford Torino before it, covers a whole spectrum of models (and

prices): Charger, Charger 500, and Charger SE. Unlike Torino, though, these are all two-doors, which, with their individual floor pan, freed the designers to "wing it," to come up with completely different styling. And this they did, coming up with the next step in Charger's evolution, the fastback. Call it sneaky, tough, or slippery, it gets a lot of attention. More than appealing style, though, each of the three new Charger series has its own distinct personality, all done, not with mirrors, but through changes in detail.

But as attractive as the new Chargers are, there is a problem... Charger is larger. To most people that would seem to be a plus, or at least the ad writers would have us think so, but not in today's hyper-crowded world. There are just too many big cars on our roads, big cars that make inefficient use of the space they take up. If you go by the specs, the figures for wheelbase and overall length, you'd have to say that opposite were true, that Charger is smaller, for as the chart shows, both of those dimensions, as well as rear overhang, are indeed less than last year. This is good. The trouble is that front overhang has been increased and overall width has been increased.

CHARGER SIZE COMPARISON

	1970	1971	CHANGE
Wheelbase	117.0	115.0	—2.0
Overall length	208.5	205.4	—3.1
Rear overhang	52.6	48.6	—4.0
Front overhang	38.9	41.8	+2.9
Overall width	75.6	79.1	+2.5
Width at			
#2 pillar	73.4	75.9	+2.5

This matter of inches may not seem like much, but the overall effect is that

E DODGE BRIGADE

the car is much larger than it has to (or should) be. Believe it or not, that's the main gripe. True, there's about an inch or more rear seat shoulder room (thanks to a 2.8-inch increase in rear tread width, which also probably accounts for some of the legerdemain by which the packaging engineers were able to chop 4 inches off the rear and still increase trunk space by 2.8 cubic feet). These things are good, but when you're driving the car those positive aspects somehow don't seem to offset the feeling that you're wheeling around one of those full-sized behemoths rather than a spritely intermediate. While we're on the subject of maneuvering, all of the cars were equipped with power steering, and anybody planning on buying one for use other than inspecting railroad tracks is advised to order that option. Chrysler power steering is not notable for its feel of the road or response, but it most certainly cuts down turning effort, especially on heavy-engined cars shod with G60 tires. The steering units in all four cars were presumably identical, but, for some reason, the unit in the SE felt markedly better than the others. As previously mentioned, each has a distinctive personality, but there were several points in common.

First, on the important subject of quality control and Dodge's avowed efforts to improve it: These cars were very early production run models, rushed to our door to meet our deadline, and so they aren't truly representative, but they did serve as general indicators, especially in the realm of paint and bodywork. Things are getting better. Pieces of interior trim were better fitted than in the past. There were no dash-

board rattles or squeaks. (On the dash and other areas where woodgrain applique is usually seen, Dodge is using a heavy, textured plastic. It's still plastic, but it's *better* plastic.) On the negative side, there were the few loose screws, particularly in the doors, balky power windows, small lumps in the vinyl tops, and improperly adjusted heater controls. Most of these gripes would normally be caught in a good predelivery prep by the dealer, but these cars were sent directly to us for cover shooting without benefit of such TLC.

Three of the Chargers had inside hood releases (a $10.55 option that makes it that much harder for those who would rob you of your spark plugs). The hood release handle, which is big and shiny, is located under the dash, just above the emergency brake release handle, which is small and made of black plastic. And, the natural thing, when starting out in the morning, after you're all strapped in and mentally prepared to go, is to pop the hood, when all you really meant to do was release the parking brake. It only takes three or four turns at unstrapping, getting out, opening the hood all the way, slamming it closed, getting back in, and buckling up again, before you learn which handle is which. Actually, the problem is that you can't see the brake release because of the steering wheel rim. The same thing holds true on the right side, where the rim blocks a lot of the good instrumentation that Dodge bothered to put in: oil pressure, fuel level, water temperature, and alternator, arranged in two neat dials. But even if you can't easily see them, they are attractive and legible, and they are there, as they ought to be.

All of the cars exhibited a great deal of road and tire noise, which became quite pronounced on rough surfaces, at which time vibrations would be transmitted to the steering wheel. There were no adverse handling or control characteristics, only the increased noise level in the car.

Rear seat legroom and headroom haven't grown, but they are better than average, as is knee room, and two adults can travel quite comfortably back there. Front seat accommodations are likewise good, and the optional high back buckets are comfortable, though the seat portion could use more padding to make long stretches behind the wheel more bearable. The sweeping design of the roof creates a blindspot in the right rear quarter, making it good practice to check the right hand outside mirror before changing lanes. Visibility to the front and sides, with the new ventless side windows is generally very good, through the placement of the oversize rear view mirror can also produce a blindspot on right turns, particularly on tight ones.

On to specifics.

CHARGER 500

This is the middle series Charger, corresponding to last year's Coronet 500. Its two variants, the Super Bee and the R/T, constitute Charger's members of the Scat Pack. Base engine in the 500 is the 230 hp 318-2V, with 383-2V (275 hp) and 383-4V (300 hp) as options. All of these are designed to operate on regular fuel. Being interested in performance, we selected the four-barrel engine, but rather than a 4-speed or Torqueflite opted for the standard, all-synchro 3-speed manual trans, with floor

The Chargers of the Dodge Brigade

Charger 500 was equipped with 3-speed trans and good floor-shift linkage, performed very well with 383 engine. All Chargers feature clean dash layouts, but steering wheel blocks key gauges.

shift linkage. Though the economic advantage of this choice, from the standpoint of new car prices, was considered, the choice was more heavily based on a series of tests we ran last spring. Thanks to the cooperation of Jack McFarland, Dodge's gravelly-voiced West Coast p.r. rep, we were able to obtain two identically-equipped 340 Dart Swingers, one with a 4-speed, the other with a 3-speed. Basically, we found that the 4-speed car, not surprisingly, was about .2-second quicker in the quarter-mile and got the same maximum gas mileage on the highway as the 3-speed. The 3-speed, on the other hand, was much more pleasant to drive, especially in city traffic, where it delivered a little more than 1 mpg better fuel economy. Since we were anxious to give the 3-speed some of the exposure it deserves (as devices like the "crime-fighting steering column," which may be getting its own TV show next season, replacing Adam-12, have captured most of the limelight), we specified the "3-at-the-knee" setup for our 383, the biggest engine it is available with. The results didn't disappoint us in the least.

The shift lever is straight and direct, with a plain, functional knob that fits your palm. There's no Mickey Mouse pistol grip handle, only a shiny black ball that falls right where your hand is. There is one drawback though. You must forget that you're in the Now Seventies, break the ingrained 4-speed habit, and drop back to the less complicated Then Fifties, to resurrect (or learn) the pattern from a '39 Ford box. And remember — you must always remember — where first is, and where reverse is. Even so, you might as well resign yourself to the fact that you'll

botch it at least twice the first day you drive it; after that you'll be O.K.

The transmission features a 2.55:1 first gear, 1.49:1 second, and 1.00:1 high, which is roughly identical to a Torqueflite (2.45, 1.45, and 1.00). Shifting action is clean and the throws short. There was a slight gate between first and second, which bothered us during the acceleration testing, but this eventually smoothed out as the linkage loosened up. As it was, the car ran a 15.15 elapsed time, with a trap speed of 94.8 mph, which isn't bad for a regular fuel sub-400-cubic-inch engine. Some improvement in performance can be expected from use of the optional 3.55:1 rear axle ratio with Sure-Grip differential, as our car was carrying the standard 3.23:1 gear set, without limited slip. For maximum acceleration, it was necessary to use a starting line rpm of 2,500-3,000, requiring judicious use of the throttle to prevent excessive wheelspin. Full-throttle starts below this rpm level produced a bog just off the line. Shifts were made at 5,200 rpm in each gear, with good clutch action. In normal driving, good clutch feel and pedal leverage contribute greatly to making smooth starts and shifts. Part throttle response in top gear is also very good.

In hard cornering, the 500 exhibited considerable body roll, more than any of the other three test Chargers, something that was almost as uncomfortable to watch as to experience. This reflected its lower torsion bar and rear spring rates, although it did have the .88-inch front stabilizer bar. The rear springs on the 500 had 4½ leaves on each side, while the others, as a function of their 426/440 engine options carried stiffer

CHARGER 500

Base price	$3,196.
Bucket seats	105.
Disc brakes	24.
Power brakes	45.
Console	57.
3-speed	14.
383 4-bbl.	144.
Left mirror	16.
Right mirror	11.
AM/FM multiplex	213.
Power steering	111.
Rim blow horn	28.
Vinyl roof	95.
Invoice	$4,065.

SUPER BEE (440)

Base price	$3,245.
Bucket seats	100.
Concealed headlamps	65.
Super Track Pak	219.
Console	57.
Torqueflite	237.
440-Six Pack	262.
Headlamp washer	29.
Hood tie down pins	16.
Tachometer	52.
AM/FM multiplex	213.
Power steering	111.
Vinyl roof	90.
Invoice	$4,702.

SUPER BEE (HEMI)

Base price	$3,245.
Super Track Pak	219.
Torqueflite	237.
Hemi	883.
Left mirror	16.
Right mirror	11.
Hood tie down pins	16.
Inside hood release	10.
Spoiler	35.
Tachometer	52.
Power steering	111.
Tuff wheel	30.
Vinyl roof	95.
Invoice	$4,966.

CHARGER SE

Base price	$3,396.
Bucket seats	105.
Disc brakes	24.
Power brakes	45.
Console	57.
Torqueflite	237.
440-4 bbl.	281.
Right mirror	16.
Left mirror	11.
Air conditioning	383.
Headlight warning	5.
Power windows	110.
AM/FM multiplex	213.
Power steering	111.
Vinyl roof	28.
Invoice	$5,029.

SPECIFICATIONS	CHARGER 500	SUPER BEE	CHARGER SE	SUPER BEE HEMI
Engine	90° OHV V8	90° OHV V8	90° OHV V8	90° OHV V8
Bore & Stroke — ins.	4.25 x 3.38	4.32 x 3.75	4.32 x 3.75	4.25 x 3.75
Displacement — cu. in.	383	440	440	426 (Hemi)
Advertised gross HP @ RPM	300 @ 4800	385 @ 4700	370 @ 4600	425 @ 4600
Advertised gross Torque: lbs.-ft. @ rpm	410 @ 3400	490 @ 3200	480 @ 3200	490 @ 4000
Compression Ratio/Fuel	8.5:1/Regular	10.3:1/Premium	9.1:1/Premium	10.2:1/Premium
Carburetion	1 4-bbl	3 2-bbl	1 4-bbl	2 4-bbl
Transmission	3-speed	Automatic	Automatic	Automatic
Final Drive Ratio	3.23:1	4.10:1	3.23:1	4.10:1
Steering Type	Recirculating ball power-assisted	Recirculating ball power-assisted	Recirculating ball power-assisted	Recirculating ball power-assisted
Steering Ratio	15.7:1	15.7:1	15.7:1	15.7:1
Turning Diameter (Curb-to-curb-ft.)	40.8 ft	40.8 ft.	40.8 ft.	40.8 ft.
Wheel Turns (lock-to-lock)	3.5	3.5	3.5	3.5
Tire Size	F70-14	G60-15	G60-15	G60-15
Brakes	Power, front disc/drum rear	Power, front disc/drum rear	Power, front disc/drum rear	Power, front disc/drum rear
Curb weight — lbs.	3879	3945	3764	4083
Front suspension	Independent; lateral nonparallel control arms with torsion bars	Independent; lateral nonparallel control arms with torsion bars	Independent; lateral nonparallel control arms with torsion bars	Independent; lateral nonparallel control arms with torsion bars
Rear Suspension	Parallel longitudinal semi-elliptic leaf springs	Parallel longitudinal semi-elliptic leaf springs	Parallel longitudinal semi-elliptic leaf springs	Parallel longitudinal semi-elliptic leaf springs
Body/Frame Construction	Unit	Unit	Unit	Unit

PERFORMANCE	CHARGER 500	SUPER BEE	CHARGER SE	HEMI SUPER BEE
Acceleration (2 abd.) 0-30 mph	3.2 secs	2.9 secs	3.2 secs	2.5 secs
0-45 mph	5.2 secs	4.7 secs	4.9 secs	4.2 secs
0-60 mph	8.1 secs	6.9 secs	7.0 secs	5.7 secs
0-75	11.5 secs	9.9 secs	9.9 secs	7.6 secs
Standing Start ¼-mile MPH	94.8 mph	97.3 mph	96.4 mph	104.0 mph
Elapsed time	15.15 secs	14.74 secs	14.93 secs	13.73 secs
Passing speeds (2nd gear) 40-60 mph	3.8 secs	2.9 secs	3.3 secs	2.9 secs
50-70 mph	3.8 secs	3.6 secs	3.4 secs	3.0 secs
Speeds in gears* 1st ....mph @ rpm	47 @ 5200	42 @ 5500	46 @ 5200	42 @ 5500
2nd ....mph @ rpm	83 @ 5200	73 @ 5500	80 @ 5200	70 @ 5500
3rd ....mph @ rpm	109 @ 4500	106 @ 5500	114 @ 5000	104 @ 5500
Mph per 1000 rpm (in top gear)	24.2 mph	19.3 mph	22.8 mph	18.9 mph
Stopping distances (panic) From 30 mph	32.6 ft.	27.0 ft.	32.2 ft.	28.8 ft.
From 60 mph	123.0 ft.	119.1 ft.	122.3 ft.	115.1 ft.
Stability	Fair, moderate rear wheel hop	Good, no wheel hop	Fair, moderate rear wheel hop	Good, no wheel hop
Gas mileage range	12.1-13.5 mpg	9.1-11.2 mpg	10.4-13.0 mpg	11.0-12.0 mpg
Speedometer error Electric speedometer	30 45 50 60 70 80	30 45 50 60 70 80	30 45 50 60 70 80	30 45 50 60 70 80
Car speedometer	33.5 48.5 53 63 73 82	31 46 51 61 72 82	32 46 51 61 70 80	31 45 50 60 70 80

*Speeds in gears are at shift points (limited by the length of track) and do not represent maximum speeds.

The Chargers of the Dodge Brigade

springing, achieved through the use of 6 leaves on the left rear and 5 leaves plus 2 half-leaves on the right. This increased the spring rate from 138 pounds per inch (on 383-powered cars) to 150. At the front, torsion bar diameter is .020 greater, boosting the rate from 111 lbs./in. to 118.

During the brake tests, which some believe is more a test of tires than brakes, the F70-14s did a good job despite late-stage wheelhopping antics in the panic stops from 60 mph, laying down black streaks for 123 feet. There was a slight tendency for the car to turn left toward the end of each high-speed stop, but it was easily counteracted by normal reaction on the steering wheel. The rear wheelhop can occasionally get quite severe, but it doesn't seem to hurt stopping distances or directional stability. In normal stops from 60, attempting not to lock the brakes, the car took 145 feet to stop and there was no wheelhop.

On the whole, the car was quite adequate performance-wise. The engine is flexible, the transmission easy to work. The fuel economy is nothing like a Honda's, but it was the best of the group. The ride is good, the accommodations comfortable, and all vital controls (including the center-mounted vent controls) are within easy reach of the driver. The chief shortcoming is in the handling, and here use of the beefier suspension components, addition of an accessory type rear stabilizer bar, or possibly a larger front bar, would cut down on the body roll. The stiffer rear springs, plus stiffer (S25) shocks, would probably go a long way toward eliminating that wheelhop on braking that has became a trademark of Chrysler products.

SUPER BEE 440-6

Our first representative of the Scat Pack was equipped with the torquey 440-Six Pack, one of the four premium fuel engines still offered by MoPar. (The others are the 340, the high compression 440-4V, and the Hemi, all of which are options in the Super Bee. Standard engine is the regular fuel 383-4V.) In addition to a Torqueflite transmission and "Slap Stik" positive stop shifter, it was equipped with the Super Track Pak. This package, available with the three top engines, includes a Sure Grip limited slip differential, Dana 4.10:1 rear axle with 9¾-inch diameter ring gear, 7-blade torque-drive fan, dual breaker point distributor, standard Hemi 26-inch high performance radiator with fan shroud, and power disc brakes. The price for this is $219.30. There is also a "plain" Track Pak option which differs in that it includes a 3.54:1 axle ratio and leaves out the power disc brakes.

The Six Pack is rated at 385 hp this year, down 5 from last, due to changes

Top: Unique canopied roof distinguishes Special Edition, which turned out to be a surprisingly good runner with 440-4V engine. Above: Although wheelbase and overall length have been cut for '71, front end is excessively long, car's chief fault. Trunk space is up despite reduced rear overhang. Below: Super Bee is one of two Scat Pack representatives in the new Charger lineup.

Left: Hydraulic cammed Hemi proved itself on strip with runs of 104.04 mph in 13.73 secs. Above: 440-6 Pack is now rated at 385 hp, is one of four remaining premium fuel engines.

DODGE BRIGADE

for emissions purposes. The best quarter-mile e.t. it could muster was a 14.74, with a trap speed of 97.3, though it only had been run-in just a little over 800 miles, as were all the other cars except the Hemi, and hadn't had the benefit of a pre-test tune-up. When the engine was hot there was occasional slight pinging at part throttle between 2,000 and 3,000 rpm, but this didn't occur during full-power runs, and might be attributable to the decreasing availability of good premium fuel in the L.A. area. Traction is the key to getting good times in this car — and the problem — even with the wide G60-15 tires. Starting with the engine at about 1,100 rpm, releasing the brake, smoothly adding more throttle, and making the gear selections manually between 5,400 and 5,500 gave the best results.

During normal cruising, the engine operates on the center two-barrel carb. The vacuum-actuated auxiliary carburetors are sensitive to engine demand, coming on like a transmission kick-down when they flop open. In other cars we've tested with this system there is usually a severe torque reaction associated with both the opening and closing of these carbs, as their operation is almost instantaneous, but this was much less pronounced in the new Charger. The only adverse effect was encountered when suddenly getting completely off the throttle while making a turn at high power (admittedly an uncommon maneuver). Here the car would go into a momentary period of oscillation as the chassis unloaded and reacted. The result was a few seconds of directional uncertainty. The point of this is that it behooves drivers of Six-Pack cars to learn to be extra smooth on throttle transitions.

Handling is otherwise satisfactory for a car of this type, though it seemed that the shock absorbers lacked the bounce control of the other cars in the group. The natural propensity toward understeer is easily, almost too easily, changed to oversteer by pressing on the gas pedal. The Sure Grip differential was generally well-behaved, though there was some rear wheelhop on sharp (right angle) turns from a stop when entering a cross street.

There was no wheelhop during the braking tests, however, and stability was very good. Panic stops from 60 produced average distances of 119.1 feet, second only to the Hemi. Normal stopping from 60, without locking the brakes, resulted in straight ahead stops in a quite respectable 136 feet. Toward the end of our testing sessions, the brakes got pretty hot, but there was only a slight hint of fade, thanks to the 8:1 pressure boost ratio supplied by the power assist, though the already low pedal was noticeably lower.

This Super Bee was a "fun" car to drive and be seen in, but one wonders at its relevance, in view of its size, 10 mpg fuel economy, and 4.10 gear ratio, doubly dubious in light of its performance figures.

CHARGER SE

Corresponding to last year's Charger 500, the Charger SE (Special Edition) is the top line, with canopy-styled roof and concealed headlights standard. The 318-2V is the base engine, but both the two- and four-barrel 383s, the Hi-Perf 440-4V, and the 440-Six Pack are available options. Ours was equipped with the 370 hp four-barrel 440, which proved itself a surprisingly agile performer, even with the standard 3.23 rear axle, automatic, and air conditioning. Cracking the 15-second barrier with runs in the 14.90s, this supposed luxury vehicle was not too far behind the drag strip times of the Six Pack Super Bee. Another surprise was the ride and handling, which also seemed superior to the "hot dog" model (despite identical suspension), though those looking for softly-sprung comfort might be disappointed. The ride is firm, the feel of the road positive. The steering, as already mentioned, felt much better than usual, perhaps due to the extra front end weight of the air conditioning unit, as well as the wide tires.

One of the nice interior touches was combination ribbed cloth and vinyl upholstery, which turned out to be standard issue in SE models. For Mr. and Mrs. Firstnighter there's a leather and vinyl combo that's optional. Intruding into all this luxurious splendor was engine noise under acceleration, chiefly exhaust "tinkles" from the head pipes. This, and the tire/road noise, spoiled what is basically a quiet car.

The SE established itself as a truly interesting car. It had the look and feel of a luxury car, yet the performance and handling were about the equal of a basic muscle car. The brakes were fine, although high-speed panic stops produced the customary rear wheelhop syndrome. Like all the Chargers, its styling drew laudatory comments wherever people saw it, but the special vinyl top and solid white paint somehow imparted a touch of class that set it apart, making it seem a totally different vehicle than the the wildly striped Super Bee or the somewhat plain Charger 500, though for all purposes they were identical cars. It looked different, felt different, and sounded different. And, driving it, you couldn't help but have a different outlook, the certain coolness of a high roller. Interesting.

HEMI SUPER BEE

If the SE was interesting, the Hemicar was remarkable. Loaded with $1,340 worth of dual-quad Hemi, Super Track Pak, and column-shift-controlled Torqueflite, but no radio, it had to be the goer of the quartet. And it was, to the tune of a 13.83/104.04 clocking for the quarter-mile right in off the street (partly attributable to a check-out 400 miles earlier, by "racing grandfather" Norm Thatcher, who made sure that everything was right up to specs). That it ran a second quicker than the 440-Six Pack was unexpected; that it was also the quietest, solidest feeling of all the Chargers was *totally* unexpected. It also stopped best, making a straight, wheelhop-free, hands-off-the-steering wheel panic halt from 60 in 115.1 feet. Average fuel mileage, with the 4.10 gear and G60-15 tires, was also surprising: 11.4 mpg. What made this miserly economy possible was a very stiff detent in the throttle linkage before the four secondary throats of the two Carter AFBs swung open. This made it possible to operate on just the primaries (which are ¼-inch smaller in diameter than the secondaries) 99 percent of the time, which still permitted over-70 mph cruising on the freeway (at 4,000+ rpm).

The same detent that kept the Hemi's thirst within limits, made it more difficult than normal to drive on the strip. With cars of this type traction is always a problem, necessitating smooth throttle control on the starting line if you seek to do other than incinerate the tires. The detent, which occurs at about quarter-throttle, complicates all this, making it very difficult to get consistently good times. Our runs ranged from a quick 13.725 e.t. (obtained with Ramcharger scoop open and top of air cleaner removed, but element in place) to a "slow" 14.180. The trap-door hood scoop appeared to be good for about 2½ mph on the top end, and best results were obtained by doing the shifting yourself at 5,800 rpm. Leaving the selector in drive produces automatic 5,500 rpm shift points. When making your own shifts, moving the lever at 5,500 produces the desired gear change at 5,800. (The 4-speed we had opted for got sidetracked in the paperwork of ordering).

The funny thing about the Hemi Super Bee was that, even before testing it, we had the feeling that it was going to be strong. The result was that there was never any need to cob it just to impress the other guy. It was a Hemi and you knew it...that was enough. That notch in the throttle linkage didn't hurt either.

Ah, now which is best? There's no doubt that the most sensible package is the 383-4V with 3-speed. It's also fun to drive. This combination in a Super Bee (in which it happens to be standard) would make a lot of sense for the average Charger buyer. The Charger 500 is O.K., if plain, but really needs the big engine suspension. For a little healthier performance, certainly the premium fuel 440-4V is quite adequate, even with automatic. And, if you seek to break away from the supercar image, but aren't quite ready for a four-door Imperial, the SE is the obvious choice. There are really enough variations for everybody. 　　　　　　　　　　/MT

440 charger six-pack

With a few simple modifications, Dodge's latest Charger will carry home its share of the bacon.

CAR CRAFT MAGAZINE DRAG TEST

THERE WAS A TIME NOT TOO LONG AGO, WHEN A NEW DODGE WAS RECOGNIZED ONLY BY ITS OWNER, MEMBERS OF THE IMMEDIATE FAMILY, AND PERHAPS BY THE BANKER WHO FINANCED THE CAR. These functionally sound vehicles were great studies of engineering reliability, but were about as aesthetically appealing as an "Our Gang," orange crate, buggy-wheeled, Soap Box racer. Performance wise, they were as equally inspiring as the flat-head six that powered them, registering 0-60 times that made a sun dial seem fast in comparison. Sales curves revealing public acceptance were equally apathetic, so to forestall extinction, corporate policies were changed to seek a new image.

One of this month's Drag Test cars, a '70 Charger, is part of that new image, and there's no mistaking it for anything but a Dodge. Looks, performance and a youth market are the current keys to the top of today's automotive sales charts, and if our

car is any indication the execs in Hamtrammick have done their homework. This car looks fast, and don't be surprised if the "Man" pulls you over for "operating a racing-type vehicle inside the city limits." As far as being fast, it is and it isn't. The PR guys would have you believing that a Charger with the optional "... big fo' forty Six-Pack engine and four-speed tranny" is the hottest thing ever to hit the street or strip. This is stretching the truth, if you evaluate the car in its dealer-delivered form; but, with the addition of a few tricks, the gap is considerably narrowed.

Our first look at the R/T Charger brought a variety of favorable comments from the staff members and secretaries alike. The Sub-Lime paint job is anything but reserved, making the car immediately identifiable wherever we went. Styling changes have been evolutionary, rather than revolutionary, with a new nose and grille the primary change. Sometimes, for rea-

sons unknown to us, styling changes are made for the sake of change, whether they add to the existing lines or not. In the case of the Charger, simulated air scoops, looking more like gills from a beached flounder, have been tacked to the forward portion of the doors.

The R/T is the most expensive model in the Charger lineup. With a $3711 base price, and a thousand dollars worth of accessories, it's not cheap; but in comparison with other "loaded" pony cars, the price is comparable. Among the included optional equipment is a Super Track Pack kit — $235.65 suggested list price. This includes the Dana rear axle (9¾" ring and pinion) with Shur-Grip differential, 7-bladed viscous-drive cooling fan, heavy duty radiator, dual-point distributor and power disc brakes on the front. This kit is available only on Chargers equipped with the 440 or 426 hemi engine and four-speed manual transmission. This is in addition to the standard R/T handling

luxe handle on the Hurst shifter is more ornamentive than functional, as it has more bends and angles than a dog's hind leg. Coupled with a long throw between the gears, you are never quite sure whether the trans is in gear, as the handle will flex on fast shifts.

Releasing the twin hood-pins and raising the hood reveals the 440 Six-Pack engine. Underneath the air cleaner are three Holley two-barrel carbs. The center carb, rated at 250-cfm, has an automatic choke and accelerator pump system. The 390 cfm end carbs have no choke or pump system, and are opened by engine vacuum, operating through a diaphragm control valve. Internally, there are changes to complement the additional carburetion. The connecting rods are hand selected for uniform bearing size and length. The valve train included Street Hemi valve springs with increased tension for higher rpm's, and special bevel-faced lifters with more surface contact to minimize camshaft wear.

The next couple of weeks were spent familiarizing ourselves with the car and logging-in needed break-in mileage. Unlike many hi-per cars we've tested, the Six-Pack Charger does not have a rough idle, balky low-end throttle response or a tendency to foul plugs in bumper-to-bumper traffic. Gas mileage is better than most big-engined pony-type cars, as long as one doesn't open the end carbs excessively. The Charger is no sports car when it comes to handling, but it's a lot better than most cars that emerge from Detroit. It understeers (show us one that doesn't), but there's enough power and throttle control to keep out of trouble. The power steering doesn't help this condition, but, on the other hand, it's a necessity for parking in tight places.

After logging-in a thousand miles, it was time to head for the drags for some initial timed runs. The first few attempts were miserably disappointing. A no-traction condition off the line, coupled with a "wandering" shifter and a set of end carbs that opened way too late, netted 15-second elapsed times and low 90-mph trap speeds. Compared to the automatic version we had seen at the press previews, our Charger was more than a second and a half off the pace. Off the line starts could be improved with practice, as could the shifting, but the carburetion problem was a different situation. Luck was with us, however, as Ralph Johnson from Holley Carburetors had come with us. We put him to work.

One of our problems became apparent when we found the throttle shafts in the end carbs binding. The

ABOVE — Carbs with accelerator pumps and mechanical linkage worked the best.

MIDDLE — Prototype equal-length Cyclone headers add h.p. throughout rpm range.

BOTTOM — "Tricking" up stock vacuum-operated end carbs requires plugging off the kill bleed hole with lead shot, and installation of "brown" diaphragm spring.

stock gaskets between the carbs and manifold are too thick, and improper tightening of the mounting bolts will cause the shafts to bind. (Note: Carburetor gaskets from Tri-Power Chevrolets work perfectly.) The end carbs were modified to open sooner for improved throttle response. Ralph removed the diaphragm housing, plugged the kill bleed hole with a piece of lead shot, and replaced the housing. This procedure, by itself, makes the carburetors too sensitive to the vacuum signal, so the stock (purple) diaphragm spring was replaced with a stronger Holley (brown) spring to delay the opening time. With this combination, the setup is virtually foolproof in its operation, and the car started to perform as advertised. The elapsed times dropped a

package, consisting of heavy-duty springs, shocks and sway bars. Complementing these components is a set of F-60 x 15 Goodyear Polyglas tires. Our only criticism here is that these tires should be standard on a car with this much power and weight. From past experience, one would be lucky to exceed 15,000 miles on the standard 14-inch tires, regardless of their driving habits.

Inside the cockpit, the driver has the advantage of a six-way adjustable seat — sort of a dial-your-own comfort setting. A full console separates the high-backed bucket seats, which may be great as a protective device in the event of a rear end collision, but prove to be difficult to see around when backing up. Most of the gauges are easy to read with the exception of the combination tach and clock. You have to look twice to make sure it's the tach you're reading, and not the sweep second hand. On top of this, there are occasions when the tach is a little slow in counting the rpm's (this proved to be somewhat troublesome during the strip phase of our testing). Also, the de-

full second, and the mph topped the century mark. With a car that tipped the scales at 4070-pounds, these marks were deemed acceptable for base line figures.

If we were going to improve on this performance, it would be necessary to increase horsepower, get it to the ground, and improve the shifting situation. Limiting ourselves to bolt-on modifications, the car was taken to Cyclone Automotive Products in Burbank, California, for a set of their equal length, under-the-frame headers. A prototype set was fashioned for the car, along with a complete muffler system of minimal restriction. Next, the car was taken to Dick Landy's headquarters in Van Nuys. In order to meet emission requirements the factory installs lean metering plates in the carburetors, along with a retarded ignition curve. Since the headers would allow more efficient breathing, the end carbs were modified by carefully hand drilling the metering plates .003" larger than stock (use a .092" drill for this). Next, the ignition curve was modified by changing the springs that control the advance weights. In stock form there is one heavy spring and one light one. Remove the heavy spring and replace it with another light one. This does not change the total advance curve, it just makes the rate faster. Full mechanical advance should be obtained between 1600-1800 engine rpm. With this set-up the vacuum advance is disconnected, and the hole in the manifold is blocked off.

To solve our shifting dilemma, we contacted Hurst Performance Products and ordered one of their Competition Plus shifters (see CC, December '68). This particular model has a special mounting bracket that moves the shifter 9-inches closer to the driver. Heavy duty shift rods are also included. Part of the console and a section of the floor must be trimmed in order to install the shifter. Once in, however, the efforts are well worth it. The shifter is ideally located, but the throw is almost too short for a stock transmission. This shifter was designed for the "crash box," non-synchro Super Stock transmissions, and plenty of "beef" is required on gear changes to compensate for the drag of the synchros in the stock trans.

To handle the traction requirements, a set of Goodyear 8.90 x 15 slicks were installed on stock 6-inch wide MoPar rims. These will fit the stock wheel well openings without modifications. One final trick was to install a fiberglass scoop to the hood. With the high rise Six-Pack manifold, there isn't sufficient air space between the top of the carbs and the hood. Mid-year Chargers will be available, from the factory, with a hood scoop for similar fresh-air induction.

The fruits of our labors could only be determined by running the car, so we headed for Lions Drag Strip once again. The headers were uncorked, the slicks were installed, and the power steering belt was disconnected. Removing the belt was done primarily to keep from over-revving the power steering pump; it is questionable whether we were gaining any power with this procedure.

After a few burnouts, it was apparent that the car was getting a grip on the ground. Five-thousand-rpm starts bogged the engine, making full throttle starts mandatory. Shifting at 6200, our best runs were 13.18, with a top speed of 106.54. The bogging problem was not so much a condition of too much traction, as it was a lack of low-end power. Advancing the timing to a total of 40 degrees helped, but the power was still short. We contacted Ralph again, and he replaced the end carbs with #4783 Holley units. These carbs do not have the vacuum diaphragms. Instead, they have accelerator pump systems. Consequently, a mechanical throttle linkage is needed to replace the vacuum system (Edelbrock Equipment Company is in the process of making a linkage kit for this conversion).

With this setup, we had increased throttle control off the line, along with an increase in power. Tire pressures were lowered to ten pounds, with neck snapping starts a welcome feeling. The timing slips registered the increase, as the Charger dipped into the 12-second bracket, and the speeds jumped past the 109 mark, recording a best of 12.87 at 109.54. The best part was the fact that our modifications had not affected the on-street reliability. You might say that we had the best of both worlds — a 12-second strip machine, and a docile grocery getter. ⓒ

Goodyear slicks, size 8.90 x 15 are needed for high-rpm starts and 12-second e.t.'s.

DODGE DAYTONA
CONTINUED FROM PAGE 72
credit for the economy boost.

There are many things we like and dislike about the Daytona. First off the bug-eye recessed headlights look great when they're hidden, but completely ruin the frontal styling when they're brought into view. The rear wing treatment is downright ugly, but super functional from a racing viewpoint. We really missed the normal front bumper, especially when parking. But the word is that the full productionline models will sport some frontal protection. And, we really can't hack the mating surface between the streamlined nose and the stock fenders. The rubber molding gets kind of sloppy and looks cheap. The rest of the car—performance, comfrot, appointments—is Charger R/T and certainly competitive with the current market. At first we hated it, but as time went on we learned to groove on it. If it were only available in some conservative colors . . .

CHARGER 440 R/T

Two old friends—the Charger and the 440— strike up a friendship of their own.

IT IS WRITTEN somewhere that a car must be small and sporty to be right for enthusiasts. It's a good thing that the guys at Dodge haven't read that. They keep making the Charger go like stink and handle better than a lot of the so-called sportsters.

For our '70 Charger road test, we specified the 440 engine one step up from the standard 318-cid V-8. We have tried the big gun, the 426 Hemi, but we wanted to sneak up on the road, not bludgeon it. We happen to believe that the Charger can be had with finesse and not just brute force.

Our test Charger, painted metallic tan came with an alligator roof (plastic alligators), and a hydraulic lifter 440 Magnum packed under the hood, a 3.55:1 rear axle ratio out back and TorqueFlite. Glued on the side were R/T emblems (we like to think these are in honor of our sister publication, *Road & Track*) indicating that the car had been fitted with heavy-duty drum brakes, special torsion bars, firmer shock absorbers, heavy-duty rear springs and a front anti-roll bar.

The 440 is a hefty hunk of iron

(rated at 375 bhp) that accounts well for itself in the performance league. It has good porting and a streamlined exhaust. It is modest in its fuel consumption, imbibing at the rate of only 15 miles per gallon. It'll wind to 5000 rpm all day long if you want and has potential to meet much greater demands.

The 440 Magnum engine uses a Carter AVS four-barrel. This carb is adequate for the demands of street driving, providing plenty of torque and tractability in the lower gears and permitting you to sharpen your low end performance as precisely as you want.

More power is available with the 440 Six Pack. As we see in the power chart on page 10, the Magnum's single carburetor is on the small side. The triple twos add an honest 50 horses. In most driving, though, they aren't needed, and we'd settle for the Magnum.

The interior was as comforting as granny's afghan. Ours had the SE package which means Special Edition and includes leather facings on the front buckets, a simulated walnut

steering wheel, special interior lights, chrome dress-up moldings and map pockets on the doors. The high-backed buckets had *soft* headrests—the first we've actually been able to rest our heads against. The driver's bucket had the 6-way adjustment for angle, increasing the driveability of the car for different sized drivers.

The Charger is, in size anyway, an Intermediate. With its long wheelbase, the designers don't need to pinch the passengers (as they did in the Challenger, for one example). Here, the 6-way adjustable driver's seat works. There's hip and head room for driver and passenger, and even room for adults in the back. It's no limousine, mind, but it can serve four people for the average trip. The same goes for the trunk; unless you're a gypsy tribe, everything you need will fit.

Purposeful is the word we'd use to describe the instrument panel. Set into test-tube-born walnut were gauges for water temp, an ammeter, oil pressure and a tach. The tachometer, oddly enough, was almost completely obscured by a large clock set smack-dab

CHARGER interior was super roomy. Tall buckets were comfy. Elastic topped map pockets we liked.

CHARGER'S dash was neat; orderly. Tachometer was difficult to read because of clock placed on top.

on top of it. We suppose Dodge stylists didn't want to cut another hole for the clock but, really, we like to see *all* of our tachometer.

One good thing was the elastic-topped map pockets in the door. If you're like us, you like to keep maps around. With the Charger's regular glovebox, console glovebox *and* door pockets, we were equipped to drive from

California to Peru by map, anyway.

As far as ride, the Charger was a bit stiff on the highway, just as you would expect with a heavy-duty option package like the R/T. The front anti-roll bar is a good idea, increasing handling ability without making the ride stiffer. Rough road ride, the real test of a heavy-duty suspension, was not any bumpier, indicating the sus-

pension was a good all-around set-up.

The Charger's big wheelbase, 117 in., is one of the best things it has going for it in terms of ride. One thing that always hurts the sporty cars is the short wheelbase. Sure, the shorter the wheelbase, the more maneuverable the car but, in going over bumps, you have a shorter distance between the tires to absorb the shock.

1970 CHARGER R/T
DODGE

DIMENSIONS

Wheelbase, in.	117
Track, f/r, in.	59.7/59.2
Overall length, in.	208
width	76.6
height	53.0
Front seat hip room, in.	22x2
shoulder room	56.6
head room	37.4
pedal-seatback, max.	42
Rear seat hip room, in.	53
shoulder room	55.9
leg room	33.4
head room	36.4
Door opening width, in.	46
Trunk liftover height, in.	30.5

PRICES

List, FOB factory............$3711
Equipped as tested...........$5546
Standard equipment included: Torque-Flite transmission, 440-cid Magnum engine.
Options included: Air conditioning, $358; stereo tape with AM radio, $196; power steering, $105; vinyl roof, $100; power windows, $105; special edition package, $162; performance axle package, $92; F60x 15 tires, $63; power brakes, $54; disc brakes front, $43; tachometer with clock, $68; auto speed control, $58; evaporative control system, $38.

CHASSIS/SUSPENSION

Frame type: Unitized.
Front suspension type: Independent by short-long arms, torsion bars, anti-roll bar.
  ride rate at wheel, lb./in. 118
  anti-roll bar dia., in. 0.88
Rear suspension type: Live axle, leaf springs.
  ride rate at wheel, lb./in. 150
Steering system: Recirculating ball with integral power assist.
  overall ratio...............18.8:1
  turns, lock to lock............3.5
  turning circle, ft. curb-curb....40.9
Curb weight, lb...............4170
Test weight...................4545
  distribution (driver)
  % f/r.................57.3/42.7

INSTRUMENTATION

Gauges: 120°-250° water temp., fuel level, 0-8000 tach, 0-150 speedometer, −40 to +40 alternator, 0-80 psi oil pressure.
Warning lights: Brake warning lights, high beams.

WHEELS/TIRES

Wheel rim size	15x7JJ
std. size	14x6JJ
bolt no./circle dia. in.	5/4.5

Tires: Goodyear Polyglas GT.
type	fiberglass belted
size	F60x15
std. size	F70x14
Test inflation	33/33

ENGINE

Type, no. of cyl	V-8
Bore x stroke, in.	4.32x3.75
Displacement, cu. in.	440
Compression ratio	9.7:1
Fuel required	premium
Rated bhp @ rpm	375 @ 4600
equivalent mph	96
Rated torque @ rpm	480 @ 3200
equivalent mph	67

Carburetion: 1x4V Carter AVS.
  throttle dia., pri./sec. ...1.69/1.69
Valve train: Overhead valves, rocker arms, pushrods, hydraulic lifters.
  valve dia., in.
  int./exh. 2.08/1.74
  lift, in.
  int./exh. 0.450/0.465
Cam timing
  deg., int./exh. 21-67/79-25
  duration, int./exh. 268/284
Exhaust system: Dual, reverse flow mufflers.
  pipe dia., exh./tail.......2.50/2.25

DRIVE TRAIN

Transmission type: 3-speed automatic TorqueFlite.
Gear ratio overall
  3rd (1.00:1)...............3.55:1
  2nd (1.45:1)...............5.15:1
  1st (2.45:1)...............8.7:1
1st x t.c. stall (2.0:1)........17.4:1
Shift lever location: Console.
Differential type: Hypoid, limited slip.
  axle ratio..................3.55:1

TILTING the spare gives a bit more room, though high lip makes lifting luggage a chore with the Charger.

440 MAGNUM. It's no Hemi, but it's tough enough. With R/T Package, you get choice of TorqueFlite or 4-speed.

Any skier who has ever switched from the long skis to "shortie" skis knows what we're talking about. The short ones are fine for maneuvering *around* moguls but if you ever schuss straight down the hill, the short ones aren't long enough to be able to withstand the pounding of bump after bump.

Along with the bouquet, a thorn.

One trouble with the Charger, as well as a lot of other big cars, is that—with the wider wheels and tires—unsprung weight has suddenly loomed as a villain. There's no doubt that wide wheels and wide tires offer superior handling. The only thing is, wide steel wheels, like the Charger's 15-inchers, and big gumbos like the Charger's F60 x 15s, weigh more than

the old skinny wheels and tires, representing an increase in unsprung weight. This weight reacts *against* the car's two tons plus weight, diminishing ride quality.

For an analogy, think of match-shooters. They choose a heavy stock and a small calibre bullet so that they won't have recoil throwing the rifle around, causing them to re-calibrate

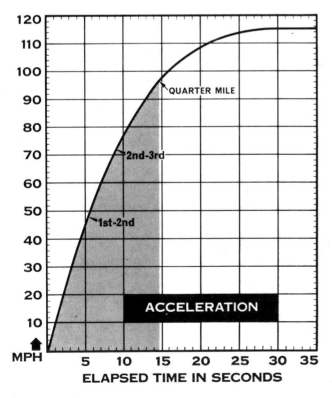

CAR LIFE ROAD TEST

ACCELERATION

QUARTER MILE

2nd-3rd

1st-2nd

MPH — ELAPSED TIME IN SECONDS

5 10 15 20 25 30 35

CALCULATED DATA

Lb./bhp (test weight)...........11.8
Mph/1000 rpm (high gear)......20.9
Engine revs/mi. (60 mph)......2870
Piston travel, ft./mi...........1795
CAR LIFE wear index..........51.5

SPEEDOMETER ERROR

Indicated	Actual
30 mph	.29
40 mph	.38
50 mph	.48
60 mph	.58
70 mph	.68
80 mph	.76
90 mph	.85

CAPACITIES

No. of passengers.................5
Luggage space, cu. ft...........11.4
Fuel tank, gal...................19
Fuel consumption, mpg.........11.6

MAINTENANCE

Engine oil, miles/days.....4000/90
  oil filter, miles/days....8000/180
Chassis lubrication, mi........36,000
Antismog servicing: 12,000 mile
  replace PCV valve and tune engine.
Warranty period, mo./mi., 12/12,000
  entire vehicle, 60/50,000 power
  train
Spark plugs: Champion J-11Y
  gap, in......................0.035
Basic timing, deg./rpm:.0-5BTC/800
Ignition point gap, in.....0.016-0.021
  cam dwell angle, deg.....28.5-32.5

PERFORMANCE

Top speed (5500), mph..........115
Test shift point (rpm) mph
  2nd to 3rd (5000)..............72
  1st to 2nd (5500)..............48

ACCELERATION

0-30 mph, sec...................3.3
0-40 mph........................4.5
0-50 mph........................5.8
0-60 mph........................7.2
0-70 mph........................8.8
0-80 mph.......................10.7
0-90 mph.......................13.1
0-100 mph......................16.2
Standing ¼-mile, sec...........14.71
  speed at end, mph...........96.67
Passing, 30-70 mph, sec.........5.5

BRAKING

Type: Power assisted disc/drum.
Front rotor, dia. x width, in...10.7 x 1.8
Rear drum, dia. x width.....10 x 2.5
  total swept area, sq. in.........358
Max. deceleration rate and stopping
  distance from 80 mph...........
  ft./sec./sec..................n.a.
  distance, ft..................317
Rate and distance after six ½-G
  stops from 80 mph.............
  rate, ft./sec./sec..............18
  distance, ft..................395
Control loss? Yes.
Overall brake performance......poor

CHARGER 440

sights, re-aim, etc. Similarly, Mercedes has been putting small wheels and tires on their cars for years, knowing their customers prefer ride to extreme cornering power. They don't want the tail wagging the dog and all that.

One solution for Charger might be to offer genuinely *lightweight* wheels as an option instead of the heavy steel ones they presently offer.

Do Chargers handle? Are trees made of wood? As we found in our Hemi Charger road tests, two tons of weight don't have to be a drawback if suspended properly, which it is on the Charger. You could go into a corner

at too high a speed, tap the brakes yet experience no brake hop, get on the power again and come out aiming right, without the weight transfer interfering.

The front anti-roll bar did its job well. It still allowed some plow—a condition where the front tires deviate some from their path but hang on for the most part. But the front tires didn't stumble, causing the back end to come around.

Why not hang an anti-roll bar on the back? It wouldn't work. Dodge already has the rear leaf springs doing double-duty—soaking up shock and locating the rear axles so they won't

wind up under the massive torque of the 440. The high spring rate was determined by the engine. If you added an anti-roll bar to an already stiffly sprung set-up, you would have so much anti-roll resistance that the whole car would pick up and skitter across the pavement sideways as soon as you put any sideloads on it.

The Charger 440 is basically a milder understeerer. You can go into what is a low speed corner for ordinary cars at a high rate of speed with the Charger without experiencing large amounts of understeer. The 440 engine is flexible enough within its 5000-rpm limit rev range, to permit gradual applications of rpm to power the tail out, inducing mild oversteer.

The steering wasn't exceptionally fast, but you don't run out of steering because of having to crank too much lock at the front part of a turn. Steering depends a lot upon the characteristics of the car. If the car handles well, as the Charger does, you're not going to have to be over-compensating with the steering. Consequently, it's not as critical. The steering definitely had road feel. You knew what the tires were doing.

This degree of controllability in a Charger while cornering is something that must continually prove embarrassing to the drivers of smaller cars who try to keep up with a Charger 'round a curvy expressway entrance.

Enough on handling? What was its E.T., ask the dragstrip fans. How about a 14.7 E.T. at 98 mph? For a car the size of a Charger, this is an accomplishment.

The Charger brakes were two different stories. The first story, out on the highway, is that they were efficient and didn't take a lot of pedal effort. There was no locking, swerving and a minimum amount of fade upon repeat applications in traffic. The second story came with the maximum effort stops we made on the test track. Our first one resulted in a brakes-locked skid that almost left the Charger's profile on the test track wall. The next seven ½G stops resulted in quite a bit of fade, losing about one-fourth the brake's effectiveness by the time we pulled our last maximum effort stop. The drums on the Charger, then, *do* fade, but only after extremely hard use. We're still hoping, though, that like the '70 Camaro, Dodge will make front discs *standard*.

Overall, the '70 Charger 440 R/T is an extremely roadable concept in big car packaging. If you want good ride, lots of room, punch in your engine and mileage to boot, we'd recommend it. There's another plus—with its distinctive body styling, we think the Chargers got "special interest" built into it. ∎

GOING INTO turn, Charger R/T leans some, but anti-roll bar and excellent Rallye suspension save it.

DODGE
CHARGER CORONET

Both Dodge and Plymouth have innovatively given their intermediate models distinct and separate styling themes. Dodge, however, has the easier-to-understand naming system which is predicated on the fact that the new 2-door hardtops replace the specialty Charger line of the past. The 4-door models are called Coronet as before.

One economy achieved by these otherwise expensive changes is eliminating the need for a special Charger roof designed just for super-speedway racing. The tunnel roof style helped the appearance of previous Chargers but it had poor aerodynamic characteristics. This gave rise to the special Charger 500 and Daytona models with a semi-fastback roofline minus the "sails" at each side. The necessary production of street models for homologation never paid back the costs of tooling the special roof.

Whether the wedge-nosed Daytona model with its elevated spoiler will appear in '71 is problematical and aside from roof shapes. The aerodynamic characteristics of this car were and are superb and the roadholding side effects could be felt even at legal turnpike speeds. However, the elongated nose without any form of protection was totally impractical around town, not to mention the attraction this equippage had for highway patrolmen anywhere. Dodge and Plymouth (which had an equivalent "Super Bird") could continue racing their '70 models or sacrifice some aerodynamics by racing the new configuration in conventional form. This latter will be the probable route because as of January 1, 1971, NASCAR rules call for reduction of maximum engine displacement to 366 cubic inches with a consequent reduction of

race speeds. The present 426-cubic-inch Hemi, incidentally, will have a revised bore and stroke to meet this new limitation but it won't be changed in street form.

The new Charger coupes will have a 115-inch wheelbase and the Coronet sedans 118, but the difference in overall length is only 205.4 versus 207.0 inches, respectively. Coronet wagons are quite a bit longer at 213.4 inches but they use the sedan wheelbase. About the only dimension shared between Chargers and Coronets is front seat leg room at 42.3 inches.

The lowest price Charger (the company has so far stated only that "Charger prices will be reduced to the former Coronet hardtop level . . .") is a coupe with fixed rear quarter windows. Matching it is the base Coronet in 4-door sedan and 2-seat wagon form. In these three, the 225-cubic-inch slant-6 of 145 hp is standard but you can get optional engines ranging up to the 383 4-barrel.

At this point the Charger Super Bee fits in with the 383 4-barrel standard, and the Hemi or Six-Pack optional. The Super Bee is Dodge's version of the Road Runner concept: namely, high performance coupled with relatively austere trim. Body color bumpers are optional, front and rear, and the car is cluttered with decals. Coronet Custom models are not counterparts in concept, being re-

latively luxurious cars with a standard 6-cylinder engine except for the 3-seat wagon.

The '71 Coronet wagon body is equally new and has attractive lines. It has a standard 2-way "hardtop" tailgate which can be opened or closed with the glass in any position. On 3-seat models an electric interlock system is provided which prevents, for safety reasons, the door from being unlatched from inside the car whenever the ignition is on. Another useful accessory is a spoiler to keep the tailgate window clean that can be ordered with or without a built-in roof rack. Other makers generally combine this spoiler with the rack, which makes it an expensive add-on as the spoiler is needed all the time and the rack only occasionally.

A hardtop called simply Charger is the equivalent of the Coronet Custom both in engine availability and trim. The Charger 500 is similar except that it has a standard 318-cubic-inch, 230-hp V-8 as does the Charger S.E. The latter features a different grille with concealed headlights and a vinyl top applique that covers only the flat portion of the roof. The Coronet Brougham sedan and Crestwood wagons have equivalent trim standards but the headlights are exposed. Then finally, there is the Charger R/T with its standard 440-cubic-inch, 370-hp premium fuel engine and

CHARGER SUPER BEE

single 4-barrel carburetion. This model and the Super Bee are the only ones in which the Six-Pack and the Hemi may be optionally installed, at least by the factory.

Availability of the manual 3-speed transmission stops with the 383 4-barrel engine, after which the 4-speed box becomes standard. Automatics are optional on all. Charger and Coronet models share a common instrument panel which is complete except for an oil pressure gauge. Unlike Challenger, no "rally cluster" is listed, but tach may be applied to any V-8 engine in any body style in this series.   •

CORONET/CUSTOM/BROUGHAM/ CRESTWOOD/CHARGER/SUPER BEE/ 500/ R/T /S.E.

ENGINES: 225 cu ins (145 hp). 318 cu ins (230 hp). 383 cu ins (275, 300 hp). 426 cu ins (425 hp). 440 cu ins (370, 385 hp).

TRANSMISSIONS: 3-spd manual, 3-spd auto, 4-spd manual.

SUSPENSION: Torsion bar front, leaf rear.

STEERING: Manual std, power opt, curb-to-curb 40.8-40.9 ft.

BRAKES: Drum std, front disc opt, power opt.

FUEL CAPACITY: 21.0 gals.

DIMENSIONS: Wheelbase 115-118 ins. Track 59.7-60.1 ins. front, 61.6-63.4 rear. Width 78.6-79.2 ins. Length 205.4-213.4 ins. Height 52.2-57.4 ins. Weight 3355-3480 lbs. Trunk 14.2-15.9 cu ft.

BODY STYLES: 2-dr cpe, 2-dr hdtp, 4-dr sdn, 2- and 3-seat wgns.

CHARGER S.E.

1971 DODGE CHARGER,
TOP PERFORMANCE CAR OF THE YEAR

The Dodge Boys' latest effort boasts tasteful styling, excellent
handling and ride characteristics plus as much performance
as anyone could ask for

BY MARTYN L. SCHORR

Dodge General Manager, Bob McCurry, right, explains the high speed streamlining qualities of the Charger to CARS Editor Marty Schorr.

IN THE PROCESS of choosing the Eleventh Annual Top Performance Car of the Year, the CARS staff tested and evaluated no less than 23 high-performance '71 supercars, mini-musclecars and super ponycars. Some had four-speeds, others had automatics. Some were geared for the quarter-mile, others geared for commuting between Salt Lake City and Wendover, Utah. Some had bucket seats and others bench seating. We ran the full gamut. The test and evaluation program was a six-week affair and staffers logged over 6900 road test miles. Candidates were checked out over the road, on

the skid pads and drag strips at the various Proving Grounds and in typical urban traffic situations. The job of picking the "Top Performance Car of the Year" has been getting tougher and tougher each year, as model lines are expanded and new models introduced.

The words *Top Performance* mean many things to many people. To the street racer or drag enthusiast they mean lowest elapsed times and top miles per hour. To the sporty car buff, they mean lean and roll-free performance and suspensions as stiff as those used on in-transit cement mixers. To the drive-in "tire-chirper"

they mean noisy exhausts, lots of stripes and scoops, big cube emblems and mod colors. To us, they mean "Total Performance" which encompasses street performance, road handling, comfort and appointments, styling and, to a much lesser degree, quarter-mile acceleration and top end. That's why the award is *never* given to the quickest accelerating car or the one with the ultimate road racing suspension or highest horsepower rating. That's not where it's at.

The Eleventh Annual award goes to the Dodge Division of Chrysler Corporation for its exciting line of Chargers. This year the Charger is all-new,

Dodge completely covers the two-door hardtop market with its new Charger line. Shown here L to R: Charger 500, SE and Super Bee.

as is Dodge's Charger marketing and merchandising policies. For '71 you can get a budget-priced economy Charger (Six-cylinder), a dressed-up Charger 500, a youth market performance Charger Super Bee, a maximum-image, maximum-performance Charger R/T, and an ultra-luxurious Charger SE. The basic Charger is available with choice of Six or Eight cylinder power, while the Charger 500 and top-line SE can be had only with V-8 power. The Scat Pack Chargers —Super Bee and R/T—come stock with 383 four-barrel and 440 four-barrel engines, respectively. The 426 Hemi and popular 440 Six-Pack wedge are optional. Thus the Charger line covers a broad segment of the market, offering something to satisfy the buying habits of anyone who's interested in a two-door hardtop.

"In the past we have been locked into a compromise position between our hardtops and sedans," said Bob McCurry, Dodge general manager. "With our new product marketing approach for '71," McCurry explained, "we will be able to give sedan buyers all of the advantages of a full-sized car without trying to get adequate leg room and trunk space into a hardtop floor plan." "And by

the same token," he said, "we'll be able to give the hardtop enthusiast sleek styling and sporty appointments without having to employ an extended trunk and elevated roof line." McCurry pointed out that both cars—Charger and Coronet—will be built on separate floor pans, which is the determining factor in the usual design lock-in between the sedans and hardtops. The Charger has a 115-inch wheelbase, while the Coronet

Ramcharger hood scoop is vacuum-controlled and really blows minds at traffic lights!

checks out at 118 inches.

So much for the Charger marketing program. The third generation Charger is a far cry from the original which debuted in 1966. It, too, was radical for its time and, because of its unique styling, suspension and power packages, got our vote for Top Performance Car of the year in 1966. The latest version represents a deliberate extension and refinement of the highly popular wedge shape first introduced in 1968. The '71 Charger has soft, smooth and gracefully flowing lines, accentuated by ventless side glass and hidden windshield wipers. Its styling can best be described as tasteful. It's a together car. Both the chrome loop bumper treatment or the optional color matched application works into the overall design. They don't look like bolt-ons or afterthoughts. The rear is tastefully styled with a slight spoiler influence.

Performance packaging has long been a plus-feature in Dodge's marketing policies since the first high-performance wedges rolled off the line. The latest Charger is a perfect example of what we're rapping about. There's no way you can get a performance engine without also

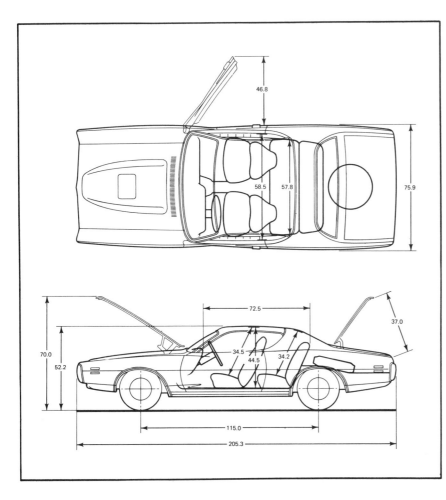

Best engine choice for top street/strip perf is tri-power **440** Six-Pack wedge with super lower end, good cam. Schematic, left, reveals full dimensions of new hardtop layout.

View from the open sunroof shows new race-type wheel, full gauges, four-speed changer.

getting a matching heavy-duty suspension and related running gear component parts. And, while Dodge still offers a high-compression ratio for the performance enthusiast, it doesn't saddle the *average* buyer of a Charger R/T or Super Bee with the high ratio. If you order a straight Super Bee you get a regular fuel 383 wedge. With a straight R/T you get 440 Magnum cubes with a compromise ratio of 9.7-to-1. The top line 426 Hemi checks out at 10.2-to-1 while the 440 tri-power Six-Pak goes right to 10.5-to-1.

The enthusiast who wants to keep costs down to a bare minimum and still go the supercar route, can afford the Super Bee. The standard equipment Super Bee comes with the 383 Magnum V-8, performance hood, Ralley instrument cluster with 150 mph speedo, carpeting, Ralley suspension (HD torsion bars, rear springs and sway bar, shocks), floor shifted three-speed stick, HD brakes (11x2½ inches), F-70x14 bias-belted tires and dual exhausts. What you end up with is a respectable performer with top eliminator status.

The other performance choice is the R/T which comes with stock 440 Magnum V-8 power, full instrumentation package including 150 mph speedo, carpeting, buckets, Torque-Flite shifter, Extra Heavy Duty suspension which includes special springs with an extra leaf on the right side to offset engine torque, HD brakes (11 x3-inch front and 11x2½-inch rear). G70x14 raised white letter bias-belted tires and dual exhausts. It's more potent and even more of a head turner than the Super Bee. That's the basic Charger performance story.

Super Bee and R/T with 440 tri-power mill are super impressive road handlers and straightline performers. Note fat 'glass shoes.

But, that's not where Dodge leaves off. There are a multitude of performance and dress-up options which can be applied to the Super Bee and R/T, as well as the super-lux models. There are mag wheels, Ramcharger hood treatments, a tach, racing mirrors, hood pins, fat tires, four-speed Hurst setups, *ad infinitum*. And, if you want to go one step beyond, Dodge has a Hustle Stuff program which makes it possible for owners to purchase the right cam, headers, ignition setup, drag gears, manifolds and Holley carbs, etc., for maximum off-road performance.

Another interesting Dodge innovation is the packaging of HD component parts with high performance gearsets. This type of program insures reliability whenever someone specifies a hot ratio. The mildest is the A-36 package for 383 models with stick or auto and 440 and 426 Hemis with auto only. It consists of HD 3.55 gears, Sure-Grip differential, seven-bladed torque fan, extra HD suspension (440 and 426 only) and a 26-inch HP radiator and fan shroud. The next step up is the A-31 package for 383 cars only. It consists of HD 3.91 gears, Sure-Grip, seven-bladed torque fan and the radiator assembly. Next up is the A-33 Track Pak for 440 and 426 cars with four-speed sticks. It includes an HD 9¾-inch Dana 3.54 rear, Sure-Grip, seven-bladed torque fan, dual-point distributor (Six-Pack and Hemi

Charger with SE package is one of sleekest machines on the '71 specialty car scene.

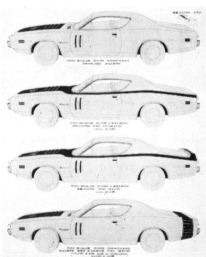

If stripes and tape goodies turn you on, check Dodge for the widest selection.

only) and the radiator assembly. The top dog setup is the A-34 Super Track-Pak for 440 and Hemi cars. It consists of the big Dana rear with 4.10 gears, Sure-Grip, seven-bladed torque fan, dual-point distributor (Six Pack and Hemi only), radiator package and power disc brakes. Dodge is interested in safety, reliability and in keeping warranty costs down.

The '71 Charger line offers something for everyone. Packages and options can be interchanged so that the R/T buyer can get SE (Special Edition) luxury features if so desired. It's this type of flexibility that helps build an impressive sales picture and a pride in ownership. Anyone interested in a sporty hardtop should be interested in a '71 Charger. It's *that* kind of car.

Color-keyed bumper treatment and Super Bee package turns the Charger into a supercar.

DODGE CHARGER SE

By far and away it's 1971's best styled new car

"Heigh ho, Lance. This is Rob. You know, *Rob*, I met you over at Samantha's during the Tactile Encounter session. I had on the purple Yves Saint Laurent jump suit and was sitting between that tacky copy of Oldenburg's "soft hamburger" and the dynamite Ernst Troler original. Right . . . right, we were rapping about the relevancy of Dusty and Marty Balsam's pivotal encounter in *Big Little* when she turned on the whale thing, right.

"Yea, well what I was calling about, really, was to see if you'd like to fall by my digs sometime this weekend. I just picked up on· a dynamite, *really* dynamite new sculpture that I figure you'll be into, too, as soon as you see it.

"Right, *right on*, Tom Owen is going to go out of his gourd on this one.

"It's called 'Charger' and it's—are you ready for this?—it's made by Dodge.

"Hello? . . . Lance? . . ."

That's the way it goes nowadays, Rob old buddy. Had you said that *Playboy's* sculptor laureate, Frank Gallo created the Charger from ground-up polyurethane coffee cups, Lance would have been rattling your blue anodized aluminum doorknob instead of leaving you standing there in front of your Lucidity clear plastic phone with his curt *ciao* still searing across your eardrum.

A Dodge Charger? A piece of sculpture? What the hell kind of individual artistic statement can that be when

50,000 people a year make the same statement? Besides, you've got to admit that an *objet d'art* created by a guy with a name like Gallo, or Toler, or Quasar (who everybody knows works in a vital environment like Ibiza or Johnson's Pasture, or St. Tropez) has a bit more of a cachet than anything Bill Brownlie can slap together out of modeler's clay in gay, romantic Hamtramck, Michigan.

But that does not alter the fact that Brownlie and his
(Text continued on page 107. Specifications overleaf)

The new Dodge Charger SE
proves
that a marketing compromise
need not result
in·a styling disaster

NATURAL OPOSSUM COAT PROVIDED BY GEORGES KAPLAN FURS

ACCELERATION standing ¼ mile, seconds

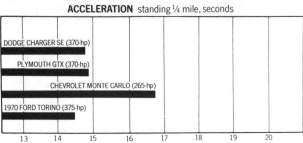

- DODGE CHARGER SE (370-hp)
- PLYMOUTH GTX (370-hp)
- CHEVROLET MONTE CARLO (265-hp)
- 1970 FORD TORINO (375-hp)

13 14 15 16 17 18 19 20

BRAKING 80-0 mph panic stop, feet

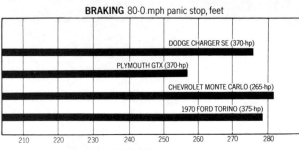

- DODGE CHARGER SE (370-hp)
- PLYMOUTH GTX (370-hp)
- CHEVROLET MONTE CARLO (265-hp)
- 1970 FORD TORINO (375-hp)

210 220 230 240 250 260 270 280

FUEL ECONOMY RANGE mpg

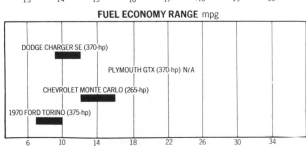

- DODGE CHARGER SE (370-hp)
- PLYMOUTH GTX (370-hp) N/A
- CHEVROLET MONTE CARLO (265-hp)
- 1970 FORD TORINO (375-hp)

6 10 14 18 22 26 30 34

PRICE AS TESTED dollars x 1000

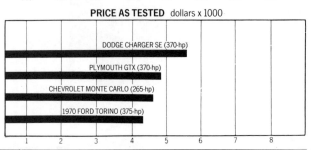

- DODGE CHARGER SE (370-hp)
- PLYMOUTH GTX (370-hp)
- CHEVROLET MONTE CARLO (265-hp)
- 1970 FORD TORINO (375-hp)

1 2 3 4 5 6 7 8

Dodge Charger SE

Manufacturer: Dodge Division
Chrysler Corporation
Detroit, Michigan

Vehicle type: Front engine, rear-wheel-drive, 5-passenger 2-door Hard top

Price as tested: $5670.75

(Manufacturer's suggested retail price, including all options listed below, Federal excise tax, dealer preparation and delivery charges, does not include state and local taxes, license or freight charges)

Options on test car: Base car, $3422.00; leather bucket seats, $52.50; front disc brakes, $24.45; power brakes, $45.15; console, $57.65; 6-way adjustable seat, $35.00; automatic transmission, $237.50; limited-slip differential, $45.35; 440 4-bbl. V-8, $281.25; tinted windows, $43.40; right outside mirror, $11.75; remote control driver's outside mirror, $16.25; rear window defogger, $31.45; air conditioning, $388.00; headlight washer, $29.30; variable speed windshield wipers, $5.85; undercoating, $22.60; fender mounted turn signals, $11.60; time-delay headlights, $25.05; front and rear bumper guards, $33.70; engine block heater, $15.55; exhaust tips, $21.90; automatic speed control, $60.90; power windows, $121.75; AM/FM radio and stereo tape recorder, $366.40; microphone, $11.70; power steering, $116.25; special steering wheel, $30.50; wire wheel covers, $42.90; G70x14 tires, $63.10

ENGINE
Type: V-8, water-cooled, cast iron block and heads, 5 main bearings
Bore x stroke ....4.31 x 3.75 in, 109.2 x 95.2 mm
Displacement ....440 cu in, 7200 cc
Compression ratio ....9.7 to one
Carburetion ....1 x 4-bbl.
Valve gear ....Pushrod operated overhead valves
Power (SAE) .....370 bhp @4600 rpm Net (305 @4600)
Torque (SAE) ..480 lbs/ft @ 3200 rpm Net (400 @ 3200)
Specific power output ....0.84 bhp/cu in, 51.5 bhp/liter
Max recommended engine speed ....5500 rpm

DRIVE TRAIN
Transmission ....3-speed, auto-synchro
Max. torque converter........................2.02 to one
Final drive ratio ....3.23 to one

Gear	Ratio	Mph/1000rpm	Max. test speed
I	2.45	9.9	54 mph (5500 rpm)
II	1.45	16.6	91 mph (5500 rpm)
III	1.00	24.1	110 mph (4570 rpm)

DIMENSIONS AND CAPACITIES
Wheelbase ....115.0 in
Track, F/R ....59.7/62.0 in
Length ....205.4 in
Width ....79.1 in
Height ....52.2 in
Ground clearance ....4.7 in
Curb weight.................................4092 lbs
Weight distribution, F/R................58.5/41.5%
Battery capacity ....12 volts, 70 amp/hr
Alternator capacity ....444 watts
Fuel capacity ....21.0 gal
Oil capacity ....6.0 qts
Water capacity................................15.5 qts

SUSPENSION
F: Independent unequal length control arm, torsion bars, anti-sway bar
R: Rigid axle, semi-elliptic leaf springs, anti-sway bar

STEERING
Type ....Recirculating ball, power assist
Turns lock-to-lock 3.5
Turning circle curb-to-curb ....44.5 ft

BRAKES
F: ....10.7 vented disc, power assist
R: ....11.0 x 2.5-in. cast iron drum, power assist

WHEELS AND TIRES
Wheel size ....14 x 6.0-in
Wheel type ....Stamped steel, 5-Bolt
Tire make and size ....Goodyear 670 x 14, Polyglas
Tire type ....Tubeless, Belted
Test inflation pressures, F/R ....26/26 psi
Tire load rating.................1620 lbs per tire @32 psi

PERFORMANCE

Zero to	Seconds
30 mph	2.3
40 mph	3.4
50 mph	4.8
60 mph	6.5
70 mph	8.5
80 mph	10.8
90 mph	13.5
100 mph	16.2

Standing ¼-mile ....14.8 sec @ 95.7 mph
Top speed (at redline)........................133 mph
80-0 mph ....276 ft (0.78 G)
Fuel mileage ....9-12 mph on premium fuel
Cruising range ....189-252 mi

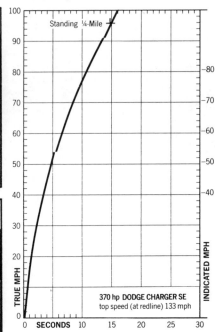

Standing ¼-Mile

370 hp DODGE CHARGER SE
top speed (at redline) 133 mph

TRUE MPH — INDICATED MPH

SECONDS

associates at Dodge have come up with the best-styled new car for 1971. Or that Dodge, not Georg Jensen, is selling it. Dodge? The company that gave the world such exquisite creations as the original Charger—a tribute to the ever-popular Rambler Marlin; the station wagon that has a rear silhouette like a drain culvert, and has pursued the evolution of the neo-DeSoto design school with the fervor that only graduates of such an academy could muster. But even before the '71 Charger there have been signs that someone in Dodge Division was doing more than mimicking whatever trend the GM Styling Center was into. The second generation Charger was the first significant departure. It was so far out of the Detroit styling mainstream that it remained unique throughout its three-year model run despite its public acceptance—which, in light of Detroit's copycat styling syndrome means it was radical. And, it turns out that Brownlie was also responsible for that car with its high, wide hipline and small tunnelroof greenhouse.

Subsequently, a corporate reorganization had Brownlie working for both Dodge and Plymouth and one can see the embryonic lines of this year's Charger taking shape with the 1970 Plymouth Barracuda and Dodge Challenger. And actually that experience probably proved most valuable as, for the first time this year, the Charger series of Dodge's intermediate line-up has lost its exclusivity. When you buy a 2-door Dodge intermediate it's automatically a Charger. No more separate sheetmetal as in the past when the Coronet was available as a 2-door and a 4-door in addition to the sportier-imaged Charger hardtops. What this new policy meant was that the stylists had to come out with a car that retained some of its sporting flair but was not wild enough to turn off middle-aged, middle of the road, middle Americans. In other words a compromise between a Charger/Pontiac Grand Prix/Chevrolet Monte Carlo-type car and a plain-jane business coupe or 2-door sedan. Incredibly, given these parameters, Dodge has pulled it off, and done so with élan. Meanwhile Dodge's sister division, Plymouth, attempting the same marketing gambit with its Sebring model (which uses the same basic under-the-skin hardware) ended up with a compromise that looks just that.

The Charger comes off as anything but a styling compromise. Not only is it apparent to people viewing the car from the outside but the driver is aware that he is controlling something far from normal as well.

From the driver's seat you find the front part of the Charger sloping down and away, giving the impression that there's a set of Honest Charley extended spring hangers jacking up the rear. The raked impression is also reinforced by the upward sweep of the sheetmetal at the roof's rear corners. It may make for great exterior styling but it does little for rear corner vision, leaving large blind spots that only the Charger's extreme tunnelroof predecessor outdid in recent memory. And although proper positioning of the inside rear view mirror has alleviated most of the visibility problem in normal driving conditions both driver and passenger-side outside mirrors should be considered mandatory options on the Charger.

One of the more enjoyable aspects of the third-generation Charger is its feeling of compactness. The wheelbase has been reduced by 2 inches and overall length by 3 inches, but in one of those curious juxtapositions of fact over feeling, a dimension which has actually grown, makes the car feel smaller. This is the width: the '71 Charger is over 2 inches wider than its im-

By Brownlie out of Hamtramck, Dodge's Special Edition Charger is, on styling alone a desirable car, and a wave of the option list will make it do handsomely, too.

mediate predecessor but you feel more secure. The older Charger with its narrow greenhouse and bulging side sheetmetal, made you feel that you were sitting in the middle of the car and you were never quite certain how much side clearance was required. The new styling, although physically wider, eliminates this feeling and also provides more hip and shoulder room for the driver and passengers.

The driving position has also been improved by repositioning of the steering-wheel. Previous Charger styling required that the driver sit low in the car, however the steering wheel was mounted relatively high in relation to the driver's arms. The result was an automotive equivalent of a Chopper seating position—an ape-hanger steering wheel if you will. Our Charger also came equipped with an optional small fat, leather covered steering wheel. We can certainly live without the breathless appellation—Dodge is calling it the "Tuff "

steering wheel—but it represents a vast improvement over the standard version by offering the driver a firm, non-slip grip. However, just because you can buy a steering wheel that looks like it came out of a Formula One car, don't get carried away and start thinking of the Charger SE as a sports car.

Our test car was loaded down with nearly every conceivable option known to exist which caused this "intermediate" to weigh over two tons and resulted in a front to rear weight bias of 58.5/41.5%. Consequently it should come as little surprise that the Charger SE was victim of massive understeer. For normal expressway driving this presents no problem as the car will track beautifully, and is predictable to the extent of being boring. And for this type of driving the optional 370-hp 440 cu. in. engine performed effortlessly and was surprisingly responsive. But on New York National Speedway's extremely tight handling course the Charger was anything but graceful. It would plunge into turns with its front wheels on full lock but the rest of the car maintaining a stubborn desire to continue on its previous course. The wide G70 tires screamed in their painful attempt to change the car's direction—both front *and* rears as the fronts would be doing most of the work in altering course while the rears would be trying just the opposite—and for their effort they were also getting their outside tread shaved off because of a combination of body lean and insufficient wheelwell clearance.

Normally, this type of problem can be overcome by inducing power oversteer but with our test Charger this was hardly the solution because of the suddenness with which the secondaries would come in. One second your foot would be progressively applying more power via the primary barrels of the 4-bbl. carburetor, the next the floodgates were thrown wide-open and all hell broke loose. Most often the result was a spin—its suddenness and severity depending on what degree the tires were able to maintain traction through this surge. The reason for this problem probably lies in the fact that Dodge's engine development department is still having problems in adapting certain engines to smog-control equipment. This would seem to be reinforced by the fact that the recent 440 engines we've tested, particularly with automatic transmissions, have a tendency to "stumble" coming off idle, and will occasionally backflash through the carburetor under hard acceleration from low rpm.

And although our Charger SE came equipped with massive 10.7-in. vented front disc brakes and 11.0-in. drum rears, there was little to inspire confidence. The brake pedal had a spongy feel, which may have resulted from some flex in the system, making it hard to modulate, and during both the braking and handling portions of our test procedure we experienced brake fade and overheating. In fairness it should be mentioned that our test car had less than 1000 miles on it and the brakes may not have been broken in at that point. A similarly equipped Plymouth GTX we tested (*C/D*, November) did not have this problem.

While the Charger did not perform up to expectations in the extreme conditions we created during the track evaluation testing portion of our road test procedure, it came into its own in the over-the-road evaluations where it proved to be predictably competent and comfortable.

In this latter respect, the car had damn well better be comfortable! Take a good look at the specifications page—you'll discover that the Charger SE which sailed into our garage had a two-page window sticker telling why it should cost $5670.75. Attsa some expensive automotive sculpture you got there, art lover. For that money you'd figure that Brownlie or Dodge's General Manager Bob McCurry ought to sign each model of this Special Edition (that's what SE stands for, not super expensive). Things get a little more reasonable when you consider that you can get a 318 cu.in. V-8 Charger for a base price of $3422—if your life style will permit a depradation of things like a high-performance 440 cu.in. V-8, speed control power windows, paint strips, automatic headlight washers, wire wheel covers, leather upholstery that has been sprayed with color-coordinating paint to make it undetectable from genuine vinyl, or a vinyl "canopy" roof that has been embossed to look like real leather. The point is that all this trash is available and, in fact, dealer's love to have you check it off on the order form—some of them are even nice enough to check it off for you—because that's where the highest percentage of profit comes in. Which accounts for an "order to build" form that provides spaces for 220 different entries. *Car and Driver* has long been an advocate of special ordering any car you buy in preference to taking whatever is lying on the dealer's floor at the moment (no matter how friendly a price he'll let it go for), but when $3500 cars can easily come in with $2200 of whipped cream on top it's time to issue a warning. You damn well better cast a judicious eye over the order form and know exactly what you want and

what you can afford beforehand because a slip of the pen is liable to win you a convertible top with a sunroof sewn in it. No questions asked, no excuses accepted.

For instance with the Charger SE, the base 318 V-8 just isn't going to provide the type of performance that any enthusiast will want. But going to a 440 in a car of this type comes close to cubic inch overkill, in between lies two versions of the 383—although inexplicably no 340 is presently available—which offer a proper level of performance and economy both in terms of fuel mileage and purchase price, and, with most companies, insurance classification.

In particular with this Charger it's difficult not to fill up every box in sight with a check mark. After all, if you want to make an individual artistic statement you can create it yourself through the option list. If 50,000 or 100,000 or 1,000,000 Chargers are built the combinations and permutations of possible options almost guarantees that yours will be unique. It's just a matter of how unique you can afford to be—and $2200 worth is a bit steep.

The Charger SE, on its styling alone is a desirable car. It has a completed look that has been sorely missing from many Detroit cars since the advent of making everything except the chassis and seats extra cost options. This even extends to the interior wherein the options look like they were custom designed for a particular model and not just universal parts that can be bolted into anything from a Demon to a Polara.

That this isn't a false impression is brought hope by the fact that the car feels and sounds solid. The theorem that "The greater the number of options, the greater the number of things to rattle and go thump in the night" just doesn't work with this car. Despite its taut ride quality, and a considerable amount of road harshness transmitted through the tires, the Charger SE was one of the quietest cars we've recently tested. The only rattles came from the cassette tape recorder which, coincidentally, was the only item that didn't look like it had been specifically designed for this car (being clumsily perched on the front console—an open invitation to theft). With a little self-will and discretion in the face of a sales form that makes the menu in the Russian Tea Room look barren—and unimaginative—you can come out with a spectacular looking American-style grand touring car for around $4000. Which is no bad price to pay for a combination of practicality and individuality these days. ●

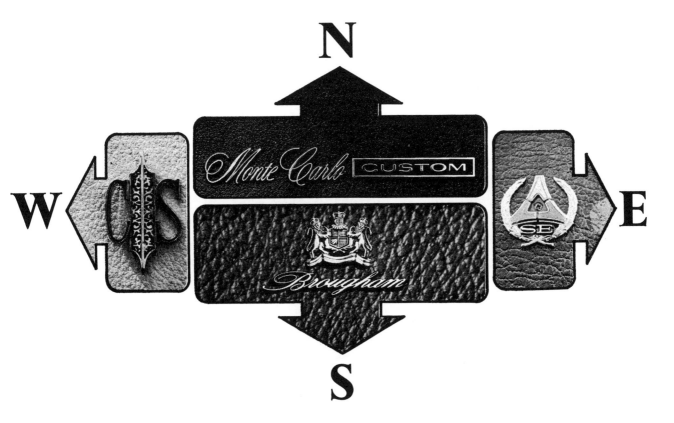

MONTEGO, MONTE CARLO, CHARGER, CUTLASS
Are they coming or going?

By Jim Brokaw

Comparison

Industry leaders hailed 1970 as the dawn of the intermediate era. Two years later we are still waiting for the sun to rise. Instead of kicking down the gateway to the 36-easy-payment promised land, the intermediates got into the loose stuff and spun going into turn one. Sales plunged in '70, and were just beginning to show signs of survival in the latter stages of the past model year.

The dip in sales is a bit surprising inasmuch as the intermediate, particularly the two-door version, is a personality car. It is too big to make the bold statement of a Corvette or Pantera and not quite expensive enough to rank as a "personal" car, but it very definitely caters to that intangible within each of us that says, "Here I come."

It is a personality car for the man whose family must ride with him on occasion, or whose profession demands he haul a few things around with him. In most cases, a four-door or a full-sized

sedan would better suit the owner's needs, but he doesn't want a four-door; he doesn't want a wagon; he wants "his" car to suit "his" taste.

A clue to the decline of the intermediate can be found in the amount of loose walking-around money most of us wind up with at the end of the week. Lately, it has been jingling instead of rustling. The penalty for owning a racy looking machine with a bit more "schmaltz" than is really necessary is found on the window sticker. These "me" cars are costly after you bolt on all the neat little options that make it truly your car. Price may be the primary reason for the dip in sales. Much of the exodus from the intermediates has been toward the compacts, which tend to fulfill the same function at a much more manageable price. Passenger space is a bit cramped, but the individual spends most of his driving time alone in the car.

With the advent of the President's hammerlock on inflation, it is entirely possible the middle-sized "I Am" car will make a return to the joyous hearts of your local new car salesmen.

In order to assess the prospects of the

various entries in the assault to recapture the intermediate car buyer, we lined up a few salient examples of the breed for testing. With publishing lead times well ahead of the newsstand date, our test cycle fell right between '71 closeout and '72 introduction. This generates the annual game of scramble in Detroit. Each manufacturer runs his own schedule for model changeover; and each manufacturer is committed to satisfying his dealers and customers. As a result, we were forced to spend a very short time with two of the machines being tested. Luckily, the cars in question are little changed from '71, so we were still able to be current in our evaluation.

The four cars selected are the Mercury Montego MX Brougham, Chevrolet Monte Carlo Custom, Dodge Charger SE, and Oldsmobile Cutlass Supreme. All are two-doors and all have the luxury appointment options. We had requested the new 400 cid 2v engines, where applicable, in order to evaluate the direction of our ecological migration. The 2v carburetors were specifically ordered, since the smaller block 2v engines exhibited some very lively response characteristics in the

Charger, Dodge's styling masterpiece, was slow off the line in '71 with sluggish sales until the spring thaw sent the numbers up the chart. Wisely leaving a good thing alone, Dodge made only superficial changes in the grille and some side striping for '72. Altered roof line, exclusive in the SE model, permits increased rearward visibility as well as more distinguished profile. Fully instrumented dash panel is among the best in the industry. Comfortable interior offers new colors.

low end of the performance spectrum.

Due to the previously mentioned scheduling difficulties, Monte Carlo was only available in the 402 cid version with a 4v carburetor, and since Oldsmobile does not have an engine in the 400 cid range, the Cutlass was equipped with a 350-4v. This turned out to be a fortunate turn of events, allowing a direct comparison with a size above and a size below the target.

If the Chrysler and Ford 400 cid engines are bellwethers of the smog engine market, then we are all headed for a nostalgic trip to the days of yesteryear when passing on a two lane highway was the second greatest thrill obtainable in a car. In all fairness, total judgment should be reserved until we have a chance to examine in detail, the 4v versions of the clean power plants. Unlike the small block engines, the 2v configuration did not produce an abundance of low end torque. In fact, they did not produce an abundance of anything. Economy was respectable, but not inspirational, in the Mercury with an average of 13.69 mpg. We didn't have the Charger long enough to get a mileage reading, so we'll assume reasonable mileage until proven otherwise.

In spite of their distinct lack of responsiveness, the 400's are most adequate in normal driving circumstances. They go up and down hills without laboring, enter and exit traffic without scaring the garbage out of you, and are acceptable, if not exciting, for the high-speed freeway maneuvering which is often precipitated by sleepy drivers and sluggardly trucks. The area of performance that opens your eyes and sweats your palms arrives when you punch the gas pedal to the floor to pass on a short stretch of two lane rural road. The desmogging process eats heavily into the response time and acceleration parameters.

On the other hand, Chevrolet's 402-4v was a lively road grabber, answering the call of the right foot in a positive and forthright fashion. It is also not available in California. The Golden State has more restrictive smog requirements than the other 49, so the manufacturers have simply tagged the offending engines as non-Californian in some cases, or added specific smog accessories in others. The Ford 400 cid is an example of bolting on the made for California hardware.

The Cutlass engine, although only a 350 cid, performed on a par with the two 400 inchers, courtesy of the 4v carburetor. Adequate, but not exciting. It too has been detoxed. Naturally, there are more powerful engines in the inventories of all marques tested, and some discreet inquiry could produce a more responsive rear end ratio, however, the intent of the test was to examine the 2v

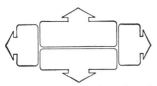

desmogged engines. Ecology is going to cost each of us a very distinct penalty. The big boys in Detroit have been the prime target until now. We will soon find out why they didn't detox the engines a long time ago. No one would have bought them. The time has come for us, the little people, to make our contribution to the crusade for clean air. Engines are just like women; if they're really pure — they aren't very exciting.

In spite of mixed emotions under the hood, the interiors were top quality, and very much a matter of taste. The most luxurious of the people packaging was in the Montego. Their Flight Bench seat with wide, folding arm rest was the most comfortable by a distinct margin. Rich tricot brocade cloth sets a very elegant tone, but the actual seat construction was the dominant factor. Full-range support, comfort and lateral retention are combined with the utility of a full-width bench seat. The center seating position would be awkward for long hauls, but most satisfactory for local transportation.

Monte Carlo came equipped with bucket seats and a center console. The buckets were well upholstered and configured for good lateral retention. A fully instrumented dash panel was set in a rich, burled wood grain applique. One of the best features in any Chevy is the small-diameter sport steering wheel. In this case it was also a tilt wheel which adds quite a bit to driver comfort — a safety factor.

Cutlass was laid out in bright white vinyl. The split-back bench seats approached those of the Montego for comfort and retention, but didn't quite make it. Although the three-pod instrument panel didn't have a full set of gauges, it did have an engine temperature gauge along with the fuel quantity indicator. In fact, all four machines had a functioning temperature gauge in addition to the normal complement of idiot lights. We have long suggested that a temp indicator was mandatory in order to take corrective action in an overheating situation before the old girl cooked off in the middle of the road. We are most pleased to see that the manufacturers finally agree.

The Charger also had a complete vinyl interior. The color was a combination of avocado green and a subdued gold, which was as pleasing to the eye as any seen. Seats were the old reliable Charger buckets of last year, which means that they hold you snugly during all maneuvers. The instrument panel was compactly laid out right in front of

Olds Cutlass Supreme, credited with providing much of the sales impetus to the entire division, received minor upgrading for '72. Basic car remains unsullied, with only a grille change and the addition of crash protection devices. Side molding, recessed parking and taillights, plus optional bumper guards round out the package. Three-pod instrument panel contains direct reading temp guage as well as full array of idiot lights. Relocation of right engine mount reduced vibration.

the driver containing a full bag of direct reading gauges.

A lot of planning has gone into the operation areas of all four vehicles. Instrument panels are all clustered in front of the driver, all controls are clearly labeled and within no-stretch reach. Seats are designed for retention as well as seating comfort, be they buckets or benches. We did however find one area of criticism. In all cars except the Charger, the driver's hands blocked one or more instrument pods when placed at the 10 and 2 driving position. This problem can be solved, but the logical approach would leave all instrument panels looking very much alike. Neither the customers nor Detroit are quite ready for this.

Front-seat head room, leg room and ease of entry/exit, were excellent in all four cars. Rear seat entry was no strain in all, but not so for exit. Regardless of who makes it, getting out of the back seat of a two-door requires a little arm and leg coordination and a very long and careful step outside.

Rear-seat leg room is deceptive. From the outside, it appears that an adult just wouldn't fit. However, the designers have cleverly opened some secret foot space under the base of the front seat. Montego has hollowed out more foot space than the other three, but the kick plate on the rear base of the front seat is plastic. It is also located at precisely shin-bone level. By merely lurching heavily out of the back seat, instead of dexterously shuffling out, you will rake the stout plastic kick plate across your unsuspecting shins, inducing instant pain. This is not all bad. You don't have to be concerned over stiff muscles after a long trip, one rake across the seat back and you're wide awake.

Wind noise with the windows up was quite low, but the real surprise came with the windows down. Wind blast and noise is minimal. It is actually possible to drive with the window fully retracted and hear the radio. Charger and Montego had a slight edge in the open car quiet ride department.

In the area of interior sound deadening, Montego and Monte Carlo have gone one step further than Charger and Cutlass. Sound control was one of the primary considerations in Ford's switch to a separate body chassis for the intermediate line. This year, Monte Carlo has included a considerable amount of sound-deadening material in its Custom option. Neither Charger nor Cutlass permit a great din of outside noise, but their level of control simply hasn't reached the degree of refinement attained by Monte Carlo and Montego.

In the area of ride and handling, each machine has its own unique method of dealing with the bumps and

Monte Carlo, Chevrolet's luxury intermediate standard bearer, retains same quality of assembly and grace of line as in '71. External changes consist of a revised grille, recessed head and taillights and very little else. Fully instrumented, wood grain dash panel complements new Custom option package. With the demise of the SS option, Chevrolet is offering the suspension and dress-up items without tying them into an uninsurable engine. Good news for Chevophiles under twenty five.

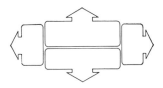

Mercury's all-new Montego Brougham is FoMoCo's final statement in two-door intermediate luxury. Split-back Flight Bench seat is the most comfortable in the industry. Rich brocade tricot cloth blends harmoniously with unique leatherized elbow panel door insert. Five-pod instrument panel is backed by Velino grain applique which almost comes off as leather. All lights are recessed to reduce minor impact damage. The overall effect gives the intermediate Merc a new image.

curves. The Custom option on the Monte Carlo, which replaces the previous SS package, contains special suspension provisions. A heavier 1 1/8-in. front stabilizer bar coupled with the additional 7/8-in. rear bar provide excellent roll control. Wide 7-in. wheel rims put more of the G70 X 15 belted tire footprint on the ground. The net result is a firm stable ride with excellent control. Monte Carlo attacks the road like a fullback rumbling along on short driving legs, whereas Cutlass with the same basic suspension, more lightly structured, dances over the rough pavement much as a halfback making it through the secondary on his own. Oldsmobile makes much noise about their tuned "G" Ride; in the case of the Cutlass Supreme, the noise is justified. Handling in both GM offerings is quite satisfactory. Monte Carlo goes through the turns flat and crisp, while Cutlass employs the principle of the working suspension, leaning slightly to the outside going into the turn, and rolling smartly back to level when exiting the turn under a full head of steam.

Charger is neither light on its feet, nor is it a churning tank. It lies somewhere in between with rock steady cornering capabilities. The positive response of the torsion bar front suspension, balanced by the leaf spring rears give the driver much confidence in the machine's capacity to negotiate the most devious of rural roadways. The ride in the SE is a bit firm, almost harsh, but the sacrifice is well worth the premium in handling.

Montego is different from all three. FoMoCo's new separate body chassis is liberally cushioned with tuned mounts and rubber spring caps to eliminate all possible noise and vibration, with coil fronts and 4-link coil rears for ride control. The engineers did their work well. It is possible to motor along at speeds in excess of the legal limit, 70 mph in Michigan, in perfect comfort and control. Short, sharp bumps are barely noticed. Unfortunately, there had to be an area of compromise somewhere in the soup. Those long, loping bumps caused by frost heaves, generate some undesirable oscillation. The damping of this action is a bit slow. Handling of the Montego is excellent, but somewhat short of the ultimate. The Dearborn suspension engineers have designed the understeer to occur at a point where the driver still has control over the car. Sort of a built in *dummheiten* factor.

Quality control is one of the gratifying features of the entire group. For a change, everybody has it. Charger makes a greater use of preformed plastic pieces than the other three, but it is well executed and properly fitted. All of the upholstery, whether cloth or vinyl, was of high quality and neatly fitted.

Nothing made by man is perfect, and these neat little ego-boosters are no exception. The common fault is in the rear-quarter sail panels. Their size and location create a formidable blind spot. An outside mirror on the right will solve traffic visibility problems, but nothing short of an alert passenger is going to help when entering traffic in a 45-degree left-hand turn. Oncoming traffic approaching from the right is totally obscured. The price of styling.

Price information is a trifle shaky. At this writing we are going in with 1971 prices less the excise tax. They may or may not be in effect when the book hits the newsstands.

Picking a winner, in all fairness to the competitors, would require more time with each car than was available. Cutlass Supreme has the best sales record, followed very closely by Monte Carlo, however, Montego is completely new, therefore negating the importance of 1971 sales figures. Montego gets the nod for overall luxury, Cutlass has the best balanced suspension as to ride and handling, Monte Carlo had superb overall handling and an excellent dash panel, and Charger had the best instrument layout and displayed the top cornering characteristics. As for styling, it is a matter of taste. Montego is the most elegant, but Charger is by far the most exciting. Price would seem to be the prime determinant as to which is the winner.

/MT

SPECIFICATIONS

	MONTEGO	MONTE CARLO	CHARGER	CUTLASS
Engine	OHV V8	OHV V8	OHV V8	OHV V8
Bore & Stroke — ins.	4.126 x 3.76	4.00 x 4.00	4.34 x 3.38	4.057 x 3.385
Displacement — cu. in.	402	400	400	350
HP @ RPM	240 @ 4400	180 @ 4400*	190 @ 4400	180 @ 4000
Torque: lbs.-ft. @ RPM	345 @ 3200	305 @ 2200*	310 @ 2400	275 @ 2800
Compression Ratio/Fuel	8.5:1/Regular	8.5:1*/Regular	8.2:1/Regular	8.5:1/Regular
Carburetion	4v	2v	2v	4v
Transmission	3-spd auto, Turbo Hydro	3-spd auto, Select Shift	3-spd auto, Torqueflite	3-spd auto, Turbo Hydro
Final Drive Ratio	2.73:1	3.25:1	3.23:1	2.73:1
Steering type	Variable ratio power	Power	Power	Variable ratio power
Steering Ratio	18.5-12.4:1	21.7:1	18.9:1	18.8-15.3:1
Turning Diameter (curb-to-curb-ft.)	42.0	40.13	40.8	41.2
Wheel Turns (lock to lock)	2.9	3 5	3.5	3.4
Tire size	G70 x 15	H78 x 14	G70 x 14	F78 x 14
Brakes	Power disc/drum	Power disc/drum	Power disc/drum	Power disc/drum
Front Suspension	Coil/stabilizer bar	Coil/stabilizer bar	Torsion bar	Coil/stabilizer bar
Rear Suspension	4-Link coil/stabilizer bar	4-Link coil/stabilizer bar	Leaf springs	4-Link coils
Body/Frame Construction	Welded perimeter	Perimeter	Unit body	Welded perimeter
Wheelbase — ins.	116	114	115.0	116
Overall length — ins.	206.5	208.1	205.4	207.6
Width — ins.	75.6	78.6	76.9	76.8
Height — ins.	52.9	51.8	52.1	53.5
Front Track — ins.	60.3	62.8	59.7	59.7
Rear Track — ins.	59.3	62.9	62 0	59.0
Fuel Capacity — gals.	19	22.5	21	20
Oil Capacity — qts.	4(½)	4(1)	4(1)	4(1)

*Information approximate, not available from manufacturer

PERFORMANCE

	MONTEGO	MONTE CARLO	CHARGER	CUTLASS
Acceleration				
0-30 mph	4.1	3.5	4.0	4.3
0-45 mph	6.7	6.5	7.2	7.4
0-60 mph	9.5	11.0	11.5	11.3
0-75 mph	14.3	17.2	17.2	17.2
Standing Start ¼-mile				
Mph	89 0	77.31	76	77.8
Elapsed time	17.1	17.7	17.6	18.4
Passing speeds				
40-60 mph	4.5	5.7	5.8	5.9
50-70 mph	5.3	7.2	7.0	6.9
Speeds in gears*				
1st ... mph @ rpm	52.4 @ 4500	42 @ 4320	50 @ 4000	51 @ 4500
2nd ... mph @ rpm	88.0 @ 4500	71 @ 4350	71 @ 4000	86 @ 4500
3rd ... mph @ rpm	116.0 @ 4000	96 @ 4000	98 @ 4000	100 @ 3650
Mph per 1000 rpm (in top gear)	26.3	24.0	24.5	24.8
Stopping distances From 30 mph Normal/Panic	38 ft. 1 in./32 ft. 6 in.	30 ft./23 ft. 4 in.	36 ft./32 ft.	45 ft./41 ft.
From 60 mph Normal/Panic	157 ft./140 ft. 9 in.	145 ft. 10 in./132 ft.	134 ft./123 ft.	181 ft./161 ft.
Gas mileage range	12.2-16.6/13.7	13.05-14.33/13.69	NA	NA
Speedometer error Car speedometer	30 45 50 60 70 80	30 45 50 60 70 80	30 45 50 60 70 80	30 45 50 60 70 80
Electric speedometer	28.8 45.3 50 61.2 71.8 82.8	28 42 46 55 62 71	28.5 43 49 59.5 69.5 79	28 42.5 47.5 57 66.5 76.5

*Speeds in gears are at shift points (limited by the length of track) and do not represent maximum speeds.

CHANGING MODES

**Trading performance for luxury, the Dodge Charger
loses some of its former image but gains much in the transition.**

Not too many years ago the name Dodge Charger was synonymous with high performance. The automobile was bred for racing and it, along with its brother the Plymouth Road Runner, ruled the high-banked ovals of NAS-CAR. Racing created further engineering developments which ultimately led to specialty vehicles like the 1970 winged Daytona Charger. The engines which powered these cars were big honking monsters with names like the 426 hemi, 440 Magnum, and 440 6-pack. The Charger was king to professional and street racers alike. And then the roof fell in. The behemoth motors were crippled by high insurance rates and finally killed by government-instigated emissions laws. Performance became a dirty word as auto manufacturers tooled up to meet smog and safety regulations. Out of all this has emerged a new Charger which embodies only a shadow of its

former performance image and depends heavily on luxury for its appeal.

Now don't get us wrong about the Charger's transition to luxury for it remains a fine automobile; we just miss the old gut level sensation of power which was so much a part of the car. Today's Charger is more refined in many ways than its predecessors and somehow manages to combine exuberance with restraint.

Since its restyling of a couple years ago, the Charger has been one of the best looking intermediates on the market and the few changes made in 1973 enhance, rather than detract from, its dynamic design. It has an extremely long hood and short rear deck with undulating side body panels and a severely raked windshield which leads to a gently sloping top. It seems as though opera windows are the current styling fad and the S.E. (for Special Edition)

version of the Charger has its own modification of this concept with three vertically louvered openings in the rear quarter panel. Combined with a grained landau vinyl roof and chrome accents, these treatments give the car a very plush appearance. In front is a cross-hatched deep-set grille and full-width bumper incorporating three-inch thick rubber guards while the hood is adorned with a wreath surrounded S.E. insignia ala Mercedes.

The interior of the S.E. is very comfortable and shows the lengths Dodge went to in providing a high amount of luxury. High-back bucket seats give adequate support and have enough travel to accommodate even the tallest of occupants although passengers in the rear seat may find themselves crowded if a six-footer is driving. A graceful center console with arcing plastic panels contains the low-profile shift lever and di-

Opera windows are in vogue today and the Charger S.E. possesses its own tri-sectional version in the rear quarter panel. Visibility, though, is not improved.

Charger could really smoke the tires during hard acceleration. Full-width cross-hatched grille accentuates the car's width. Front bumper has thick rubber guards to protect against damage.

vides the two front seats. The dashboard, although made primarily of plastic, is well-assembled and looks good. In front of the driver are three dials including the speedometer, electric clock, gauges for fuel, oil pressure, engine temperature, and alternator. To the lower right of the steering wheel is the superb AM/FM stereo radio while the heater/air conditioner controls are located on the left. All controls are placed so the driver can manipulate them effortlessly.

Riding in the Charger S.E. is a remarkably pleasant experience since Dodge engineers have undertaken the task of removing all extraneous noise through additional sound deadening material and a mofified suspension. They have succeeded admirably. Since the car weighs 4,180 lbs., it has practically unswerveable directional stability in cross winds but what is surprising is the manner in which it rides over road imperfections. There is absolutely no "floating" sensation since the suspension provides more than adequate rebound control and you never feel out of touch with the road. Silence is another characteristic of the new Charger's ride. In addition to the rubber-buffered suspension, further chassis and drivetrain noise has been reduced by using spool-type motor mounts to lessen engine vibrations and road shocks through the steering wheel are lowered via a double coupling inserted between the steering column and steering gear. Further sound isolation is achieved by placing noise barriers in the "C" pillars, covering the floor pan with foam mastic, and insulating the car's

Large taillights give other drivers plenty of warning while dual exhausts pump out delicious engine sounds.

Plastic dominates the interior but it is well constructed. Seats are comfortable and legroom is excellent.

dual exhaust system. All of this acts to prevent excess noise from entering the passenger compartment and results in a sound level reading of 73 dB at a speed of 70 mph.

Although the Chrysler performance engines are no longer with us, the new Charger still retains a goodly amount of power. Our test vehicle came equipped with a 440 c.i. engine and a Carter 4-bbl. carburetor. The cast iron cylinder block has a bore and stroke of 4.32 x 3.75 inches, tin plated aluminum alloy pistons, forged steel crankshaft, and hydraulic valve lifters. The compression ratio is a low-lead gasoline satisfying 8.2:1. A new addition to the Charger's powerplant this year is a standard electronic ignition system which eliminates the need for contact points and condenser thereby reducing maintenance costs. Smog equipment includes induction hardened exhaust valve seats to minimize the effects of no or low-lead fuel, a vacuum advance chamber in the distributor, and a refined exhaust gas recirculation system. Even with this paraphernalia, the 440's power output is rated at 280 net hp at 4,800 rpm with 380 lbs. ft. of torque at 3,200 rpm. With a 3.23:1 rear axle ratio, the Charger S.E. turned the quarter mile in 15.0 seconds and 93 mph, extremely good perform-

Oversteer was the order of the day during handling tests. For a big car, the Charger corners quite well despite very light power steering.

The Charger's hood bears a wreath-surrounded S.E. emblem as proudly as a Mercedes wears its three-pointed star.

ance for a heavy car with an anti-smog engine. The power is so evident at the low end that wheelspin is often encountered if too much pressure is applied to the accelerator pedal. However, you have to pay for this performance and the 440 exacts its price by averaging a mediocre 10 mpg fuel economy.

Straight line performance is greatly aided by the superlative 3-speed TorqueFlite automatic transmission which incorporates one of the best shifters around. The major improvement in the transmission is a hydrodynamic front pump seal to reduce the possibility of fluid leakage to increase reliability. The shifter is Chrysler's "Slap-Stick" which automatically prevents skipping gears when you shift manually and works as quickly as any 4-speed in the business.

The suspension modifications designed primarily to improve ride and reduce noise have also greatly enhanced the Charger's handling characteristics. Up front are independent nonparallel control arms, torsion bars, stabilizer bar, and isolated cross members which are separated from the body by six rubber

mounts. The rear suspension consists of a live axle, parallel longitudinal semi-elliptical leaf springs with rubber iso-clamps, and a stabilizer bar. This system allows the chassis to "work" thereby fully utilizing the suspension's capabilities. On the skid pad at Orange County Raceway, the Charger S.E. generated .703 lateral "g," very respectable for a large luxury-oriented automobile. Transitional handling qualities tend towards oversteer when the vehicle is pushed through a corner but, it is easily controllable and once mastered can be confidence-inspiring. This tendency to an oversteering attitude is surprising in a car of the Charger's size and can probably be attributed to the vehicle's power and the .86-inch diameter rear sway bar. If there is one fault with the automobile's handling it is the Chrysler power steering unit. Although steering reaction is fairly quick with a gear raio of 18.82:1, the power assist unit makes wheel effort almost negligible and robs the driver of adequate road feel through the steering column.

For 1973, Dodge has made vented

The huge 440-4v engine produces 280 hp and gives the car good performance by today's standards. Fuel economy, though, is very low.

invariably produced rear wheel lock-up only, thereby making braking performance somewhat erratic and, at times, hair-raising. The stops were short with a test distance from 60 mph of 127.2 feet but, since the rear brakes would lock, excessive fishtailing was encountered and on one occasion the automobile actually spun out. If there is a saving grace to the Charger's braking capabilities, it is that fade could not be attained through our test of 10 panic stops.

To summarize the 1973 Dodge Charger S.E., it is evident that the automobile has achieved what the engineers at Chrysler Corporation wanted. It is quiet, comfortable, good handling, and powerful by today's standards. There are points which deserve needed improvement; most notably the power steering and braking system. However, we must conclude that the car is refined and updated in many ways over its ancestors. And as much as enthusiasts may regret the passing of the Charger's performance image, we can safely say that the emergent product is the next best thing. ●

front disc brakes standard equipment on all Charger models with a power assist booster offered as an option. The discs have a working diameter of 10.84 inches while the rear drums measure 10.0 inches resulting in a total swept area of 365.2 sq. in. Although the brakes are proportioned 71/29 to accommodate the vehicle's nose-heavy weight bias of 59/41, our panic stops

DODGE CHARGER SE

SPECIFICATIONS AS TESTED

Engine	440 cu in., 4-bbl OHV V-8
Bore & Stroke	4.32 × 3.75 ins.
Compression ratio	8.2:1
Horsepower	280 (SAE) at 4,800 rpm
Torque	380 lbs-ft at 3,200 rpm
Transmission	3-speed automatic
Steering	3.5 turns lock-to-lock
	41.2 ft, curb-to-curb
Brakes	Disc front, drum rear
Suspension	Torsion bar front, leaf rear
Tires	G70×14

Dimensions (ins.):

Wheelbase	115.0	Rear track	62.0
Length	212.7	Ground clearance	8.1
Width	77.0	Height	52.5
Front track	61.9	Weight	4180 lbs

Capacities:

Fuel	19.5 gals	Oil	5 qts
Coolant	16.5 qts	Luggage	14.3 cu-ft

PERFORMANCE AND MAINTENANCE

Acceleration:	Gears:
0-30 mph	3.0 secs, 1st
0-45 mph	4.2 secs, 1st
0-60 mph	7.0 secs, 1st, 2nd
0-75 mph	10.0 secs, 1st, 2nd
0-¼ mile	15.0 secs, at 93 mph
Ideal cruise	75 mph
Top speed (est)	120 mph
Stop from 60 mph	127.2 ft
Average economy (city)	9 mpg
Average economy (country)	11 mpg
Fuel required	low-lead
Oil change (mos/miles)	3/4,000
Lubrication (mos/miles)	36/36,000
Warranty (mos/miles)	12/12,000
Type tools required	SAE
U.S. Dealers	2500

BASE PRICE

Base price: $3,336.00

$ 294.90 440-4v V-8
$ 125.00 Bucket seats
$ 378.45 A/C
$ 144.15 AM/FM stereo
$ 30.75 Rear defog
$ 119.10 Pwr. windows
$ 42.45 Tinted glass
$ 561.35 Easy order package (TorqueFlite, pwr. steering, pwr. brakes, AM, vinyl roof, WSW tires, bumper guards, 3-spd. wipers, remote mirror)

$4888.00 TOTAL

1973 Dodge Charger Rallye.
For the hard driving man.

If you're the kind of man that responds to the pulsating beat of a performance car, grab hold of Charger Rallye. Charger's got the low, lean look that tells you exactly what it is—a performance machine that enjoys being on the road. Go ahead, get in. Settle your frame into Charger's optional, soft bucket seats. Turn the switch on this beautiful baby. Charger's new Electronic Ignition System will give you surer starting because it delivers up to 35 percent more voltage to each spark plug. Then pop the clutch on Charger Rallye. That optional floor-mounted, four-speed Hurst shifter and 440 four barrel will let you put this Rallye through its paces. Charger's rugged Torsion-Quiet Ride and front and rear sway bars can take it. This go anywhere, do anything Charger Rallye can be an expression of whatever you want it to say. And those no-nonsense Rallye instrument gauges say a lot about the car and the man who uses them. When you take off with that power bulge hood and those raised white letter tires, there's one thing sure, you'll be remembered . . . as the hard driving man.

Extra care in engineering makes a difference in Dodge...depend on it.

The Paper NASCAR Street Machines

Chevelle, Charger, Grand Am and Torino

Droop-snoots and door numbers do not a race car make, but on the street that's another matter.

By Jim Brokaw

Ten years ago, Fred Lorenzen, Junior Johnson, Joe Weatherly, Richard Petty and Fireball Roberts electrified thousands of NASCAR fans dueling wheel-to-wheel on the oval, high-banked Southern tracks. As a by-product, thousands of Fords, Chevys, Plymouths and Pontiacs were sold. The axiom came to be: "Win on Sunday, sell on Monday."

The fiercely loyal customers of the white whiskey country were still naive enough in 1963, perhaps knowingly, to believe that the cars they drove off the lot at such dealers as LaFayette Ford were just as good, if not quite as swift, as the similar looking racers on the left-hand expressways. When Junior Johnson picked off the checkered flag at Charlotte, all the Chevrolet dealers in the Carolinas rejoiced and broke out the sales orders for the Monday morning rush.

The factories were so sure of the sales boost by winning a few races that millions of dollars were spent by Ford, General Motors and Chrysler in an effort to get the right car first across the finish line.

In the late Sixties, NASCAR went national with the addition of races in California, Michigan, Texas, and New Jersey.

Unfortunately, like Confederate money, the win-on-Sunday, sell-on-Monday principle was not good "up north," if it ever really had been in the south. GM headed for the barn in '64.

In early 1970, Ford pulled out of racing. Chrysler cut back to one team the next year and withdrew completely in 1972. Racing did not sell cars—or did it?

Some deeply analytical reasoning, plus a peek at some of the hanky-pank sliding out of the back door at Milford Motors in Michigan, leads us to believe that even if racing *doesn't* sell cars, styling and aerodynamics *do*.

Two years ago, Junior Johnson, who now builds race cars, brought a Chevrolet Monte Carlo to Charlotte Motor Speedway. Every seat in the house was sold. A month later, David Pearson trundled around Michigan International Speedway in an under-powered Pontiac GTO and got more ink in the local press than the front runners.

Last year, the blunt-nosed Monte Carlo won big on the intermediate tracks (165 mph or less) and drew thousands of hungry Chevy lovers. Pontiac was nowhere in sight.

While neither Chevrolet nor Pontiac are back in racing, the new crop of intermediates out of GM's styling studios are curiously aerodynamic. They are also curiously competing on the NASCAR circle tracks, and selling as fast as they can be hauled into the dealerships.

Whether racing sells cars or not can only be answered by the buyers themselves.

To judge for ourselves, we acquired a 454 Pontiac Grand Am, a 455 Chevelle Laguna, a 440 Charger SE, a 351 Torino fastback and took them to Riverside Raceway to test the high-speed handling and stability. It was quite a revelation. So was the street test.

Each car tested had a unique and distinct personality. The Grand Am and the Laguna are large, "small" cars. Nimble, quick and responsive. The Torino is a small, "big" car, with a solid, heavy feeling. The Charger is the only true intermediate from the standpoint of driver feel. It has solid straight-line performance and positive cornering, but it needs a tickle of power to get it cleanly through a turn. This is all a trick on the senses played by the various suspensions since all four cars weigh within 150 pounds of each other. The "lightweight" Chevelle weighs 65 pounds more than the "intermediate" Charger.

The Pontiac Grand Am represents a radical change in styling for a GM intermediate. The closed, pointed-nose section is vaguely reminiscent of older GTO and Firebird snoots, but only vaguely. A sharply raked windshield cuts wind resistance. The roofline curves back in an aerodynamic sweep into an equally gracefully curved rear deckline. Pontiac avoids the penalty of reduced visibility inherent in this configuration by inserting a set of very ample rear sail panel windows. They don't do much for the esthetics, but the visibility is great.

The pointed snout is pliable urethane and everyone who passes by pinches it.

Handling is very smooth and stable under most conditions, better than a lot of so-called good handling foreign sedans. But, while steering is precise, at higher speeds the machine feels a little nervous. That is, you tend to feed in more steering input than is necessary and you

wind up making some minor corrections.

There is one other shortcoming to the otherwise superb suspension. While it eats up small bumps, it tends to overreact to larger ones. Damping is immediate, but there is quite a bit of rebound in some of the larger swales; not distressing, mind you, simply noticeable.

The real wood veneer instrument panel is the best we've seen on a U.S. production car. The tach is to the left, putting the critical high rpm range in clear view. Miraculously, the engine monitor gauges are stacked in the center of the dash, between the tach and speedometer. All are easily read.

The adjustable, small-diameter steering wheel has a fat, soft rim for firm grip.

Another Pontiac innovation is the adjustable lumbar support in the seatback of the six-way power seat. A cylindrical pad is vertically adjustable with a roller wheel at the side of the seat back. The concept is brilliant, but it doesn't quite come off. The roller sticks out too far and never seems to find the correct spot on the spine. A bit of refinement could do the trick.

The seat itself is great. Just enough resilience to mold to body contours, with excellent support and lateral retention but too short under the thighs. To say the 455, four-barrel engine is strong would be the understatement of the year, it propels the car along like a rocket. In traffic, response is crisp and immediate. Under a full head of steam, however, the shift from second to third was a bit slow.

Brake response is very good. The brakes do begin to fade after four or five strong stops, smoking quite heavily, but there is still enough grabbing power to make a safe stop.

As good as the Grand Am was, the Dodge's Charger 440 SE is even faster with the strongest engine of the lot, with excellent low end power and a quick, positive downshift for rapid passing. Charger utilizes torsion bars for the front suspension and leaf springs for the rear. The result is an excellent balance between ride and handling, with a slight penalty paid in roughness. Understeer can be avoided by applying just a taste of power as the apex of the corner is reached. Exiting under power brings the Charger smartly in line without any hunting or seeking by the rear end.

Charger bucket seats are excellent. Their height is right on, support and comfort strike the correct balance, and

Chevelle

Charger

Grand Am

Torino

lateral retention is all one could expect. Chrysler's sport steering wheel becomes almost mandatory in the Charger, since the skinny rimmed stock version is totally out of context with the rest of the car. Power steering is very good, but like GM's there is no detectable centering force. Under city or suburban driving conditions, this is no handicap, but on the expressways, where it becomes easy to drift out of your assigned lane on warm, sleepy days, positive centering is essential.

Charger's dash panel is located on the right side of center and two dials are blocked by the right hand on the wheel.

The simulated wood-grain plastic panel needs modernizing. The current trend is to achieve at least a facade of quality to interior appointments. Chrysler's plastic is no better or worse than anyone else's, but the wood grain is so obviously an imitation it's almost embarrassing.

The little vertical slot windows in the SE sail panel are more than decorative. While they don't allow scenic, panorama vistas, the presence of another vehicle off your right rear quarter is instantly detectable. It's an excellent innovation.

Although Chrysler is proud of its new "torsion quiet" ride, it isn't as quiet as the competition. And, although the Charger's brakes are good, they are not spectacular, giving straight sure but average stops.

The Chevelle Laguna has many features shared by the Grand Am, plus a few of its own. The front cowl piece is a rubberized plastic, but very firm and solid. The basic body styling from the front fender well back is virtually identical, with the same graceful curve to the roof and rear deck.

This Chevelle was powered by a 455 cu. in. engine—more than just a cubic inch away from Pontiac's 454. The Chevy engine has a wider bore, shorter stroke and a higher torque peak rpm. This gives better passing response at cruising speed, but less hustle at the lower rpm range.

Laguna has the same sense of balance and quickness as the Grand Am, but the reaction of the front suspension to small bumps imparts a slight rolling moment to the front end. The first reaction is to correct for this, but that is not necessary. The movement is only in the body, not the steering system. The Laguna's brakes give sure straight stops, but heat up and fade after four cycles from 60 mph.

Like the Pontiac, the Laguna's visibility is excellent, but unlike the Pontiac, the dash panel has the temperature and amp gauges out on either side of the center panel. The layout is an improvement over previous years, but two instruments are obscured by the driver's hands.

Laguna's new swivel bucket seat is a bit of an enigma. Memorabilia from Plymouth's Flite sweep '50s. It still takes some getting used to, particularly when getting into the back seat because the seat doesn't tilt forward at all. The swivel release latch works well, but not as easily as one would like.

I still haven't decided if I like to sit in it. It is more like a living room chair than a car seat, which I'm sure was the intent. But it is more comfortable to sit in, than drive in. It makes you feel isolated from the car's movement, which may have been great in the boulevard cruisers of the '50s but wasted with such a responsive suspension and steering system. It's a little like playing a quadrasonic stereo record on a monaural system. The trans-

Despite radical styling individuality, all four vehicles share common ride height, profile.

MOTOR TREND Test Data

Torino, Laguna, Grand Am and Charger have distinctive rear end treatments. Torino sports steepest rake angle, Grand Am cleanest tail, Charger has spoiler.

SPECIFICATIONS	LAGUNA	TORINO	CHARGER SE	GRAND AM
Engine	V-8	V-8	V-8	V-8
Bore & Stroke—ins.	4.251 x 4.00	4.00 x 3.50 ins.	4.32 x 3.75	4.15 x 4.21
Displacement—cu. in.	454 cu. in.	351 cu. ins.	440 cu. in.	455 cu. ins.
HP @ RPM	245 @ 4,000	246 @ 5,400	220 @ 3,600	250 @ 4,000
Torque: lbs.-ft. @ rpm	375 @ 2,800	312 @ 3,600	350 @ 2,400	370 @ 2,800
Compression Ratio	8.25:1	8.0:1	8.2:1	8.0:1
Carburetion	FOUR BARREL	FOUR BARREL	FOUR BARREL	FOUR BARREL
Transmission	3 spd. Automatic	3 spd. Automatic	3 spd. Automatic	3 spd. Automatic
Final Drive Ratio	2.73	3.25:1	3.23:1	3.23
Steering Type	Variable power	Power	Power	Variable Power
Steering Ratio	17.9-13.0:1	21.73:1	18.82:1	17.5-14.2:1
Turning Diameter (curb-to-curb-ft.)	39.60 ft.	41.6 ft.	41.20 ft.	39.5 ft.
Wheel Turns (lock-to-lock)	6.64	3.5	3.5	3.3
Tire Size	Bias belted G-78x14B	G70-14 Polyglas steel belted	Bias belted G70-14	Steel belted radial GR 70-15
Brakes	Power disc-drum	Power disc-drum	Power disc-drum	Power disc-drum
Front Suspension	Coil springs w/stabilizer bar	coil springs w/stabilizer shocks	Torsion bar, shocks	coil springs, stabilizer bar, pliacell shock absorbers
Rear Suspension	Linked salisbury axle fixed by control arms	4 link rubber insulated	Leaf springs & shocks	4 link stab. bar coil w/pliacell shock absorbers
Body/Frame Construction	All welded perimeter type	Body on torque box perimeter type frame	Unit body	Independent body frame
Wheelbase—ins.	112.0 ins.	114.0 ins.	115.0 ins.	112.0 ins.
Overall Length—ins.	202.9 ins.	208.0 ins.	212.7 ins.	208.6 ins.
Width—ins.	76.6 ins.	79.3 ins.	77.0 ins.	77.7 ins.
Height—ins.	53.1 ins.	52.2 ins.	52.2 ins.	52.9 ins.
Front Track—ins.	61.5 ins.	62.8 ins.	61.9 ins.	61.9 ins.
Rear Track—ins.	60.7 ins.	62.9 ins.	62.0 ins.	61.1 ins.
Curb Weight—lbs.	4,225 lbs.	4,240 lbs.	4,160 lbs.	4,090 lbs.
Fuel Capacity—gals.	22.0 gls.	22.5 gls.	21.0 gls.	25.0 gls.
Oil Capacity—qts.	4.0 qts.	4.0 qts.	6.0 qts.	5.0 qts.
Price as tested	$5251	$5110	$5145	$6153

PERFORMANCE

Acceleration				
0-30 mph	3.6	3.4	2.8	3.2
0-60 mph	8.0	8.8	7.4	7.9
0-75	11.8	12.6	10.4	11.4
Standing Start ¼-mile				
Mph	88.4	86.5	92.9	88
Elapsed time	15.7	16.3	15.2	15.7
Passing speeds				
40-60 mph	4.0	4.6	3.9	4.3
50-70 mph	4.9	4.8	4.2	4.8
Speeds in gears*				
1st . . . mph @ rpm	57 @ 5,000	45 @ 5,000	38 @ 4,000	48 @ 4,500
2nd . . . mph @ rpm	94 @ 5,000	77 @ 5,000	62 @ 4,000	78 @ 4,500
3rd . . . mph @ rpm	99 @ 3,500	87 @ 4,000	93 @ 4,000	102 @ 4,000
4th . . . mph @ rpm				
Mph per 1000 rpm (in top gear)	28.54	21.75	23.25 mph	25.5 mph
Stopping distances				
From 30 mph	37.9'	36.0'	37.9'	37.9'
From 60 mph	184.9'	159.7'	165.8'	160.3'
Gas mileage range	10-12 mpg	10-12 mpg	10-12 mpg	11-13.5 mpg
Speedometer error				
Car speedometer	30 45 50 60 70 80	30 45 50 60 70 80	30 45 50 60 70 80	30 45 50 60 70 80
True speedometer	31 46 51 61 71 81	28 43 47 57 67 76	30 45 50 61 71 82	30 45 50 60 70 80

*Speeds in gears are at shift points (limited by the length of track) and do not represent maximum speeds.

mission shift handle and the ignition system components are too far back in both GM cars. The "click-shifter" enables the driver to manually upshift the auto trans by simply moving the handle smartly outboard and forward. It moves one position only. A nice idea, but it's set too far back on the console.

Charger also has a click shift, but it is a direct throw on a much shorter handle. It is correctly located, but tends to work loose and rattle.

Torino, the small "big" car, is totally different from the other three. The four-coil suspension eats up the big bumps, but overreacts to the small ones, giving a continual thumping and bumping as you drive. The steering is not as responsive as GM's or Chrysler's, but it has a firm centering position which helps a lot.

Torino's shifter is at the farthest end of the console, but the handle curves back toward the driver. The only improvement would be to use the positive lock feature shared by the other three. In this day of smog-choked engines, it often becomes desireable to shift for yourself to maintain a feeling of performance.

The high-back bucket seats are comfortable, but the angle of the seat gives you the feeling you are going to slide off

The 351 cu. in., four-barrel engine finally made it through emissions testing and into the hands of the public. This used to be a strong engine with gobs of torque, but now it has breathing problems when any power is needed. It just isn't the 351 of old, but then neither is anything else.

The Pontiac Grand Am had the best balance, best combination of ride and handling, and was the most comfortable to drive, lumbar lump notwithstanding.

On the track it was a different story. While none of these machines expected to operate much above 70 mph, because they are some of America's most exciting cars, we wanted to do some high-speed driving. Both the Grand Am and the Laguna became light on their feet above 90 mph. The comfortable pliancy of the suspension is too pliant for control at 100 mph.

Charger was most stable and remained glued to the ground, until we hit a slight bump and got that slope nose up in the air. Once the nose lifts, Charger's down force evaporates and the front end loses its firm grip on the ground.

Torino was the big surprise. With the particular combination of spring and shock rates on our test car, it appeared the Torino was designed more for the demands of high-speed operation than the city freeway.

Under heavy cornering up through Riverside Raceway's esses, the Torino was the most stable. While the Laguna and Grand Am did not give any trouble, neither did they inspire as much confidence. The Charger oversteered, which could be corrected by a little opposite lock steering and feathering the power. By contrast, Torino came whipping through solid as a rock. On a sharp lane change, the rear of the body made one short, quick cycle to the outside before settling. There was no body roll and the rear tires remained firmly on the ground, but the movement was there. That was peculiar to an abrupt wheel movement and not to hard cornering.

Torino is the enigma of the bunch, with an operating envelope too high for anything but a track.

All were fun to drive, all benefitted from reduced wind resistance credited to their aerodynamic contours. Less wind resistance means less wind noise and more stability as well as reduced drag and better gas mileage. With gas mileage deteriorating yearly and prices climbing monthly, every reduction in drag helps a little.

On balance, the Pontiac is the best automobile of the four, the Charger is a close second and the Laguna and Torino are tied for third. The important point, though, is that the NASCAR street machines are the new generation fun sedans that can be purchased for styling and performance without worrying that you won't be able to live with them over the long term like the super-cars of the '60s. They handle well, ride nicely and are the cars of the '70s. ∎

New Charger from Dodge

CONTINUED FROM PAGE 39
is by the Chrysler's Cleaner Air System, which consists primarily of carburetter modifications for a leaner mixture at idle, and a special distributor to retard the spark at idle. Cars with manual transmissions have a sensing valve to advance the spark during deceleration. Combustion chamber alterations have been made on the 318 and 440 V8 chambers for 1968 to reduce the surface area, thus minimizing the unburned hydrocarbons remaining after combustion.

Transmission choice is very wide. All engines can be fitted with Chrysler's excellent TorqueFlite automatic, with three forward speeds and a torque converter. The 318 V8 may have a 3-speed manual transmission with a column shift, while the 426 and 440 engines are offered with a four-speed manual gearbox with a floor lever. The four-speed's indirect ratios are 2.65, 1.91 and 1.39. The 383 engine is available with all three transmissions. Axle ratios offered range from 2.76 to 3.55. At the front of the Charger propeller shaft is a shock damper consisting of two moulded rubber rings driven by an inserted steel shaft which has proved effective in reducing drive line noise.

Burt Bouwkamp's men made the engineering contributions; Bill Brownlie now had to come up with an exterior design that, in Bill's words, "looked like 'go'. We wanted a car that people would look at and say, 'Wow!'" The primary target had to be the Pontiac GTO, the automobile that sets the standard for medium-range performance-oriented cars in the U.S., both inside and outside General Motors. He urged his four stylists and six clay modellers to give the car a clean, straightforward, functional look with an aerodynamic line and shape. This is often attempted but not often successfully.

Central to the Charger's conception is the high, "hippy" look over the rear wheels, essentially a modern GM theme which here is used in a completely new way, giving the car a wedge-like air-penetrating look. The lines are stretched very tight from front to rear, giving the fender shapes great strength and authority. In only one way is the concept carried not quite far enough: there's too much lateral body overhang, tending to undermine the car's "tight" look. Pontiac scores here with its "wide-track" styling look, which puts more emphasis on the wheels as design elements.

All the Charger's surface detailing is neat and handsome. The very wide, recessed grille is pressure cast, for the first time at Dodge, of plastic. On previous Chargers, the hidden headlamps were mounted on an axis which rotated them into position. The 1968 model has fixed headlamps, covered by doors which lift out of the way when the lights are switched on.

Indented sections on the hood and sides of the Charger are obviously not functional air vents, but they add surface interest at the right areas. The side marker lights and quick-release fuel tank filler are also handsomely handled, as is the trim rear end with its spoiler-like ducktail. The recessed rear window is unabashed in its good use of a GM-sponsored styling trend.

Brownlie's stylists gave the Charger's interior a bold, simple look, with vinyl plastic trim materials for the seats and doors, which carry flexible map pockets in the European manner. The upper structure of the front seat back has foam padding and a hat-section member, to absorb crash impact from a belted rear-seat passenger. Safety is also emphasized in the dashboard controls, which are rocker-type switches or recessed thumb wheels. A thoughtful small touch is an optional time-delay switch which illuminates the ignition key cylinder for 30 seconds after the driver enters the car.

With its extreme fast-back design, the previous Charger was thought likely to be very fast on the stock car circuits, where lap speeds now reach and exceed 180 m.p.h. It was fast, but its handling on fast banked turns proved to be very poor. Chrysler built an accurate 3/8 scale model of the car and tested it in the wind tunnel of Kansas State University, confirming that substantial lift was being developed over the tail; this was reduced by a small spoiler across the rear deck which transformed the handling qualities.

In July this year, Dodge engineers began a tunnel test series to find out how good their 1968 aerodynamics are. Their first step is to conduct scale model tests of both the Charger and the standard Dodge Coronet to find out which has the most promising combination of low drag and high stability. The scale tests are to be followed by tunnel checks on full-size vehicles, and finally by track testing. When the NASCAR season gets under way, we'll know by the entries which body was aerodynamically more efficient.

The 1968 Charger has already markedly influenced Chrysler's other cars. So many interesting new ideas were generated in the studio while the Charger was created that more than a few were borrowed by the Chrysler and Plymouth stylists for their 1968 models. If the Charger is a market success, its influence will be even wider in an industry that is very much in need of new styling directions.

124

Charger

One of the Dodge intermediates, the 115-inch wheelbase Charger, will be available with 2 body styles, a coupe and a hardtop, both 2-door models, with 3 levels of trim, the Coupe, Charger, and top-of-the-line Charger S.E. (Special Edition).

Both six and 8 cylinder engines are available for the line except the six is not supplied as standard for the S.E. model or on cars slated for California registration. Standard for all is the 318 CID V-8, with the new 360 CID high performance engine as an option along with both 2 and 4-barrel carbureted versions of the 400 CID and 440 CID power plants. Solid state electronic ignition and voltage regulators are standard on all engines.

With the exception of slightly different front and rear bumper configurations to meet the new impact standards, the Chargers are little changed in overall styling for 1974. There are unseen improvements in the method of mounting the suspension system to reduce transmission of road noise to the passenger compartment, front disc brakes are standard with power assist for them and the steering optional, and the Rallye pack and instrumentation option can be ordered with Chargers.

Standard transmission is a 3-speed manual with either column or floor shift, with a 4-speed manual and the Torque-Flite automatic optional. Radial ply tires are optional and a Brougham package featuring bucket, or bench seats with center fold-down arm rest, and special side trim, are also available at extra cost.

All of the required safety equipment, including seat belt ignition interlock system for front seat occupants, impact resistant bumpers, reinforced roof, and collapsible steering column, plus emission controls, are incorporated into the '74 Charger with little change in exterior or interior appearance. Just about every power assist and comfort item available on other models can be ordered for the Charger, including the special light and heavy duty trailer towing packages with 7-wire harness and connectors, hitch, and hitch platform.

CHARGER

CHARGER S.E.

CHARGER

You know you're in a Dodge Charger and you know you're eating up the asphalt at a damn good clip— maybe 75-80 mph, but there's something missing. You can feel it. You look around the well-laid out cockpit, check the full instrumentation on the dashboard, snug down your safety belt buckle. Everything is in order. Yet you still have the feeling that there's something unfamiliar about this Charger, that·there's something missing.

Then it hits you.

The noise. It's the noise that's missing. You're cruising at over 75 and it's still quiet inside, so quiet that it's noticeable. And for a Charger, or any Chrysler product for that matter, that is something to crow about.

Chargers and other Chrysler products have always been behind the rest of the industry in this regard. Take a Charger out on the highway and you are bombarded with a symphony of cacaphonous sounds that remain in the subconscious of your awareness for the whole ride. There are the shrill wind leaks caused by poor sealing windows, the muffled drone of the exhaust system, the rump of the tires over every tar strip, the creaks and groans of the unit body.

At least that's how it used to be.

Now, at 60 mph, the loudest sound in the car is the ticking of the clock, to paraphrase a cliche made famous by another manufacturer. The point is made, though.

The '74 Charger is a damn quiet car.

It's funny how priorities change. We've been testing Chargers since 1966. Through all those years, Chargers were pretty noisy cars. Funny how we never seemed to mind, though. Not with dual quad 426 Street Hemis and 440 tripower engines and 3.91 rear axle gears and beefed

DECIBEL DARLING

That good ol' fashioned exhaust roar is missing from the new breed of Chargers, but Dodge had better 'look-out' because Oldham doesn't like the new shock/stabilizer suspension compromise!!

Torqueflites packed into the car. All we were interested in then was seeing how many full throttle runs it would take to destroy the rear tires.

Now we're concerned with a wind leak around the front window, driver's side.

Happily, you'll find that the '74 Charger can stand very close scrutiny. It's put together perhaps better than any we've ever seen. It's still one of the best looking cars on the road. And with the 440 4-barrel engine that was in our test car, it can roll (if not blast) quite smartly away from any stoplight. And refinements over previous years make it the smoothest Charger ever.

Our '74 Charger was one of the sharpest test cars we've had in years. Somebody in the Dodge public relations office finally smartened up and realized that editors don't particularly like to ride around in test cars painted Eyeball-Shattering Orange and Pupil Piercing Purple. With 36-inch yellow stipes. This test car was a glistening black—one of the favorites of performance enthusiasts everywhere—with a black vinyl roof and a tasteful rally stripe down both flanks. We could .even have done entirely without the

stripes. The shiny black paint contrasted beautifully with the chrome road wheels and flat black vinyl roof to make a truly handsome car.

There must be a miracle worker somewhere deep in the Dodge styling studios. Where other makes have had to resort to chromed railroad ties hung on the front and rear of all '74 cars to meet the more stringent federal bumper standards, the Charger has retained its good looks with a clean, simple front end design that doesn't look like it weighs more than the Queen Elizabeth 2. The only concession is two thick rubber inserts in the small bumper guards. Other than that, the '74 Charger looks a lot like the '72 Charger and that means good. Yet, the bumpers on the Charger meet all federal requirements. Why can't all manufacturers meet the requirements and still retain some semblance of good looks?

The 440 engine is its same workmanlike self that it's been since they cut the compression a couple of years ago. If anything, driveability is better this year. We experienced no surging or flat spots because of the emission controls. Acceleration from any rpm was smooth and positive if a little weak. The only problem with the engine is keeping it lit when cold. Also starting isn't as quick as we think it could be, especially with the electronic ignition system standard. It has no points and can fire even badly fouled plugs.

The 440's power rating is the same as last year: 275 horses at 4400 rpm. Torque is rated 375 lbs./ft. at 3200 rpm. Dual exhausts are standard.

With the big Torqueflite in D all the way and with our "performance" 3.55 rear axle ratio, our test car knocked off the zero to 60 run in 7.6 seconds and the quarter mile in 15.00 seconds flat at 92 mph. This is almost identical to the performance figures of the '73 Charger we tested and shows that the tighter emission controls have not cut

performance this year.

Speaking of rear axles, optional on all 400-4V and 440 plus 360 HP powered Chargers will be a new 9 1/4-inch ring gear rear axle assembly. This is the heavy duty setup which replaces the old Dana 9 3/4-inch bulletproof setup. The new rear axle assembly should be a strong performer on the dragstrip while being about 75 pounds lighter than the Dana setup. However, axle ratios are limited right now, with a 3.23 being the highest numerical ratio currently available.

Our test car had the standard duty 8 3/4-inch axle assembly which is available with a 3.55 gearset from the factory and which makes a tremendous difference in the accelerative performance and response of the car. Cruising is a little revvy with the 3.55 but we think the tradeoff is worth it in added performance. By the way, with the automatic transmission, the 8 3/4-inch standard axle is plenty strong for all but the most maniacal of drivers.

We've already commented on the increased smoothness of the '74 Charger. Credit, in large part, must go to the suspension engineers who tailored the '74 suspension package to the optional radial tires. More rubber is used at bushings, etc. for more compliance throughout the system. Rates for the front torsion bars and rear leaf springs have been softened up slightly to decrease impact harshness. And, of course, the optional performance tire is now a G70-15 steel belted radial replacing a G60-15 fiberglass bias-belted tire.

To control body roll with the softer spring rates, Dodge engineers fit a front antiroll stabilizer bar standard and a rear bar is standard on all 440 cars and optional on other V-8 powered Chargers. Front bar diameter is 0.80-inch and the rear bar measures 0.86 inch.

All this works out fine on the road except for one thing which we'll get to in a minute. The fiberglass tires were always a very harsh riding tire. Not so the radial. The radial is a much softer riding tire. The soft sidewall absorbs much of the road shock that would normally be transmitted into the passenger compartment. You get the feeling that you're riding on a continuous track with no road irregularities at all. The softer suspension helps reduce shock, too.

All this is fine and we approve up to a point. However, the engineers were out to lunch when they picked the anti-roll bar rates and the shock absorbers. Ou test car rolled quite a bit when pressed on the road course, which is quite understandable with a relatively softly sprung car. However, to compensate for the low spring rates, heftier anti-roll stabilizer bars are called for.

Out on the open road or on back roads with chopped up surfaces, the soft shocks simply didn't do the job. Dodge uses 1-inch diameter shocks across the board regardless of engine size or suspension equipment. Internal valving is modified for heavy duty use. But the small shock just doesn't make it. We experienced wallowing and front end float over any kind of rough road, even on large dips on the New Jersey Turnpike. This lack of shock absorber control is uncalled for in a performance oriented car like the 440 Charger Rallye. At least make large capacity, flat shocks an option for those who know what to do with them.

We like cars with soft spring rates. They don't knock your kidneys into your throat. However, soft springs must be teamed with hefty stabilizer bars and shock absorbers —else you have a flabby car that bounces down the road rather than glides down. Come on Dodge. You can do better than this.

The radials themselves are a fine tire which we really like. They grip like Nick Buonoconti on a quarterback blitz. Cornering power is high on both wet and dry roads. They don't look as hairy as the old G60-15 fiberglass bias-belted tires. Nowhere near so. The tread is about an inch and a

DARLING

half narrower. But maybe it's time we all grew up and *admitted* that *looks aren't everything.* These radials are a case in point. Their on-the-road performance is far superior to wider, bias-belted tires and should be the first choice of any real enthusiast .

Last year, in our test of the '73 Charger, we spoke of the fine interior layout and proper use of ergonomics to put the driver in the precisely correct relationship to the automobile's controls. Happily, Dodge hasn't fooled around with the interior, and except for a few trim changes, it's identical to last year's.

What's the Charger's rationale for existence? It's no longer the tire shredding supercar of the '60s. Instead, it has evolved into a refined intermediate-sized road car that can deliver sporty transportation and still have room for the edibles from Stop 'N Shop and the kids. And if you're a swinging single, the Charger in Rallye trim still puts over more macho image than any ten men could ever live up to. Perhaps it's an anchronism in light of the energy crisis. But it's an anchronism that lots of people like.

Photography: Peter Robain

MUSCLE DEFINITION

Pumping iron to improve fitness and strength will give you bigger biceps, but late '60s Detroit iron came with all the muscle you could handle — straight from the factory!

There's an unforgettable scene in the 1968 Steve McQueen film 'Bullitt' as part of the build up to the most famous film car chase of all time. It's when the bad guys in the black Dodge lose track of McQueen in his Mustang and you see this shot looking in their rear view mirror — I can still recall the shiver of excitement that ran up my spine as that mean, green Ford loomed over the brow of a hill the first time I saw the film.

Those climactic few minutes of cinema hyper-action were probably responsible more than any other single event, for bringing the reality of high performance American cars to the attention of the British public. Smoking tyres, roaring V8 engines and high speed leaps down the steep San Francisco streets had the audiences clinging onto their seats.

When I began setting up this feature, it really wasn't my intention to recreate the movie chase pairing. I wanted to get together a couple of muscle cars that would illustrate the different approaches by manufacturers to this automotive phenomena. But first a really tasty 1968 Shelby Mustang GT500KR came to my attention and then I was informed about a Dodge Charger 440 R/T of the same vintage and it all seemed to click into place. Sadly, we weren't able to go 'on location' to California and ride the roller-coaster humps of San Francisco, instead we gathered at the much flatter, but considerably less tropic, environs of Santa Pod Raceway in Bedfordshire.

Furthermore, we were not about to thrash these two fine machines in order to determine which is the quickest — in any case the Charger driver refused point blank to crash it into a petrol station, so that killed that idea!

As well as showing how the factories built muscle cars in wildly varying guises, this dynamic duo also have two totally opposite, but equally typical, case histories. One, (the Mustang) arrived in this country as a possession of a USAF serviceman, was wrecked in a crash and left behind when he returned home; the other, (the Charger), was imported in 1988 from Colorado with a genuine 29,000 miles showing on the clock and having had only one owner.

From a purely descriptive point of view, the Shelby Mustang story makes a more interesting narrative, so let's begin with that. Bought new by a man named Jarvis in Missouri, it saw plenty of drag strip action at the local tracks. Later on he passed the car on to his brother who also liked to canter down the quarter mile, unfortunately his right foot was rather too heavy on one pass and the engine let go. Sold on to the youngest of the Jarvis boys, who subsequently rebuilt the engine and used the car regularly, it was brought to the UK when he was transferred to USAF Bentwaters in Suffolk as part of his tour of duty.

As so often happens, not long after he arrived, one icy winter morning on his way to work young airman Jarvis lost control and put the Shelby into a ditch hitting an oak tree at the same time. This excusion, not surprisingly, severely damaged the front end of the Mustang.

So the year is now 1976, and a fifteen year long repair and restoration epic is about to get underway. The car was sold in its damaged state to another US airman who stripped off all the bent and broken front end, then lost interest when he discovered how expensive it was going to be to repair. Living next door to him at the time was Russell White, a boat builder who had taken an interest in the project and helped his neighbour dismantle the wreck. Eventually, after laying idle for some time the Shelby was bought by Russell for a mere £375!

He started the restoration work, replacing the inner and outer wings, front chassis box sections, suspension and steering components as and when he could afford to. The engine was removed, steam cleaned and repainted. The rest of the Shelby was stripped to the bare shell, found to be completely rust free, so the underside and engine bay were painted in black. This work all took place over a period of three years, during which time the suspension and running gear were all cleaned, refurbished and refitted at a cost of several hundred pounds.

Progress then came to a halt due to Russell buying a house and other committments. The Shelby remained, virtually untouched, stored in a rented garage until August '89 when the owner of the garage decided he needed the space for his own use. Having nowhere to keep the car, Russell contacted Tim Brundle, a friend since schooldays and a fellow American car nut, asking him if he would be interested in restoring the car and becoming joint owner. Tim, a 33 year old HGV truck mechanic, jumped at the chance and within a week the car was moved to his home.

Tim's first step was to undertake some intensive research, double checking the VIN number with the Shelby records and tracking down books and magazines — gathering all the relevant information together to ensure the car could be 100% authentically restored. Once again, the Mustang was completely stripped down and every part, down to the last nut and bolt, was painted the correct colour or replated. Any components not up to standard were replaced and the pair found themselves ordering parts from the States on a weekly basis.

Two trips to Florida were also needed to come up with the goods, "It's so hard to find some genuine items and there are often no repro parts available" said Tim, "So few of these GT-500KR's were made originally, as production only lasted for the final six months of the '68 model year." Visiting almost every Mustang specialist there was he managed to pick up vital restoration information as well as much needed spares, to ensure the rebuild was as accurate as possible. They have the original factory build sheet, plus most of the appropriate sales literature and all the factory stamps, colour codes and tags have been copied.

The result of five years dedicated work, spread over a much longer period, is like a brand new automobile that's just been delivered to the dealer. Shipping tags are all in place and the lack of number plates (it is registered and some are on the way) only go to heighten this time warp. It is a beautiful sight to behold and Tim and Russell are to be congratulated on their efforts.

As we stated earlier, the Charger's story is much more mundane. It was sold new in Colorado (there's a Skyline Dodge of Denver badge on the back of the car) where it remained with the original owner until being brought to the UK by Rare Performance Motors of Aldershot in 1988. "It has been resprayed once" RPM partner Martin Savill informed me, "But apart from that it is a nice, dead original car". Indeed, it was so clean that the only work felt necessary by RPM was to pull the engine out and do some detailing. The Charger was bought by David Edwards and Martyn Piddington of Haywards Heath in Sussex and our special thanks go to them for allowing the car to be used in this feature.

THE HORSEPOWER RACE

Back in 1968, when both these cars were new, the American auto industry was engaged in a vigorous performance battle, with each manufacturer trying to outdo the other in the race tracks and drag strips across the country. This horsepower race was fought under some unusual conditions however, as often engines produced far more grunt than was admitted by the factory so that their cars could compete in lower classes.

Somewhat surprisingly perhaps, this corporate quest for more sales through speed was going on against a background of a society in turmoil. Beset by violence and protest yet at the same time faced with 'Flower Power' and the psychadelic imagery of a youth culture in full flood, the question of which car was faster, today seems almost incongruous. The Vietnam war at its bloody height; Martin Luther King and Robert Kennedy were assassinated; Lyndon Johnson refused to seek re-election and Richard Nixon won the presidency; hippy rock musical 'Hair' opened on Broadway; and Stanley Kubrick's film '2001: A Space Odessy' presented an awesome look into the future. It was a time of tremendous upheaval and change.

The auto advertising of the period used much of the vivid, luminous, wildly colourful pop art style that had been embraced by the affluent younger generation. Buying a high performance car was presented as fun with crazy little cartoon characters often used. Dodge had the 'Scat Pack' as one of its ploys and sold the Charger R/T as 'The Clean Machine' emphasising the smooth styling thus: "The clean machine effect begins right up front. With headlights that stay out of sight until summoned."

But the '68 Dodge Charger was something of an anomaly in the muscle car stakes, completely restyled from the previous year using the then in vogue 'coke-bottle' curved shape it sat on a wheelbase that was nine inches longer than the Mustang. However, its overall length stretched a further two feet and it weighed in at several hundred pounds more than the Shelby thereby hinting at the Charger's true market — the luxury end of the performance sales arena.

The interior of our featured Charger is resplendent in white to match the vinyl roof, and if you were totally ignorant of that steroid-laden 7.2 litre V8 sitting under the bonnet, you could be forgiven for thinking this was just another bloated boulevard cruiser. Appearances can be deceptive however, and while the Dodge might seem 'too large to trot' it can move out with the best of them. As has already been stated, factory horsepower ratings at the time were suspect and various sources quote figures ranging from 350 to 370 gee-gees, but the reality was probably a fair bit more.

It certainly was in the case of the 428cu. in. Cobra Jet powerplant used in the Shelby, which had a declared output of 335bhp at 5400rpm. The National Hot Rod Association weren't fooled and bumped the KR up a few classes by estimating the true horsepower figure at 400, even this didn't prevent the cars from taking home some impressive titles.

Ford had quite a line-up of hot horses for '68, but all was not well with the Shelby relationship. Manufacture of the Mustangs bearing his name was switched from Los Angeles to contractor A.O. Smith in Ionia, Michigan although the cars themselves originated from the Metuchen, New Jersey assembly plant.

In comparison then, we have the Dodge factory churning out 96,100 Chargers (of all types) in 1968, whereas only 933 Shelby GT-500KR Mustang hardtops were put together (plus 318 convertible KRs). Of course, the Mustang band wagon was still very much on a roll and total figures for Ford's pony car were over 317,000 for the year. But it's hardly fair to bracket a practically hand-built, street-going race car with lightweight glassfibre panels, strengthened suspension and improved brakes with a mass-produced monolith is it? And in all fairness to the Dodge, if it hadn't been for the film, this unlikely pairing would never have come about.

Additionally, the conditions of our two particular examples reflected their owners' attitudes towards the cars. The Shelby was almost better than brand new and arrived at the photo session on a trailer, while the Charger drove up the M1 motorway with three people on board. It so happens that the Shelby also ran out of petrol half way through the shoot and had to be replenished with a can bought from a Swedish drag racer who was at the track, Tim Brundle not anticipating doing much mileage in the car.

Performance being what these two cars are all about it might seem strange to you that we didn't get them to try a couple of passes down the Santa Pod quarter mile just to get some comparative figures, but the track was being prepped for a big meet the following weekend (including a 'grip juice' spray treatment) which put the tarmac out of bounds. Anyway, as was stated at the very beginning, it was never our intention to produce drag racing time slips which, unless the drivers were prepared to go flat out would be

pretty meaningless anyway. That said, the question of a full 'Musclecar Shootout' did come up and the RPM guys were more than happy to participate — if there's any other like-minded owners out there, get in touch and maybe we can arrange something for '92.

Right about now I suppose it's time I clambered down off the fence and gave you my choice of these two magnificent machines. Well, I've long had a thing about Mustangs and there's no doubt the Shelby is a great specimen, almost too good if anything. And I can just see myself as Steve McQueen in 'Bullitt' — racing around, having loads of fun (especially with Jacqueline Bissett as the

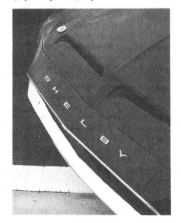

girlfriend!) but I'm practical enough to know that the four-speed manual gearbox can be a bit of a chore, so if I ever had the opportunity to take either of these home and had to pick only one, I think I'd probably go for the Dodge. If I needed to provide any more justification I could always fall back on that old adage 'There's no subsitute for cubic inches'.

In case you hadn't already noticed, it's a curious fact that both these cars are owned by a partnership and coincidentally, they are both for sale. Any serious enquiries or offers will be forwarded via the Classic American offices.

Retrospectively, 1968 was a fantastic year for high performance autos from Detroit, with a greater variety available than ever before for just a few dollars down and easy monthly repayments. Despite the social unrest, in the late '60s race-winning power really did sell more cars — it's only twenty three years ago, but it seems like forever!

Tony Beadle

Thanks to: Santa Pod Raceway and Rare Performance Motors, 36 Crimea Road, Aldershot, Hants GU11 1UE. Tel: 0252 343401.

SPECIFICATION
1968 Shelby Mustang GT-500KR
2-door Fastback

Engine	V8, OHV
Capacity	428 cu. in.
Bore	4.13 inches
Stroke	3.98 inches
Compression ratio	10.7:1
BHP (estimated)	410 at 5600rpm
0-60mph	6.9 secs
SS ¼ mile	14.57secs/100mph
Top Speed	130mph
Trans	4-speed manual
Wheelbase	108 inches
Overall length	186.6 inches
Weight	3445lbs
Factory price 1968	$4473
Production total	933

1968 Dodge Charger R/T
2-door Hardtop

Engine	V8, OHV
Capacity	440 cu. in.
Bore	4.32 inches
Stroke	3.75 inches
Compression ratio	10.0:1
BHP	375 at 4600rpm
0-60mph	6.5 secs
SS ¼ mile	14.8 secs/95.7mph
Top speed	125mph
Trans	Torqueflite auto
Wheelbase	117 inches
Overall length	208 inches
Weight	4,035lbs
Factory price 1968	$3480
Production total	17,107

FANTASTIC FASTBACK

1966 DODGE HEMI-CHARGER

by Josiah Work
photos by Bud Juneau

FOR years, the adjective that dominated Dodge's advertising copy was "Dependable." A reassuring thought, to be sure, and an accurate appraisal as well. But not terribly exciting.

Perhaps that uninspired (and uninspiring) pitch helps explain why Dodge lost its grip on fourth place in the sales race, back in 1938. There had been a time when the Dodge Brothers four-cylinder models had been, arguably, the toughest and most dependable automobiles in their price class, if not in the entire industry. But by the late thirties, dependability had come to be taken for granted. The adjective "dependable" could be used, advisedly, to describe just about any American car.

In any case, Dodge was slipping. An excellent value for the money, solidly built, well engineered, comfortable — and yes, dependable — it slid nevertheless to fifth rank in 1938, then to seventh in 1940, and to eighth a decade later.

The problem, in retrospect, isn't hard to identify. Make that *problems*, plural. For in a number of respects Dodge was building yesterday's car. It was behind the times in styling, with its boxy configuration. Behind the times in performance, with its under-powered flathead six. Behind the times in features,

too, trailing rival Pontiac by six long years in the introduction of a fully automatic transmission. And certainly behind the times in its advertising program. Stacked up against what the competition was touting, "dependable" simply didn't cut it.

It wasn't until the 1950s that somebody at Dodge (or, more likely, at corporate headquarters, since Chrysler didn't permit a lot of autonomy among its various divisions) woke up and smelled the coffee. Belatedly, the decision-makers came to realize that the Rocket engine was selling a lot of Oldsmobiles; that even Studebaker offered a peppery little overhead-valve V-8; and that there was more trouble to come from the competition.

The initial reaction was a typical Chrysler Corporation response: Whip the competition with superior engineering. So for 1953 there appeared the Red Ram V-8, a scaled-down (241-c.i.d.) version of the already legendary Chrysler hemi. Horsepower was rated at 140. That figure may have been conser-

vative, but for sure it was a country mile ahead of the 103-horsepower Dodge six, which remained in production. The "mini-hemi" was an economical engine, too. Coupled with the optional Borg-Warner overdrive, it enabled Dodge to score the best fuel mileage of any eight-cylinder car in that year's Mobilgas Economy Run, averaging 23.4 miles per gallon.

But the Dodge had its share of drawbacks. Styling, for one. The "smaller on the outside, bigger on the inside" theme, shared that year with Plymouth, went over with the public like a cast iron balloon. And again there was no fully automatic transmission, though the new Gyro-Torque unit, which hitched a torque converter to the semi-automatic Gyro-Matic, provided Dodge with better acceleration off-the-line.

An even more serious problem had to do with price. The Dodge Coronet V-8 cost nearly a hundred dollars more than the Olds Eighty-Eight Deluxe. A comparison chart became the Oldsmobile salesman's best friend, to wit:

	Dodge	Olds
Price, 4-dr. sedan	$2,220 f.o.b.	$2,126 f.o.b.
Shipping weight	3,385 lb.	3,622 lb.
Wheelbase	119"	120"
Overall length	201.4"	204.0"
Engine c.i.d.	241	303
Hp @ rpm	140/4,400	150/3,600

Driving Impressions

Clift Cullen, a Fresno, California, college instructor, learned of his Hemi Charger "through a friend of a friend," back in 1981. Family problems forced its sale by the car's original owner. Cullen was unable to learn very much about its early history, apart from the fact that it was first sold in Alamogordo, New Mexico — and that it had been raced. Given its unusually high (numerically) gearing, one assumes that this machine must have competed on the drag strips, rather than the NASCAR ovals.

The engine comes to life quickly, easily, and noisily. The idle is rough, and some smoke is laid down — all very proper, for this powerplant. The hemi was set up with fairly generous (though precise) tolerances which, in combination with the solid valve lifters, creates a distinctive sound. And not a particularly quiet one. This is enhanced by the throaty roar of the exhaust.

It is to be expected that most hemi-powered Chargers have been severely beaten over the years, which makes Clift Cullen's car a rare find. At just under 27,000 original miles, it is in superb condition both mechanically and cosmetically. It is strictly stock, and virtually "stripped": No power accessories; just a radio, a couple of trim items and the all-important Hurst shifter constitute the option list, along with an after-market oiling system that includes an eight-quart crankcase.

Despite its generous size, as compared to other "sporty" cars, the Charger is a two-plus-two, featuring four individual seats. Dodge referred to "front buckets," but buckets they're not. Little or no lateral support is afforded, a serious oversight in our view. The rear seats fold flat, revealing an enormous, carpeted cargo deck. In all honesty we found the seating to be somewhat uncomfortable. Front backrests are raked a little too much, and no adjustment of the angle is provided. The rear seat cushions are positioned very close to the floor. This creates sufficient head room, but at some cost to the back seat passengers, who find themselves riding on the ends of their spines. Leg room, however, is ample in front, adequate for the rear seat residents.

The clutch, while requiring somewhat heavier than normal pedal pressure, is smooth. Shifts, thanks to the Hurst setup, are crisp, precise and easy, though the reach is a long one. Acceleration, as expected, is simply fantastic. It would be much easier than not to get a citation with this car. Or a string of them, since the sound of this great engine announces itself to the constabulary in no uncertain terms. And in almost no time the Charger is traveling at speeds far beyond the legal limit.

There's a full set of instruments on the dash panel, including — quite properly — a tachometer. The speedometer reads to a somewhat optimistic 150 miles an hour. There's a clock on the console, but surely the driver has no time to read it.

Steering is heavy. This is a "muscle" car, and muscles are required to operate it. Brakes take less pedal pressure than we expected, and they appear to do their job well. Suspension is stiff enough to provide great cornering ability with a minimum of roll, yet the ride is not comfortable.

Clift Cullen tells us that the original lubrication system was inadequate, resulting in fried bearings at high speeds. Perhaps the fact that this was an early production unit, first sold in January 1966, has something to do with that. In any case, Clift's car has been fitted with an aftermarket Milodon oiling system, providing additional capacity.

Obviously, this is an exciting car to drive. It's not everyone's cup of tea, to be sure, but it's a machine that commands respect — and inspires awe.

1966 DODGE

Hideaway headlamps were probably inspired by Corvette Sting Ray. They lend the grille treatment a very neat, integrated appearance.

It's true, of course, that the hemi engine, with its sophisticated double rocker arm shafts, was expensive to build, and there is little doubt of its superiority from an engineering standpoint. But its advantages weren't particularly apparent to the average buyer — or potential buyer — and Dodge remained in eighth place, behind Buick, Pontiac, Mercury and Oldsmobile, as well as the traditional "low-priced three."

Somehow, Dodge managed to hang onto eighth rank for 1954, though production was down by nearly half. But at least the organization was beginning to take performance seriously. An increase in the compression ratio, from 7.1:1 to 7.5:1, boosted the horsepower to 150, and at Bonneville a '54 Dodge set no fewer than 196 AAA stock car speed records. And in the Mobilgas run, Dodge again took top class honors, averaging this time 25.4 miles per gallon.

"Flair Fashion" styling was featured for 1955. The cars were longer — by nearly 21 inches in the case of the hardtops and convertibles. A "poly" engine replaced the expensive hemi in most eight-cylinder models, and prices were much more competitive. The Coronet V-8, in fact, undercut the Olds Eighty-Eight by nearly $200. The two-speed Powerflite automatic, introduced by Dodge the previous year, was a $178 option. Performance was downplayed somewhat, though according to *Motor Life* magazine the top-of-the-line Custom Royal, fitted with the four-barrel, 193-horsepower Super Red Ram engine, was good for 107 miles an hour. The cars were well received, and a sales increase of 81 percent was posted for the model year.

For several seasons thereafter, a high-performance "D-500" package was available. In 1956, cars so equipped delivered 295 horsepower, a quantum leap over any previous Dodge, and by 1957 that figure had risen to 310. (To keep these figures in perspective, recall that as recently as 1955 the very expensive Chrysler C300 — first of the Letter series — had created a sensation in the industry by offering 300 horsepower.)

Like sister division DeSoto, Dodge dropped the "hemi" after 1957. Featured with 1958's D-500 package was a 361-c.i.d., 305-horsepower "wedge" engine, followed the next year by a 320-horsepower version of Chrysler's excellent 383. But these were modest horsepower gains at best, and although their acceleration off-the-line was excellent, the '58 and '59 models were hard pressed to keep up with the earlier

hemis at the top end. Dodge flirted with electronic fuel injection during this period, but although some horsepower gains were achieved, the system caused no end of trouble, and few cars were equipped with this sophisticated — and now common — system.

Ram induction appeared for 1960 and '61, raising the D-500's horsepower, first to 330 and then, using a 413-cubic-inch block, to 375. Two four-barrel carburetors were fitted to 30-inch intake manifolds, producing phenomenal low-end torque. As a result, Dodge became a force to be reckoned with on the drag strips.

Shorter, 15-inch rams were used for 1962's "Ramcharger" V-8. Far less troublesome than the long tubes, they provided — in combination with a 12.0:1 compression ratio — a roaring 415 horsepower. Fitted to the relatively light, intermediate-sized Dart, this unit became the terror of the NASCAR ovals, as well as the drag strips.

The hemi returned for 1964. A brand new version, this time displacing 426 cubic inches and featuring solid valve lifters. With dual four-barrel carburetors, cross-ram induction and a compression ratio of 12.5:1, this screamer was rated at 425 horsepower. Officially, that is. The true figure was evidently a good deal higher, a fact that no owner was anxious to divulge to his insurance agent. But these were competition engines, not intended (and originally not

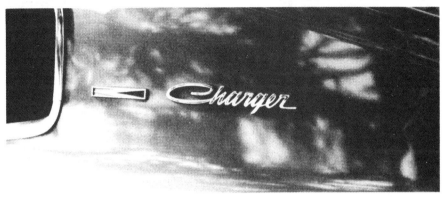

Top: The sign of a very serious motorcar. Above: Charger logos help relieve large expanse of sheet metal on fastback's roof. Below: Charger fastback is based on stock Coronet chassis and sheet metal.

1966 Charger versus Marlin

Though there was a good deal of similarity between the Dodge Charger and AMC's Marlin, there were also a number of important differences. The Marlin, for instance — though it was much larger and heavier than the stillborn Tarpon would have been — was significantly smaller and lighter than the Charger, and doubtless somewhat more maneuverable, thanks to its tighter turning radius.

There were differences in the accommodations, as well. The Dodge featured individual seats, for example, with rear backrests that folded down to provide a generous cargo area. The Marlin, on the other hand, was a six-passenger car with full-width bench seats. Perhaps the worst shortcoming of the AMC fastback was the narrow opening to its luggage compartment, which severely restricted the kinds of loads that could be carried.

For performance enthusiasts, AMC offered nothing to compare with Dodge's hemi engine, or even the 440 "wedge" V-8. But for the average motorist, perhaps the Marlin — given its substantial price advantage — deserved more consideration than it got.

	Charger	Marlin
Price (w/base V-8 engine)	$3,122	$2,707
Shipping weight (lb.)	3,499	3,210
Wheelbase	117 inches	112 inches
Overall length	203.6 inches	195.0 inches
Turning circle (curb/curb)	40' 11"	37' 2"
Overall width	75.3 inches	74.5 inches
Overall height	53.8 inches	54.2 inches
Engine c.i.d.	318.0	287.0
Compression ratio	9.0:1	8.7:1
Horsepower @ rpm	230/4,400	198/4,700
Torque @ rpm	340/2,400	280/2,600
Final drive ratio (with A/T)	2.94:1	3.15:1
Front suspension	Torsion bars	Coil springs
Brake drum diameter	10 inches	10 inches
Swept area (sq. in.)	314.2	267.1
Horsepower per c.i.d.	.723	.690
Pounds per horsepower	15.2	16.2

specifications

Illustrations by Russell von Sauers, The Graphic Automobile Studio

—59.3 inches—

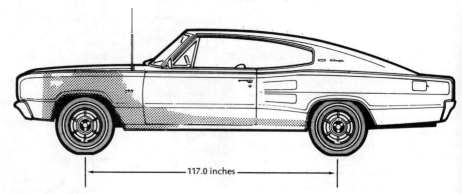

—117.0 inches—

1966 Dodge Charger Hemi

Base price	$3,128 f.o.b. factory, federal tax included
Drive train options	Hemi engine, $877.55; 4-speed transmission, $188.05
Other options on driveReport car	Radio, white sidewall tires, spinner wheel covers, Hurst shifter, after-market Milodon oiling system

ENGINE

Type	90-degree V-8
Bore x stroke	4.25" x 3.75"
Displacement	426.5 cu. in.
Compression ratio	10.25:1
Hp @ rpm	425 @ 5,000 (gross)
Torque @ rpm	490 @ 5,000 (gross)
Taxable hp	57.8
Combustion chamber	Hemispheric
Valves	OHV
Valve lifters	Mechanical
Bearing type (mains and connecting rods)	Tri-metal (copper-lead alloy with steel backing)
No. main bearings	5
Induction system	Dual 4-bbl Carter carburetors, mechanical pump, mechanical secondaries
Lubrication system	Pressure
Exhaust system	Pressure
Electrical system	12-volt

CLUTCH

Type	Single dry plate
Diameter	11 inches
Actuation	Mechanical, foot pedal

TRANSMISSION

Type	4-speed manual with Hurst shifter
Ratios: 1st	2.65
2nd	1.93
3rd	1.39
4th	Direct
Reverse	2.58

DIFFERENTIAL

Type	Hypoid
Ratio	4.10:1
Drive axles	Semi-floating

STEERING

Type	Recirculating ball nut (non-power)
Turns, lock to lock	3.5
Ratio	24:1
Turn circle	40' 9" curb/curb

BRAKES

Type	Heavy-duty 4-wheel drum type (non-power)
Drum diameter	11 inches
Effective area	234.1 sq. in.

CONSTRUCTION

Type	All-steel unitized
Body style	2-door fastback hardtop coupe

SUSPENSION

Front	Independent, .92" diameter torsion bars; link stabilizer
Rear	Conventional axle, 58" x 2½" leaf springs
Shock absorbers	Heavy duty direct-acting telescopic type
Wheels	Pressed steel, drop-center rims
Tires	7.75/14 originally; now GR 70/14

WEIGHTS AND MEASURES

Wheelbase	117.0 inches
Overall length	203.6 inches
Overall width	75.3 inches
Overall height	53.8 inches
Front track	59.3 inches
Rear track	58.5 inches
Ground clearance	6.5 inches (minimum)
Shipping weight	4,000 lb. (est.)
Curb weight	4,390 lb. (as tested)

INTERIOR MEASUREMENTS

Head room, front	37.7 inches
Head room, rear	36.5 inches
Leg room, front	41.6 inches
Leg room, rear	33.3 inches
Seat height, front	8.6 inches
Seat height, rear	9.9 inches

CAPACITIES

Crankcase	6 qt., less filter, originally; now 8 qt.
Cooling system	18 qt.
Fuel gank	19 gallons

CALCULATED DATA

Hp/c.i.d.	.9977
Lb./hp	9.412
Lb./c.i.d.	9.389
Lb./sq. in. (brakes)	17.09

(based on estimated shipping weight)

PERFORMANCE

Top speed	130 mph
Standing ¼ mile	13.8 sec., 104 mph
Acceleration: 0-40	2.8 seconds
0-50	4.1 seconds
0-60	5.3 seconds
0-70	6.9 seconds
0-80	8.4 seconds
0-90	10.2 seconds
0-100	12.8 seconds
0-110	15.7 seconds

From an April 1966 *Car and Driver* road test of a Plymouth Satellite hardtop with the same engine and transmission as our dR car, but 3.54:1 final drive.

PERFORMANCE

Top speed	130 mph
Standing ¼ mile	14.16 seconds, 96.15 mph
Acceleration: 0-30	2.7 seconds
0-40	3.8 seconds
0-50	5.1 seconds
0-60	6.4 seconds
0-70	8.0 seconds
0-80	10.1 seconds
0-90	12.2 seconds
0-100	16.4 seconds
30-70	5.3 seconds

From a February 1967 *Car Life* road test of a 1967 Dodge Charger equipped with the same engine as our dR car, but with the Torqueflite transmission and 3.23:1 final drive.

CHARGER PRODUCTION

1966 model year	37,300

1966 DODGE

available) for street use.

In competitive events this new engine did so well during the 1964 season that NASCAR established a rule to the effect that only production engines would be permitted thereafter. So Dodge and Plymouth confined their participation to drag racing during 1965, returning to the NASCAR circuit the following year.

What had happened in the meantime was that a "street hemi" had become available for 1966 as a regular production option. Two of them, in fact, one with solid lifters, the other with hydraulics. Both were rated at 425 horsepower. Or rather, *under*-rated; for Dodge, along with everyone else in the performance game — tended to be coy about such matters.

And that's where our driveReport Dodge Charger comes in, For this car is powered by the solid-lifter version of the "street hemi," driving through an excellent, close-ratio four-speed gearbox and utilizing the optional Hurst shifter. Evidently this particular car was set up for someone who took drag racing seriously, for its final drive ratio is 4.10:1, in contrast to the more common 3.54:1 or 3.23:1 cogs.

But we'll get back to that in a moment. A word, first, about styling.

The sensational popularity of Ford's Mustang set rival manufacturers to thinking in terms of sporty "personal" cars, resulting by 1967 in a bumper crop that included the Camaro, Firebird, Cougar and second-generation Barracuda — with AMC's Javelin soon to come. Nor had Dodge been sitting on its hands. Electing to use the mid-size Coronet chassis in lieu of the smaller Dart, the division displayed, for 1965, a show car called the Charger II. The public's reception was sufficiently encouraging that the car was put into production, with few changes, for 1966.

Basically, the Charger was simply a fastback Coronet hardtop, featuring four individual seats, console, concealed headlamps and a wall-to-wall taillamp. Once in the showroom, unfortunately, it drew mixed reviews, recalling AMC chief stylist Dick Teague's observation that "there has never been a successful *big* fastback" (see sidebar, page 22). Teague was mistaken, of course; witness for example the handsome General Motors B bodies of 1941-48, not to mention the 1948-49 Cadillac coupes. But the successful full-sized examples have tended, perhaps, to be more the exception than the rule. And while the Dodge Charger came off a good deal better than AMC's Marlin and Matador fastbacks, Tom McPherson wasn't far off the mark in

Above: Charger front-end styling wasn't shared with any other Dodge series. Below: Top of the line wheel covers were also used on other Dodges. Bottom: Wide, flat front buckets don't provide much lateral support.

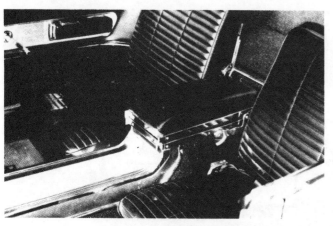

Fastback styling provides generous room for hauling passengers or cargo.

1966 DODGE

describing its styling as "rather unbecoming." Sales of 37,300 Chargers in 1966 were disappointing, and even that figure fell by more than half the following year. Not until a notchback version appeared for 1968 did the Charger really come into its own.

It is not our intent to suggest, by the way, that every 1966 Dodge Charger came with a high-performance engine. On the contrary, only a very few were fitted with one or the other of the "street hemis." Standard issue was Chrysler's familiar 318-c.i.d. V-8, rated at a comparatively modest 230 horsepower. The 361 and 383-c.i.d. engines supplied substantial extra doses of vitamins at relatively modest cost: only $130 for the

325-horsepower, four-barrel 383, for example. So-equipped, according to *Car and Driver*, a '66 Charger would do zero-to-sixty in just 7.8 seconds, which was certainly respectable enough.

But the "street hemi" was a breed apart, described thus by staffers at *Car Life* magazine:

"Its cylinder block...carries special reinforcement at the main bearing webs, and main bearings No. 2, 3 and 4 are

The Other Sporty Fastback: AMC's Marlin

Dodge wasn't alone, 20-plus years ago, in fielding an intermediate-sized fastback. American Motors had one, too. A good one. They called it the Marlin.

Unfortunately, the Marlin was both more and less than it should have been, and therein lay its downfall. It happened this way: When the Society of Automotive Engineers held its national convention in January 1964, the centerpiece of the AMC display was a flashy little fastback called the Tarpon. Built on the 106-inch wheelbase of the Rambler American, this head-turning automobile was finished in gold-flecked vermillion. It was a sensation. As American Motors' former styling chief Richard Teague later recalled, "Everybody was steamed up about it."

Note, now, the timing: January 1964. In just three months, as AMC's product-planners must surely have known, Ford would introduce the Mustang, arguably the success car of the decade. Recalling the Tarpon, Dick Teague wistfully observes, "It should have been produced."

But it wasn't, despite Teague's entreaties. Two reasons. First, AMC's V-8 engine, developed originally for the full-sized Nash and Hudson models of the mid-fifties, was too big for the diminutive Rambler American chassis. Not until mid-1966 would a smaller, lighter engine come along to take its place. Meanwhile, according to the conventional wisdom, the lack of V-8 power would be an insurmountable handicap for any car with sporting (or even "sporty") pretensions.

Probably an even more important factor was the attitude of Roy Abernethy, who had become president of American

Motors upon the departure of George Romney, in February 1962. As Dick Teague told us several years ago (see *SIA* #94), "Abernethy didn't like little cars. Never did. He liked big cars because he was a big guy...and he felt that this car was too small. So he said, 'Well, heck, Teague, why don't you just put it on the Rambler Classic wheelbase? That way you've got V-8 availability, and you've got more room inside it.'"

One can imagine how little enthusiasm Teague must have felt for the project. For, as he explained to *SIA*, in his view "there has never been a successful *big* fastback. Fastbacks have to be shorter in the wheelbase or the proportions of the car go to hell." But he did as he was instructed, with the result that the Marlin, as the new model was called, was nearly a foot and a half longer than the Tarpon. And then the final indignity came while Dick Teague was out of the country: Abernethy raised the Marlin's roofline by an inch, a further affront to the car's proportions.

Truthfully, the Marlin's design wasn't all that bad, though it clearly lacked the elan of the Tarpon. It was simply a fastback version of the popular Rambler Classic, just as the Barracuda was a derivative of Plymouth's compact Valiant. Like the Classic, the Marlin was built more for comfort than for performance, with standard power coming from AMC's excellent 232-c.i.d. six. Two V-8s, displacing 287 and 327 cubic inches respectively, were optionally available.

The first year's sales record of 10,327 cars wasn't bad, taking into consideration the Marlin's February 1965 introduction, five months into the model year.

But it wasn't what the company had hoped for, and a hefty $499 was sliced off the price of the nearly identical 1966 model. The reduction was to some extent illusory, since a number of items such as power steering and brakes were deleted from the list of standard equipment and made optional at extra cost. Even so, at $2,707 for the V-8 version, the Marlin was an excellent value. But sales, for whatever reason, plummeted to 4,547 for the year.

At Dick Teague's urging, the 1967 Marlin was fitted to the 118-inch chassis of the Ambassador. The extra length, all of which appeared ahead of the firewall, gave this Marlin — the last of the breed, as matters developed — a sleeker look, because, as Teague explained, the hood was in better proportion to the long roofline. By this time the second generation AMC V-8 had come on line, and 280 horsepower was on tap for the buyer who opted for the 348-c.i.d. version with four-barrel carburetion.

But sales tumbled again, this time to 2,545 units.

The irony of the situation, in retrospect, is that even without V-8 power (at least until mid-1966), the Tarpon could hardly have failed to exceed the sales record of the unfortunate Marlin — and by a wide margin. In so doing it would have propelled American Motors into a position of styling leadership. And who knows what the long-term effect upon the company might have been?

But that opportunity was lost forever when AMC's high command overruled its styling director and mandated that the company's fastback must be a big one.

secured with horizontal tiebolts through the sides of the block to the bearing caps. Heads have additional tie-downs by special studs and nuts that are tightened from inside the tappet chamber. Domed pistons are of extruded aluminum.

"The Hemi's crankshaft is forged from carbon steel. Added strength comes in the form of shot-peened fillets and a special nitriding dip to harden the surface of the crank to aid in resistance to fatigue. Extra-wide oil grooves in main bearings help protect this strength in high speed operation.

"The high-lift camshaft, driven off the forward end of the crank by a double roller chain, is made of hardened cast iron and is specially coated for protection from scuffing. Valve duration and timing aim not only at smooth operation at low engine speeds for normal street and highway operation, but also at efficient high-speed breathing and top power output.

"The valve train itself is made up of mechanical tappets, tubular pushrods and forged steel rocker arms, all designed for light weight with maximum strength for sustained high speed operation...."

Naturally, all this good stuff didn't come cheap. The premium, as best we have been able to determine, came to $877.55 over the price of the base Charger — though some sources quote even higher figures. At that, it's doubtful if Chrysler ever made a nickel from the sale of these engines, for each one was virtually hand-built. Critical parts were selected for optimum fit and balance, and test procedures were only a little less sophisticated than those used for racing powerplants.

Many, probably most of these cars were provided with the excellent Torque-flite transmission. *Car and Driver's* test crew actually preferred the performance of the automatic over that of the close-ratio, four-speed manual that was listed as a "mandatory option." (Whether the use of a Hurst shifter like that of our driveReport car would have changed their view, we do not know, but it evidently made a significant difference in the action of the four-speed unit.)

Chrysler's suspension system, utilizing torsion bars at the front, proved ideal for use with the "street hemi." For this application a heavy duty setup was used, identical to that which was provided with Dodge's police package. Torsion bars of 0.92-inch diameter were employed, in conjunction with a 0.94-inch anti-roll bar and heavy duty telescopic shock absorbers. Semi-elliptic springs at the rear carried two extra leaves. Withal the heavy duty suspension package provided a ride that was firm but not harsh, and cornering capability was substantially enhanced.

Above: Big, round gauges provide plenty of driver feedback. Below: Charger i.d. appears on door cappings. Bottom: Hemi V-8 is rated at 425 bhp and that's alleged to be an understated factory figure!

Above: Full-width taillamp treatment is unique to Charger. Below: A Hurst shifter was a must among top muscle cars of the sixties.

a problem. However, when front discs ultimately became available, they were a welcome improvement.

So here was an automobile that combined radical styling with superior handling and a top speed — according to *Car Life* — of 134 miles an hour. So much for Dodge's traditional image as a car for the geriatric set. □

Acknowledgements and Bibliography

Automotive Industries, *March 15, 1966; Eric Dahlquist, "Charger," Hot Rod, January 1966; Dodge Division factory literature; John Ethridge, "Dodge's Charging Charger," Motor Trend, January 1966; John Gunnell (ed.),* Standard Catalog of American Cars, 1946-1975; *Richard M. Langworth and Jan P. Norbye,* Complete History of Chrysler; *Richard M. Langworth,* Encyclopedia of American Cars, 1940-1970; *Thomas A. MacPherson,* The Dodge Story; *Alex Walordy, "390 Fairlane vs. 426 Street Hemi Dodge,"* Rodder and Super Stock, *November 1965; "Dodge Charger,"* Car and Driver, *February 1966; "Dodge Charger,"* Road Test, *May 1966; "Hemi Charger,"* Car Life, *February 1967; "Marlin and Charger,"* Motor Trend, *May 1967; "Plymouth 426 Hemi,"* Car and Driver, *April 1966; "Plymouth Street Hemi,"* Car Life, *July 1966; "Racing Cars Can Tour,"* Motor Trend, *April 1966.*

Our thanks to Dennis Boos, Fresno, California; Ralph Dunwoodie, Sun Valley, Nevada; Ben Gostanian, Fresno, California; Galen Govier, Prairie du Chien, Wisconsin; George Longacre, Stockton, California; Robert Martin, Wauwatosa, Wisconsin. Special thanks to Clift Cullen, Clovis, California.

1966 DODGE

Heavy-duty, manually adjusted drum-type brakes were provided on hemi-powered cars. Eleven-inch drums and metallic linings took the place of Dodge's standard ten-inch binders. Swept area measured 380.1 square inches, up from 340.2 in the regular brakes. *Motor Trend*, testing a hemi-powered Plymouth Satellite with these brakes, recorded a stopping distance of 183 feet from 60 miles an hour, performance that could be considered acceptable but hardly outstanding. In fairness it should be added that brake fade was not

Critique

All right; so let's get to the bottom line. What do we really think — of the Charger in general, and the "Street Hemi" version in particular?

There's a lot to like, and we'll get to that. But permit, first, a few negative observations:

• For starts, Dodge would have been well advised to pay a little more attention to ergonomics. The Charger's seats are none too comfortable at best, and when the car is driven with exuberance, its occupants are tossed about like corks on a stormy sea.

• The fastback configuration carries its own share of drawbacks. Visibility to the rear is limited, for instance, and although the Charger's cargo area is enormous when the rear seats are folded down, its utility is limited by the restricted access.

• Then there's the matter of price. The Charger cost $547 more than a comparably powered Coronet 440 hardtop coupe. Was it worth the difference? We'll let the reader decide.

On the other hand, the car deserves an ample measure of praise:

• The superiority of the Charger's (and the Coronet's) torsion bar suspension — in either standard or heavy duty form — is beyond question. Handling is excellent, and even in competition guise the ride is surprisingly good.

• Quality control, a real problem at Chrysler Corporation just a few years earlier, had made great strides by the time our driveReport car was built.

• And the engines and transmissions were really superior — whether we're talking about the garden variety 318 or the high-stepping hemi, the four-speed manual or the Torqueflite automatic. (Well, let's qualify that. For optimum performance with the four-speed, the optional Hurst shifter was a virtual necessity.)

Finally, with regard to the hemi: Is it all that it has been cracked up to be? Yes, and more. It's a fantastic piece of machinery. But was it worth several hundred dollars more than the 330-horsepower, four-

barrel 383? Probably not, to most people. For competitive purposes it was a must, for it was good for an extra ten, possibly 15 miles an hour at the top end. It could nip more than a second off the 383's zero-to-sixty time, and it would reach the century mark at least seven seconds sooner. Furthermore, it was built to withstand this sort of punishment hour after hour, something no ordinary production engine could possibly be expected to do.

But on the other hand, even apart from the initial cost of the brute, the hemi required constant maintenance to keep it in tune, while the 383 could run for months without ever having a wrench laid on it.

Car and Driver, clocking a 383-powered with the Torqueflite transmission, did the standing quarter-mile in 16.2 seconds, topping out at 88 miles an hour. Zero-to-sixty took only 7.8 seconds, and top speed was estimated at 120 miles an hour. Surely that was performance enough for any ordinary mortal.